"What I love about David, the actor, the writer, the man . . . is that there is no pretense and no desire to conform to the dictated so-called norms of society, especially when it comes to sex. He is brazen and wonderfully honest about his past, present, and future. With *Damn Shame*, the reader is in for a wild ride . . . pun intended." —Bryan Batt, actor and author of *She Ain't Heavy, She's My Mother: A Memoir*

"Who could imagine that a book which deals unapologetically with exhibitionism, LGBT ageism, and sex work could be so filled with charm and self-deprecating good humor. David Pevsner's heartfelt memoir shows how a mutual fascination with sex and musical comedy has led him successfully through the exotic worlds of Off-Broadway, Broadway, television, and erotic photography." —Charles Busch, actor and author of *The Tale of the Allergist's Wife*

"I love stories about overcoming stigma and shame, because I think shame has no place in our growth and sadly there is so much of it heaped on us everywhere, especially if you are queer. I loved David's journey to zero shame about his body, his sexuality, and himself. *Damn Shame* has my ideal combo of racy, illuminating, and idiosyncratic storytelling that transports you into a stranger's life and mind. And—or beware—there is a lot of penis!" —Alan Cumming, actor and author of *Baggage: Tales From A Fully Packed Life*

"Warning: This book is not for the faint of heart (in the best possible way). David Pevsner's voice is on the surface hilarious, self-deprecating, and sometimes outrageous. But underneath what unfolds is a candid memoir of great beauty and poignancy—the lifelong journey of being gay and learning how to love himself at long last. Deeply personal and honest, Pevsner bares his soul, and his body, over and over again as he rolls with the absurdity of it all, celebrating his choices, mistakes, and triumphs with equal measure. He effortlessly draws the reader in, bringing us along for the ride so that we too can reflect and relate and maybe even forgive ourselves for the past, love ourselves a little more, and better understand some of our universal truths as human beings on the planet." —Brian Hutchison, actor, photographer, and creator of the podcast *I Still Think About You*

"A genial host, but also a genital host, actor/writer/erotic model David Pevsner has long been turned on by Broadway musicals, hot men, and romance. His honest and emotional memoir, *Damn Shame*, sings as it takes you through his awkward coming of age, his time as a 'mature model,' and his ongoing success in erotic art, as he comes to embrace his own choices and feel comfortable in his often exposed skin. Bravo, David. Encore!" —Michael Musto, journalist

"David Pevsner assaults our 'culture of shame' by reinventing the tell-all autobiography. He actually does tell all. His honesty and the way he lays out the facts as he knows them for you to judge too, about his personal and professional life, is rare. Of course, it helps that he's had success in his varied résumé of life and work. So what we get is a thoughtful, sometimes raw, sometimes risqué, but always entertaining memoir." —Felice Picano, author of *Like People in History*

"In *Damn Shame*, David Pevsner guides us through a wonderfully appealing chronicle of his life as a performer, writer, sex worker, nude model, and a gay guy making his way on his own terms. Rather than oversharing, he's a delightful host to the most entertaining adventures." —Paul Rudnick, author of *Jeffrey*

"David Pevsner is so much more than the half-man, half-horse he played in *When Pigs Fly*. Personally, I couldn't ask for much more than a half-man, half-horse, but that's just me. Aside from being a talented actor, singer, and dancer, David is a furious social, political, and sexual activist, and altogether a one-man show. This sizzling chronicle of his ups, downs, and sideways-z will keep you entertained and inspired. And perhaps moist." —Bruce Vilanch, actor, writer and humorist

"In deft, vivid prose, David Pevsner recounts his surprising journey from awkward teen to musical theater phenom to part-time male escort and fearless sexual advocate. Written with sly humor and, at times, eye-popping candor, *Damn Shame* is a compelling portrait of one gay man's struggle for self-acceptance in a country that trumpets liberation but is all too beholden to its Puritan past." —Doug Wright, Pulitzer Prize-winning author of *I Am My Own Wife*

DAMN SHAME

DAVID PEVSNER

DAMN SHAME

A MEMOIR OF DESIRE, DEFIANCE, AND SHOW TUNES

RANDOM HOUSE CANADA

PUBLISHED BY RANDOM HOUSE CANADA

Copyright © 2021 David Pevsner

www.penguinrandomhouse.ca

Random House Canada and colophon are registered trademarks.

Library and Archives Canada Cataloguing in Publication

Title: Damn shame : a memoir of desire, defiance and show tunes / David Pevsner.
Names: Pevsner, David, author.
Identifiers: Canadiana (print) 2021025677X | Canadiana (ebook) 20210256834 |
ISBN 9781039000506 (softcover) | ISBN 9781039000513 (EPUB)
Subjects: LCSH: Pevsner, David. | LCSH: Gay men—United States—Biography. |
LCSH: Actors—United States—Biography. | LCSH: Models (Persons)—United
States—Biography. | LCSH: Gay men—Identity. |
LCSH: Gay erotic photography. | LCGFT: Autobiographies.
Classification: LCC HQ75.8.P48 A3 2022 | DDC 306.76/62092—dc23

Text design: Matthew Flute
Cover design: Matthew Flute
Image credits: Jim Cox

Printed in the United States of America

1st Printing

Penguin
Random House
RANDOM HOUSE CANADA

For Marcia Pevsner. The best storyteller ever.

When you love who you are, there is no thing unconquerable, no thing unreachable. When you truly love yourself, you live only in the light of your own laughter and travel only the path of joy. When you are in love with yourself, then that light— that mirthful state of being—extends itself to all humanity.

—RAMTHA

A little over ten years ago, I was chatting with a twenty-something kid in a bar in Los Angeles and we got onto the subject of age. He said, "Ugh. I can't imagine ever being forty years old!" I chimed in that I was fifty. He backpedaled a second, embarrassed, and I said it was okay, I understood. I asked, "Why does getting older bother you so much? It's going to happen." He said, "I know, but when you reach that age, you have to start getting pissed on and . . . yuck!" I laughed and went into Dad mode and said, seriously, "You never have to do anything you don't want to, ever. Remember that." But then I added, "But who knows? You might try it sometime and like it!" to which he gave me a look as if I just shot a puppy.

THE *PLAYBILL* BIO

Who am I?

I'm an actor, writer, composer, and singer with thirty-five-plus years in the biz: mostly doctor roles on network TV, a little bit of Broadway, larger roles in off-Broadway hit plays and musicals, a bunch of Los Angeles and regional theater credits, a couple of one-man shows, and nice parts in mostly gay independent films.

Musical comedy was my first love, so when I started writing, it was songs; the first ditties made their way into the long-running off-Broadway hit *Naked Boys Singing!* I've written and performed in various stage shows that are all pretty gay (though, I think, universally resonant about love, lust, and the search for happiness) and have strong sexual themes. This irked my mother, who told me that I needed to expand my oeuvre and write something everyone can see. As my pal Kent Gash once said, "Everyone CAN see them. They can pay their ducats and see them."

I've also done everything outside showbiz that there is to do for money. I've had gigs as a handyman, a personal organizer, a waiter, a bartender, a Christmas decorator, a house cleaner, and more.

And I mean everything: I was also a hooker. And lately what I'm known for is my erotic Internet presence. I'm naked all over the Net in photos and videos, in various states of arousal and sexual activity. I'm told I'm a bit of a "Daddy" icon and I've become an anti-ageism, anti-body-shame, pro-sex, and pro-nudity advocate, or, as a friend labeled me, a "sexual activist." Sweet.

Although this is a memoir, I wanted to include some of my lyrics because my songs are inspired by my actual life experiences. I'm not big on subtlety or the abstract; I tend to tell a story through lyrics in a direct, uncomplicated way—much to enjoy but not much to analyze. I call myself the "King of the Single Entendre." However, the great thing for me about writing lyrics is that they can start out of my reality and then I get to expound and explore the fantasies I have beyond the moment. That's my way of saying that although most of the lyrics are fairly representative of my experiences, full disclosure: not every one is the absolute truth. For example, I neither met nor had sex with a vertically challenged action film superstar in my song "The Book of Lust," but it was fun to take the list of everyone I have slept with in that direction. To be honest, I have not slept with many famous people at all, so there's not much dish there. I've had the odd reality show host, porn star, Broadway chorus boy, and TV ingenue newbie, but other than that . . . nope. However, this book is my story told through the lens of body shame and sexuality, so there will be plenty of nudity—mostly emotional, but as there are lots of photos, there will be cock. Yay!

So I've told you who I am by telling you what I do. I'm betting you still don't know who I am. That's okay. Stick with me. I am nothing if not a genial host, and though some may think I'm a minor player in the entertainment biz, I have a pretty good story to tell (but then,

I believe everyone has a story to tell). We are all more than just what we do. It took years for me to figure that out.

Okay. The pre-curtain bells are ringing. Here we go . . .

(House lights to half . . .)

PROLOGUE: CONTACT

June 1995. I saw an ad in the back of *HX* magazine, a ubiquitous, free New York City gay rag, for "Maturity Escorts," a service catering to those who desired a more, shall we say, experienced hooker experience. I was performing in a high-profile off-Broadway play called *Party* at the time, but the salary wasn't paying the bills. I was burned out on waiting tables, and I had always fantasized about being the kind of guy someone would pay money to have sex with. After transforming my former bony frame into a sculpted body with thick pecs, tight abs, and a bubbly ass, I was excited about exploring something so taboo, but also consumed with curiosity to see if I could make the grade. The ad said the company was hiring, so I called, made an appointment with the owner, Mo, and the next day made my way to the Upper East Side for my interview.

Yes, an actual interview. Like any audition, I wanted to ace it, but unlike an audition, I had no idea what to expect. I thought I knew what the stereotype escort was and what he was supposed to offer—sex on demand, open mouth and ass, a carnal glutton with a vigorous, incessant libido and cockiness—but was that the reality? Was it something I could actually do? How does one "audition" for that? And what could I bring to it, being the deep-down nice Jewish boy that I was?

At thirty-six years old, I was hardly the age one would start sex work, but the qualification was in the title—"Maturity Escorts." Part of me thought I wasn't escort material, that I wasn't enough of a fantasy man to actually get remunerated for sex, but I had been aroused by the idea of it for so long that I needed to find out. I knew I had the stamina; my sex life was pretty active and one might even say demanding, and I had built up my physique and my confidence through daily workouts at the 23rd Street YMCA and then the all-male gay Chelsea Gym on 17th Street. But like so many gay men of my generation, the scars inflicted on us for growing up "different" run incredibly deep, and though we put a Band-Aid on cancer by toughening up our bodies, the change isn't always reflected beneath the skin. Despite my ongoing therapy, inside I was still that skinny, ugly Jewish kid filled with shame and nasty voices in my head about nudity, sexuality, and my fantasies. When I saw that ad, it was like a neon sign. One of those voices began egging me on, taunting me in a deep, dirty basso profundo, sneering, "Do it! Do it!" And if I didn't act on it, well . . . shame. It was now or never.

I was anxious yet fired up about the interview, sweaty but excited as I sat in my tighty-whities in an unfussy living room on the Upper East Side—all thrift shop and IKEA—across from a heavyset, balding man with kind eyes. He offered me a cigarette, and being a pack-a-day guy at the time, I heartily accepted it as he clicked a NY Yankees lighter and shakily lit the fag. I took a long, grateful drag. He wasn't much of a talker, so I started.

"Thanks." (*puff puff*) "I bet your clients don't like smoker's breath. I should probably quit. Haha." (*puff puff*)

Nothing from Mo. The silence put me into chatty overdrive.

"I know I'm not your basic callboy type," I began to babble. "Not tall, not so handsome. Not huge . . ." I flexed my chest. "Or huge . . ."

I pointed at my crotch. "Not quite a boy, but you are looking for older guys, right? And I'm not your typical Jewish guy either. I used to say I would never date Jewish men because they can complain as much as me, but I look on the bright side these days. I talk too much, for sure, but I do listen well, I'm sort of the caretaker type, I guess I'm intelligent and . . . oh, I can be funny. I make a living, sort of, being funny in mostly musicals . . . I'm an 'actor who sings' . . . and I play all these nice Jewish boys in Jewsicals . . . y'know, *Rags*, *The Rothschilds*, *Fiddler on the . . ."*

He had no idea what the fuck I was talking about. I had to get back on track.

"My face . . . not great, but I know I'm attractive in an odd and big-nose sort of way . . . oh, I sat for this French photographer once for headshots, who said, 'You have zuch an eeenteresting face. You look like . . . like . . . an Egyptian Dog!'"

Mo cracked a smile.

"My dick's above average," I yammered on, getting back to business. "And I may have a warped idea of my worth as a sex object, but I think I can do . . . this . . . and I was hoping my brain and my sterling sense of humor might make up for the rest. Haha. Ha." I was waiting for that smile again.

Nothin'. Long pause. Then finally he said, "Not everyone wants a twenty-two-year-old *GQ* model with a big dick. Can you have sex with someone you aren't attracted to?"

Oh. That. I told him my story about Gus and what I recently did to him, how I tossed this lovely, funny guy away because of his soft, undefined body, and suddenly Mo had a lot to say. Suddenly I was getting relationship advice from a pimp. He said that I was probably a guy who demanded movie star good looks in the men I pursued, but assured me that such finds would be rare in this job. He told me to be open to other qualities in clients who weren't going to be my "type"; to look for kindness, wit, intelligence, and not to focus on the money or clock watching, to give the client the opportunity to surprise me, to appreciate that Average Joes can be sweet or smart or fun or sometimes even have a ten-inch cock (which, I won't lie, gave me a bubbly tingle in my butthole), and that though I might be a hired hand, these clients could be wonderful companions for the time I was there. Mo gave me a crash course in how to get over myself and be a good escort.

"Can I specify what I will and won't do?" I asked.

He nodded.

"Great, I can only get fucked every once in a while, otherwise my bowel movements are not my own. Rimming them is, well, out of the question, but I can pose and flex for them, they can suck or rim me, lick any old body part they want. I can fuck or massage them, maybe kiss them if they're cute . . ." I figured none of them would be "cute" in my high-bar estimation, and as looks-obsessed as I was, as diminishing as I could be regarding other positive attributes such as personality and brains, I figured I'd save the real intimacy, the kissing, only for someone who might really turn me on, as I'd heard some hookers did. "Yeah, I think I can do this. I like sex, and I'm good at it, and I think that if you do something well, you should get paid for it!" Tiny crack of a smile.

He stared at me, sizing me up, until he nonchalantly asked, "Are you into kink, bondage, S&M, that kind of thing?"

Even though I met him in my tight tank top and cock-crushing jeans, I probably seemed a tad conservative sitting there in my plain white briefs with my game show host haircut. Still, Mo suggested that if I liked, I could be marketed from time to time to guys who wanted to go beyond vanilla, who wanted older men into leather and fetish and role play. Did I have any experience with that?

Memories of getting pissed on in my neighbor's bathroom, fisting a bodybuilder at the Unicorn bathhouse in Chicago, and me in nothing but a harness, chaps, and motorcycle boots ramming into a bubble butt bottom boy in a sex party sling danced through my mind. Yeah, I had that covered. Chuckling to myself, I said, "I think I've got that. Dom, sub, any of it. As long as it's safe."

"Good. So you've never escorted before on your own?"

"No, I think I'd do better with representation." I rambled on. "Look, I know I'm not the most beautiful man, and even though it's 'Maturity Escorts,' at thirty-six, I'm probably a little more mature than your other guys—well, let's just say it, I'm old—but people still seem to want to fuck me, so why shouldn't I profit off it, right? Of course, right!"

Oy. That last part came out full Yente the Matchmaker. I was just short of breaking into "If I Were a Rich Man."

I knew I was getting into a danger zone. Besides the illegality of it all, there was the uncertainty of what would be behind each door of every call. As I sat there under Mo's silent scrutiny, my commitment faltered for a moment, unsure that I would actually follow through with the whole thing. But I kept running Mo's words in my head, that escorting wasn't just about a great body, a handsome face, or a huge cock. I sensed it was about connecting with your clients physically *and* emotionally. I always only wanted to be an actor, but the only other career that interested me at all was being a shrink. I could do this.

"Do you need to see my dick?" I asked Mo. Immediately, the blood pounded to my head . . . and to my other head. No. No. No. I wanted to show it, but I wanted to keep it soft for now. Although the notion of getting an erection in such close quarters was making my cock pulsate with anticipation, I was fairly certain that getting hard in front of him was going to be an invitation for him to suck it rather than tell me how pretty I am. I didn't want to be a trashy whore.

"Yeah, if you wouldn't mind."

I figured that Mo needed to assess the goods in order to tell his clients what I was packing, so it was time to bring out the performer in me. I'd give him a show. Part of me wanted to let loose and let go, to furiously jerk off, shoot, and impress Mo with my gigantic load (I have always been a copious ejaculator) like a geyser all over the striped rug, hardwood floor, and dirty walls. But take it easy, I thought. Keep a few cards close to your bare chest. I stood up, trying not to let on that my nerves were turning my legs into mushy noodles, and I gingerly moved around the coffee table until I was in position, facing him. Places, please!

I froze. I stood there awkwardly, feeling Mo's eyes on my crotch. *Party* was infamous for its nudity, and I was getting naked every night for the sake of comedy in front of hundreds of people. When I auditioned for the production, the final callback was simply to go in the audition room, take off my clothes, stand starkers in front of the casting director, producers, and director, say hi, get my clothes back on, and leave, just to prove that I could get naked in front of an audience. No problem. I enjoyed it, I got the job, and it was all in good fun. Now I was nervous about dropping my drawers in front of one sweet, harmless man because there was sex attached to it. Suddenly the whole enterprise had a seediness to it, the voices in my head calling out, "Dirty hooker! Dirty hooker!"

I instantly shut them down and focused. I felt that I should give a brief preshow bump and grind, flex my chest, rub my cock through the cotton, tweak my nipples, gyrate my hips, tease the reveal. I didn't need any of that. I just had to show the goods. I took a deep breath, hooked my thumbs into the waistband of my undies, and began to lower them. I intended the motion to be slow and seductive, but it became sort of spastic. As the briefs approached my ankles, I began singing to myself *la la la la don't get a boner yet la la la*. I straightened up and stepped out of them, and I was noticeably vibrating, barely keeping my balance, and my cock was fluffy, but not erect. Phew. Mo had a placid look on his face and asked me to turn around. I slowly revolved, tightening my glutes and expanding my lats.

"You really do have a lovely body," he finally said with unexpected admiration. "Not the typical muscle boy I usually see. Very natural-looking."

Thanks, I thought. Ten hours a week in the gym to get that natural look. Then my daredevil instinct kicked in: here was the line and here was me crossing it.

"Do you need to see it hard?"

"Well, um . . . sure."

Boner alert! My guard dropped full throttle and I got raging hard in one second flat. I felt a rush of air as it swept upward. I pointed to my steely erection and said, "Fast, I know. Hey, maybe THAT can be my selling point."

In that moment, I knew there was no turning back. I really wanted to do this. *Needed* to do this. Not just because I was sick of scrounging financially, living hand to mouth, a starving artist's existence. A few escorting gigs a week would more than double what I was bringing in off-Broadway. And it was also an acting gig . . . sort of . . . just on a different stage. But more important than any of that, after years of holding back, letting shame dictate my sexual limits, judging myself harshly because of my desires, I could finally rip off my conservative clothes and let out what I was desperate and even screaming to expose and explore ever since I was a little boy.

Back in the '60s and '70s, I fantasized about showing off and wearing a tight little bulging Speedo by the pool on family vacations. I wanted to swagger around the locker room with my dick flopping free after gym class. Within my weak, skinny frame, I felt I was a little slut boy, and that filled me with shame and fear. Now? I was promiscuous in real life, and I was turned on by the notion of engaging sexually with men I didn't know, letting them use my ass and cock and lips and tits for their pleasure, and I fancied the idea of getting paid for it. If it happened to include leather and S&M and pissing on each other, for god's sake, I wanted it. The Danger Zone. It was time to take a leap and fucking Do It.

Mo interjected, "I'll be in touch. Oh, it's two hundred bucks an hour, I get fifty. And we gotta get you a beeper."

A beeper. Back then, those were only for drug dealers and whores. It was all getting real.

(Lights go to black . . .)

LITTLE ME

I hate it when someone says, "I had this dream . . ." and then you have to hear about it. But I had this dream when I was twelve years old in which scrawny, awkward me was piggybacking naked on this handsome male model with dark hair and a muscular, tanned torso, and I began rubbing my hands up and down his oiled-up washboard abs, starting slowly but then picking up the pace, faster and faster, until I woke up moaning loudly, having shot a load in my pajamas. My first gay wet dream. I lay there, feeling the cum dry, confused and unable to move. Part of me was enjoying the aftershock. Part of me wanted to die and I didn't know why.

I thought of calling this book *Fancy Boy!* after *The Fancy Boys Follies*, one of the many gay shows I either appeared in or wrote. *Fancy Narcissist!* was another possibility, but I like to think I've changed. I consider myself a *recovering* narcissist. However, what's more narcissistic than an autobiography, except maybe a one-man show? I've done two!

We're Fancy Boys! Let's celebrate it!
We're proud and prance-y boys!

You too can hear a different drum
if to your instincts you sucCUM!
—from "Fancy Boys"

Shameless! was another title running around in my brain, because I am, in so many ways, as you'll soon see. But growing up, there were lots of little moments of shame that I didn't quite understand or recognize: invasive and very pervasive. PERVasive. My name's Pevsner? So of course kids called me *Perversner*. Little did they know. At six years old I was using my pillow for passionate, romantic trysts with TV actors, reenacting the love scenes I saw in my twenty-five hours of TV watching a day, with me standing in for the women. Even before I knew what sex was, all I wanted was to kiss and hug these famous men. TV was nowhere near as risqué as it is now, so that's really all I knew there was to do.

My first "boyfriend" was Brian Kelly, the father on the TV series *Flipper*. Remember him? Masculine, hairy chest, strong yet sensitive single dad to two boys. He played Porter Ricks, a park and maritime ranger in the Florida Keys, and every so often he would drive his boat wearing his khaki uniform pants, shirtless, and that solid, chiseled, furry torso made my delicate heart flutter. That, to me, was a Man. The teen fan magazines I read, like *16* and *Tiger Beat*, only featured the kids on the show, but I liked the daddy. To this day I refer to any sexy Black Irish-y-looking guy as "Flipper's Father." He was my pillow boyfriend and the love of my life until I cheated on him at seven years old with James Darren, the fit and swarthy star of my favorite TV show, *The Time Tunnel*. Through most of the series he wore a snug green turtleneck sweater and tight black pants that emphasized his lean physique. A Man. Nightly, I enjoyed romancing pillow James with all the finesse I had seen on TV . . .

"Oh, James, I love you. Kiss me. Kiss me, James! Oh, yes!" I hugged "him," cuddled "him," kissed "him" (closed mouth—I didn't know about French kissing yet), ran my hands all over "his" cushy body.

One night, in the midst of some particularly passionate pillow talk, my bedroom door opened abruptly, the hall light split the darkness, and I heard an exasperated, heavy midwest Skokie, Illinois, twang. "James? Who's James? Stahp that! Stahp it right now! Go to bed! Ohmigahd!" It was my mom. She caught us *in flagrante*, and I got the memo that what I was doing was wrong. Forbidden love. With foam. *Shame.*

I was born in 1958 to Marcia and Sheldon Pevsner in Skokie, a northern suburb of Chicago and in the 1960s heavily populated (almost 60 percent) with my peeps, the Jews. It's mostly known for the attempted Nazi march in 1978 when the ACLU defended the Nazis' right to freedom of speech, and boo-hoo, they lost. The Skokie of my childhood was very clean-cut, middle to upper-middle class, and pretty average as suburbs go, with absolutely no minorities that I knew of. I never saw any Black people around town except for our maid, Mary. She stayed with us for years and I loved her, but certain folks in our circle still referred to her as "the schvartze" (a disparaging Yiddish term for a Black person). I used to think Skokie didn't even allow Black people, that they were banned from living in our neighborhood. Nope. It was just a white-bread kind of town with very little diversity. My dad had a wholesale jewelry business with his brother-in-law in downtown Chicago and my mom was his bookkeeper, but he also had a secretary who was Black. Silver was absolutely gorgeous and classy and just fascinated me, because I didn't know anyone like her. She was so glamorous and looked and carried herself like a fashion model.

I'm the youngest of three kids. Janet is two years older and Linda four years, and though they are the absolute best and we get along great now, back then they could be typical older sisters and, at times, not very kind to me. Nothing evil or dangerous, but they liked to pick on me, taunting and criticizing, knowing how sensitive I was.

I was also a pretty smart kid, and nothing made me crazier than when someone got something wrong: mispronouncing a word, stating a wonky fact, screwing up an easy math problem, misquoting famous lines from movies. If I knew the real answer, I would offer it up. I wasn't doing it to show how smart I was; I just thought, if it's wrong, it needs to be corrected. You're welcome, I innocently thought.

When I did it to my sisters, it annoyed the piss out of them (and in retrospect, I guess I don't blame them). "Okay, Mr. Know-It-All!" they would shriek with a mocking tone, as if I were the idiot. They did that imitation thing where you say something and they parrot it back in a really demeaning, childish way. It made me nuts, but since I was the baby, I never could or would fight back, and it made me feel weak. I was a put-upon kid, too smart for my own good, but I sometimes got revenge, driving them crazy singing commercial jingles from television in the back seat of the car. Or I could sing show tunes alone in the basement and forget about them. My life in the suburbs could be summed up in two words: sheltered and innocent. But every chance I got, I snuck into my sisters' toys to play with their Barbie dolls, dressing and undressing them in various stylish ensembles and having a fabulous time. I started to understand that maybe there was something different about me. *Hello Shame!*

I learned to read at three years old when a neighbor who was an aspiring teacher made me her guinea pig, and in one afternoon she had me reading an entire volume of *Dick and Jane*, the teacher's edition. My mother was gobsmacked as I read out loud to her, and the delighted admiration in her eyes was not lost on me. I wasn't good at sports, but I had a sense my brains were going to be my armor and my way of standing out, getting attention and, well . . . love.

I felt I had to be the smartest one in the room, a straight-A kind of kid and a teacher's pet. One day in first grade it was raining and we were having indoor recess. I was watching some kids play a board game in the back of the room, and I was sitting at my desk cheering them on when I felt a tap on my shoulder. I turned around and it was my favorite teacher, Mrs. Jacobs, with a cross look on her face. She proceeded to lambaste me for having messy penmanship. It was kind of shocking. I'd never gotten that kind of criticism from anyone, least of all my beloved Mrs. Jacobs. Her disapproval immediately thrust me into a deep, drowsy depression. The energy got sucked right out of me and I wanted to crumble into the fetal position and just pass out. I wasn't used to failing at all. *Shamelot.*

I had to excel not only at East Prairie Elementary School but in Hebrew school as well, at Lincolnwood Jewish Congregation. Though it wasn't as strict as Orthodox, it wasn't as loose as Reform; it was somewhere in the middle. And the classes were an hour and a half, three times a week, with two hours on Sunday. They were lackluster and tedious, the rabbis forcing us to read and sing from the Torah and the siddur (a Jewish prayer book) without giving us an inkling as to why they were relevant to our lives. The English translations from Hebrew went on and on about God is Great, Praise to God, God is All, blah-dy blah blah, and then some guy gets eaten by a whale and I'm supposed to care? No, thank you.

Now I know that these stories are allegories, but back then they either didn't make that clear or I was asleep. As much as I hated Hebrew school, I still wanted good grades, so I listened. It was all facts to me, and I could memorize them, ace the tests, and forget them the next day. After seven years of Hebrew school, you'd think I could speak the language, but uh-uh.

Before going to Hebrew school, I'd stop at Weiner's Pharmacy to buy candy to sneak-eat during class. I'd always buy five, count 'em five, boxes of my favorites—Jujubes (or, as I referred to them, JewJewBes) at five cents apiece—and finish them off in the ninety minutes of Bible and boredom. Jujubes are translucent, colorful tidbits that used to contain gelatin, which is made from pork, and you did not bring that forbidden fruit into the Jewish Big House, let alone nosh on it in class.

I would suck on a mouthful of Jujubes, which would melt and connect the individual pieces into, ironically, a delicious little stained glass window. I'd take the candy pane out of my mouth and admire my handiwork (well, mouthiwork), then put it back in and chew on it, careful not to get it stuck in my teeth. Jujubes had a reputation for pulling out your fillings, so I had a technique for eating them that would keep me dentist free (gently bite down on them with your molars, never letting them get jammed into the grooves). The only time I ever got into trouble was when Rabbi Mlotek (who oddly slurped after every sentence he spoke) caught me and kicked me out for eating nonkosher candy. Jujubes made the class tolerable.

So many years of that fresh hell, with all the praying and crazy stories, striving to be the good boy with the best grades, pressuring myself to forge on, eventually made me resent and despise Judaism. Nothing about the religion or its traditions really resonated with me except for funny Jews like Allan Sherman (I wore out the albums of his hilarious Jewish-oriented song parodies); the food (my mom's meat blintzes, gefilte fish, matzah ball soup, and the most mouth-watering brisket on the planet made with Lipton Onion Soup mix); and the holidays and any occasion we were given presents. The booty from my bar mitzvah would later fund the entire first year of my career as an aspiring professional actor in New York City.

Chanukah was the big kahuna of Jewish holidays for presents, and I loved it until the year I was eight and my mom teased that I was getting something I "always wanted." The only thing I ever "always wanted" was a dog. I was beside myself with joyous anticipation. We lit the candles that first night and my mom brought out a sealed cardboard box. How cruel, I thought, as my dad ripped through the tape with a key. I opened the box and inside was a dog. Well, an ottoman in the shape of a dog. Leather, with tassels for eyes and rivets for toenails. For thirty-plus years that memory stayed with me and fed the resentment I had for that holiday and Judaism and rabbis and Hebrew school and traditions, but years later I wrote it as an ironic and bittersweet "'Twas the Night Before Christmas" poem called "A Chanukah Surprise!" Here's how it ended:

> *Oh, Chanukah. Oh, Chanukah.*
> *I didn't bitch or moan.*
> *She meant well and she compromised by throwing me a bone.*
> *It won't go nuts if it's not fed,*
> *and certainly, it wouldn't shed,*
> *or chew the furniture. Species don't destroy their own.*
>
> *I know it left me high and dry,*
> *and to this day I never try*
> *to celebrate or deal with the mental chazerai.*
> *So what then is the moral of this oddly epic sonnet?*
> *When I see a dog, do I pet it, or put my feet upon it?*
> —from "A Chanukah Surprise!"

Years later, when I performed the piece in my show *To Bitter and Back*, friends would tell me how horrible my mom was for leading me on like that. However, I subsequently found out that the story wasn't quite how I remembered it (more on this in a bit). But I resented it all, because my whole childhood became a self-driven, impossible quest to be the perfect little Jewish boy . . . or else. I was a nervous wreck who could not fail, and I developed the habit of chewing my cuticles down to the blood, which I still do to this day. *The Book of Shame.*

I watched way too much television for that medium not to have embedded itself in my very being, and for all the positive I got out of it—learning that I wanted to be an actor, developing my sense of humor with the help of Bugs Bunny and Lucy, and just finding great joy in my shows and everyone in them—everything was so chaste and clean-cut, and that's what I thought I was supposed to be. We never showed skin in the house, and my parents were never openly affectionate to each other like Mike and Carol Brady.

I had so many questions that I never asked. A kid once told me how babies were made, and I didn't understand what he was talking about. On TV everyone wore nightclothes to bed and I wondered, how could that possibly happen through the pajamas? Why did only pretty people get a happy ending and everyone else was either evil or pathetic? Why did the kids on my shows have no greater conflicts in their lives than being grounded for missing class or mouthing back to their parents? And as I was developing attractions to stars such as Brian Kelly and James Darren, kissing them and making love to them by pillow proxy, I got the feeling that it was not natural because I never saw guys doing that with each other on TV. From the moment I saw other people's lives play out on the screen, I felt there was something wrong with me, but even before that, something very confusing was beginning to swirl around in my little boy body. *Me and My Shame.*

My parents had a full-length mirror in their bathroom, the only one in the house, and when I was eight years old, I would sneak in and grab a glimpse of myself, fully clothed, and I wondered what it would feel like to stand there naked, to see my body reflected back at me. The thought made me tingly Down There and I was not sure why, but I was afraid to actually strip down and look. I wasn't uncomfortable being naked alone in my room, where I really couldn't see myself; it was the idea of fully exposing myself to scrutiny in a mirror or being shirtless or naked in a public place that unnerved me. *The Shame and I.*

On summer vacations, I wore various matched swim sets of colorful zippered short-sleeve shirts and matching swim trunks. When I would remove the shirt to swim or sit in the sun, my sisters would point at me, laughing, mercilessly chanting, "Woo-woo! Woo-woo!" ridiculing my skinny exposed torso at the top of their hateful little lungs as if I were a dirty boy for showing my bare chest. It made me feel so vulnerable and ashamed, without so much as a *"Sha!"* from my mother to shut them up. I suppose I could have told them that, to me, in their too-tight one-piece bathing suits, they were less Brigitte Bardot and more Totie Fields, but I valued my life. I was beginning to feel my body was only meant to be private, that being naked or even shirtless was nasty. "Shut up! Just shut up!" I'd whine at them, which would only egg them on, parroting my shut-ups and laughing as they made the "woo-woos" louder and more nefarious. I'd cover my naked torso with my scrawny arms and try to get in the pool to hide until they stopped, and after they lost interest, I could spend some time lying in the sun, turning myself less pasty white, nervous that they'd start to chant again.

Once, on a summer vacation at the Broadmoor Hotel in Colorado Springs when I was eight years old, after a very public and painful "woo-woo," I ran from the pool to our hotel room and changed back into long black pants and a short-sleeve shirt. I came back out and plopped myself on a lounge chair. On that blazing hot day I sat staring straight ahead, sweating like a racehorse while everyone else frolicked in the water. *Grand Shame.*

Changing at the JCC for swimming was so stressful that I blacked out a little every time I had to take my clothes off. I would turn and contort myself to make sure no one saw my pee-pee. I couldn't get that bathing suit on fast enough, and afterwards, the public showers were a nightmare, especially after I was old enough to start getting aroused and erect. Nudity seemed utterly wrong and kind of scary. So I stopped swimming and doing anything for which I had to undress in front of guys, anything that required me to be shirtless at all, unless it was compulsory, like changing for gym class.

When the class basketball teams were Shirts and Skins, I prayed to the Lord above to make me Shirts. Sports were humiliating enough; I didn't need to show my bony chest while I was overshooting the basket, let alone show my penis and butt in the locker room. And I dreamed of being an actor but learned that, in the theater, sometimes people had to share dressing rooms. I thought, there goes THAT career. I think of that little boy, hating his body, wanting so badly to feel the sun on him but covering up out of sheer embarrassment and shame of exposure, of being skinny, and, way deep inside perhaps, of feeling "different." And with all that shame came ridicule and torture and assumption of sexuality on the playground and in gym class. I mostly played with the girls at recess—jump rope, hopscotch, tag—because "fag" came at me on a loop from the boys as far back as I can remember, long before most kids knew what it really meant. But inside, I knew that "fag" meant me. *The Shame Game.*

In fourth grade, my friend Moses Stein and I would hang out in his bedroom after school playing board games, but one day he stood up, went to his bed, pulled the covers down, and got in, fully clothed. He looked at me as if to say, *C'mon!* So I followed his lead and got into bed with him. He pulled the blankets over us and exclaimed, "Feeley Meeley!" Y'know, like the board game? It was dark under the covers, so I couldn't see what he was doing, but I felt him stick his hand inside my pants and play with my wiener.

It was shocking—no one had given my penis so much attention since the mohel at my bris. He stopped and I figured it was my turn, so I stuttered, "F-f-feeley Meeley!" I was really reticent because I thought penises were dirty, meant to be covered up and only exposed when you peed or showered (alone), but I did the deed. We'd go back and forth like that, sort of like "Seven Minutes in Heaven" only it lasted about a minute, and as I gave in to it, it felt better and better, and it was kind of funny and we would laugh like little girls, high-pitched *tee hee hee*

hee! We did it every time we got together at his house. I don't remember either of us getting erect.

It was just a lot of innocent diddling each other's preteen penises, but it felt good and amused us, and as lovely as his hand felt on my willy, I remember that, undercover, I enjoyed touching and fondling his. Since it happened under the sheets and blankets, and since I couldn't see him or what I was touching, it seemed chaste and natural. However, when it was over, we pretended it never happened, moved on to other games, and nothing was ever said or done about it above the covers. *Les Shamerables.*

I was eleven years old when Jerry Feinberg taught me how to masturbate. We were at his house one day after school and he said, "Wanna see something cool?" Without waiting for my answer, he lowered his jeans and briefs to his upper thighs, grabbed his dick, started playing with himself, and fell belly first onto his bed and began to hump it like a dog in heat, thrusting and moaning. He flipped around on his back and began vigorously jerking off, his eyeglasses fogging up and askew. He took deep breaths through his tightened lips as if he was blowing into a tuba. I was rapt but couldn't let on. I kept rolling my eyes and tried to look really uninterested. "Come on, Jer, that's stupid. That's just . . . really . . . stupid . . ."

I faded into silence and stared at him, slack-jawed, inert, and glassy-eyed, until he started to pant out of control, got on his knees, and pumped his hips, dribbling cum all over his hand, breathlessly muttering, "Yes! Yes! Yes!" When it was all over, he fell back on the bed and looked around for his Kleenex box, leaning over to grab one from his nightstand and sopping up the juice from his hand. I continued to silently gawk at his member with my mouth hanging open, finally shutting it and stuttering, "Okay. Okay. Good, um, good, let's watch TV," and I tried to cover the tenting of my pants. He hiked his up and we did indeed watch TV.

I couldn't for the life of me tell you what program it was. I was pre-occupied with the mesmerizing show I had just witnessed, playing over and over in my head as I stared at the set. Of course, when I got home, I immediately tried it myself. Instead of just lowering my pants, I took off everything but my T-shirt. I didn't want to jerk on my dick because I thought that was nasty (remember: penises = dirty, even mine), so I just lay facedown on the bed, put a pillow under me, and began to hump it as I had seen Jerry do.

Eventually, I got hard, and after a minute or so of thrusting, I felt this sudden intense feeling overtake my body, a scary, amazing, out-of-control sensation that I'd never felt before, and it led to my very first orgasm, hands free (and awake). I kept moaning, "No! No! No!" on each ejaculation. And by "No" I meant "Dirty! Dirty! Dirty!" I looked down at the gloppy mess on the pillow, jumped up, threw on some shorts, turned off the lights, and sat in the dark for an hour before dinner, thinking to myself, I'll never do THAT again.

The next day, I told everyone at school about Jerry and what he showed me. I think I felt that if I told people in a disdaining way, if I turned him in, I would be denying to the world—and myself—how much I actually enjoyed it. I know. I suck. *The Most Shameful Fella.*

Jerry never held that against me, and he later taught me a masturbation method that he said felt better than your hand. If you rolled up gym socks, pushed a plastic bag into the center, stuffed it between the mattress and the box spring, got on your knees, Vaselined up, stuck your erection into the plastic bag/socks, and thrust it in and out, it would feel like real sex. Sort of a vintage, makeshift Fleshjack. Who knew? But I tried it and it felt awfully good. Jerry told me this was a well-known masturbation technique. So you did this, too, didn't you? You didn't? *Shame-a Mia!*

We never talked about sex in my household. In fact, my dad and I never had the conversation about the birds and the bees. One day,

I think I was maybe twelve or so, he handed me a book and said that I should read it and it would probably answer any questions I might have about "things." I had no idea what he was talking about. Even though I had been masturbating, I didn't really think much about anything else of a sexual nature except what made me erect—handsome men— and so I was glad I didn't have to have an actual conversation with him. The book was called *For Boys Only*, written by one Frank Howard Richardson, MD, and it was about adolescence and how a boy can be "not only bewildered by the physical changes he is undergoing, but by the emotional behavior caused by these physical changes." PS, it was written in 1952. But I started reading, and in the beginning it seemed fairly helpful. I thought, okay, there's a masturbation chapter, and talk about testosterone, and—oh look!—wet dreams, that's what they're called, great, and uncircumcised penises, I've never heard of them, good to know, and then—boom!—out of nowhere there was a section set off by the question: "What I can't understand is what makes older fellows, and sometimes even men that you'd think were decent people, try to get boys to let them do things to them that they know they ought not to?"

And the answer in the book went on to talk about men who tried to undress and play with young boys, how mentally "off" they were, and how they needed to be reported and removed from society so they couldn't do any more harm and . . .

That's the entire section on homosexuality.

That's it. The word *homosexuality* appeared in the index at the end of the book, leading to those entries, but nowhere within the main pages. The takeaway was: homo = child molester. Thanks, Frank Howard Richardson, MD. You were a real peach. No wonder I didn't want to talk about the feelings I was having with anyone, least of all my dad. *Damn Shame!*

PAL JOEY

I was so *not* a Man. So skinny back in my grade school days. And I was trying to figure out the signals my prepubescent body and brain were sending me while watching Brian Kelly on TV, covertly fondling Moses's penis, and watching Jerry masturbate in real life.

Whenever I would see a man wearing a tank top at the beach or on TV, I would flush with a kind of heart-pounding yearning that I couldn't explain. They were so revealing, just that little extra skin you didn't get with a T-shirt, the arm muscles on display flexing with every movement. Tank tops were something I could never wear in public, but I so wanted to, even though my arms were sticks.

When I was twelve, I sneaked two tank tops into the pile of spring school clothing we bought at Mr. Eddie's, a men's and boys' shop in downtown Skokie where every boy bought their school clothes and bar mitzvah suits. One tank top was solid burgundy; the other, navy with thick stripes of cream running horizontally. I would try them on when the house was empty and stand in front of that full-length mirror in my parents' bathroom. I'd get all flushed and excited, revealing my skinny white arms. I felt naked and alluring as I imagined walking the conservative suburban streets dressed so provocatively, but I would never have dared to be seen like this in public. Echoes of "woo-woo!" reverberated in my brain.

Around this time, I started noticing other boys' bodies, pictures in magazines of shirtless actors from the movies and TV, and the physiques of my superheroes in the comic books I collected. I'd ride my bike all over town on Friday afternoons to my various haunts to get the latest issues of the Fantastic Four, X-Men, Avengers; I was a Marvel super-heroes guy. Every super-male seemed to have the same muscular body, sinewy and chiseled and bulging out of their tights, and even the ones like Spider-Man who were supposed to be gawky still had nice tits. I was mesmerized by their strapping torsos, their abdominal muscles rippling in every panel. Sometimes there was even a bulge Down There; a simple curve drawn from the tip of a pen and my little penis would feel . . . odd.

In junior high, I'd sneak my sisters' high school yearbooks into my room and covertly but enthusiastically jerk off to pictures of the boys' swim teams—teenagers in tight little Speedos; nipples, pecs, and baskets there on page 325 for me to lust after and envy. I knew I couldn't ever show off my body like that, especially smiling in a photo with other boys in snug little swim trunks. I was skin and bones, I had braces, and stupid Jewish Brillo pad hair that I parted wet on one side the night before so I could brush it straight the next morning on the other side. The Greg Brady curly 'fro was not yet cool. I was a textbook bar mitzvah boy in training. No guts, no sex appeal, no clue, really, but at least I could try on a tank top and dream.

After my sessions in front of the mirror, I hid the tank tops in the basement among the boxes of clothing we had outgrown. They remained my private fantasy, until . . .

Joe.

Joe was a jock, all stocky muscles, perfect lustrous straight brown hair, and walking confidence. We'd had various classes together all through grammar school and became friendly, hanging out at each other's house after school. Joe always wanted to play basketball, a miserable game for me in gym class as I was a ball-dropping loser, jeered at and pushed around even by my teammates, but Joe was the only boy who had any patience at all with my fear of anything rolled, bounced, thrown, or caught. He wanted basketball, so basketball it was. I wanted to please him. He had a hoop in his driveway, and we played a couple of times a week. I didn't really enjoy it, but I got a little better, and I reveled in the presence of a manly boy giving me the attention I craved.

We'd go back to my house and into the basement to watch our giant console color TV—the kind with the built-in hi-fi that smelled like it was burning as it warmed up. His family only had black and white, and color television was all I could offer and the only reason, I'm convinced, that he hung out with me. He would sit on the floor in front of our ugly gold couch and I'd sit on the couch right beside him, my leg nearing his shoulder. I'd move it closer and closer, but never let it touch him. I wanted to, but I couldn't push past that last quarter inch. I liked Joe. Really liked him. He wasn't at all like the other boys, who constantly picked on me; he was so accepting of me, and I wanted his attention, to be closer to him, literally and figuratively. To me, he wasn't a boy. He was a Man. It wasn't a crush; it was something else. What did I want? I had no idea. Something. I wanted to seduce him without even knowing what seduction was, perhaps to do with him what I had done with my pillow boyfriends. I wanted him to know how I felt, but couldn't speak about it. Maybe showing some skin would make it all clear to him.

I had a plan. One day I excused myself during *Dark Shadows* to go to the basement's utility room, where the tank tops were hidden. Like a boy possessed, I pulled off my T-shirt, heart pounding so loud I could hear it, and rummaged through the piles of clothing. Tank tops in hand, I weighed my choice: burgundy or navy with stripes? I was jumpy as a virgin bride choosing her first negligee. This would be anyone's first glimpse of me in such scandalous clothing. I chose the burgundy—I was always a simple girl—and put it on. I remember the lightness and excitement at the prospect of being so exposed, with no one there to yell, "Woo-woo!" Joe wouldn't do that to me.

I slipped back into the TV room. I thought my legs would fall out from under me. I kept thinking the couch, the couch, just get to the couch. Nonchalant, no sign anything illicit was happening, yet here I was exposing myself to the one boy willing to spend time with me and I was jeopardizing it—why? And what, if anything besides TV, did he want from me?

I melted onto the couch. Joe's eyes never left the set. He didn't seem to be aware that I had left the room at all. He took no notice of me or my attire. I stretched my naked arms and draped myself on the couch like Cleopatra. Our heads were now just inches away . . .

"I had to change," I murmured.

Not a word from Joe.

"I had to change," I repeated. "It's too hot in here, isn't it?"

"Yeah, I guess," he answered.

I was sorta kinda making a kinda sorta pass at him in a pathetic puppy dog way. I should have just licked his face altogether because I was clue-free as to what to do next. I thought that two boys doing anything intimate the way I'd seen men and women do in movies and on TV was just not possible. I thought boys couldn't touch or physically get near each other, except to slap each other's asses after a home run, touchdown, or goal, none of which I would ever get. I didn't even know what I wanted to happen next, but wouldn't it have been a big ol' kick if he'd turned his face to mine and growled, "That shirt looks so sexy on you," as he closed in for a big wet lip lock that would have made me explode Down There. It had been raging Down There the entire time, from when I left him to get the shirts until he got up and said, "Time for dinner, see you at school."

I changed back into my T-shirt before following him upstairs, as I was not about to invite the usual verbal abuse inflicted on me by my sisters. Nothing had happened, but when I think of those moments in Joe's presence, feeling all bare in a tank top with a little stiffy in my shorts, I have to smile—at my innocence and my loneliness, but mostly at the purity of a little boy who knew what he wanted in his soul but had no idea what it meant.

MILK AND HONEY

For all the enthusiastic TV watching I did growing up, nothing matched the 1971–73 Friday night lineup on ABC. I didn't give a shit about *The Odd Couple*, but I wanted to live with *The Brady Bunch*, I wanted to be in *The Partridge Family*, I wanted to study in *Room 222*, and most of all I wanted the men on *Love, American Style* to love me.

My favorite Friday night ritual was family dinner at Normie's Delicatessen (next to Weiner's Pharmacy, which provided my Hebrew school Jujubes fix) for a greasy cheeseburger, fries, and cherry coke, then home at 7 p.m. sharp for TV nirvana. It totally retarded my social life, but I lived for it. However, if Dad arrived home from work late, my whole evening got pushed back, the miracle of the VCR being years away.

On these nights, I'd eat that burger in any condition it was delivered—red, gross, and dripping in the middle, or done to the crispness of a rice cake. I'd wolf it down, plowing fries into my mouth at breakneck speed. Dad and my two sisters were slow eaters, and I hoped that upping the eating pace on my end might charge up the ions at our table and energize them so we could all finish up and get home, but ultimately, they weren't responsible for *Brady* preemption.

Mommy, on the other hand—I'd finish my minute-and-a-half meal then have to sit for forty-five minutes and watch her slice, chew, stir, butter, and salt her food as if she were dining with the Queen. Tiny portions made it to her fork, then slowly to her mouth, and then she placed the silverware lovingly on the proper side of the plate and put her hands in her lap, because of course it's impossible to chew with your hands full. There were years between bites, and I squirmed, whined, and became that cranky kid throwing a tantrum that we all want to shoot when we eat out . . . EH! EH! EH! I knew I was doomed when it was ten to the hour and a quick jaunt home would get me in front of the tube at seven on the dot if only Mommy didn't order . . .

"Coffee!"

That word curdled my blood. It caused me to violently fling my little body in all directions in the booth . . . EH! EH! EH! I wanted to knock everything off the table with one sweep of my skimpy little arm and yell, "Let's get the fuck out of here!" embarrassing my family in their weekly hot spot where everyone knew their name and every Jew in Skokie would know "That Pevsner Boy" was just full of *meshugas*. But no, I had to sit as she began her coffee ritual . . .

As soon as the cup hit the table, Mommy raised the cream container and said, "Milk, please." While our waitress Shoshana or Naomi fetched the moo, Mommy poured in two heaping spoonfuls of sugar in slow motion streams. The deli goddess returned with the "less rich" dairy product, and Mommy poured with abandon.

She languidly picked up her spoon to stir the coffee . . . clink, clink, clink. She cleaned the spoon on the saucer with another clink and laid it next to the cup. Clink. She raised the cup to her lips carefully, and took staccato slurps . . . two, three drops' worth . . . then lowered the cup into its little saucer circle, leaving a red imprint of her lips on the rim.

Her hands met, folded, and settled on the table, at rest until it was time to take the next sip, oh, some two or three minutes away.

In the interim, she stared straight ahead, fixed her hair and lipstick, waved at anyone she knew, anything to quietly eat up time, which I was made aware of by the sweep-second hand of the clock on the wall taunting me, "*The Brady Bunch* is *DEAD* to you!" This went on maddeningly until the cup was two-thirds empty. Finally came her signal to "the girl." Was it a quick index finger check mark for the bill? Or was it a gesture toward the cup, asking for a refill? If it was the latter, you could find me slipping under the table, kicking my legs and keening a double-desperate "EH EH EH!"

Eventually, it was time for "Check, please," and I scrambled out of the booth, rushing past the checkout with the gum and candy that I usually desired, ignoring the cashier who tried to say a jovial "Goodbye!" but never got past "G—" as I stormed out the door, not caring that I had just knocked over Mrs. Goldenbergenschwartzensteinman.

I stood at the car waiting for my family, futzing with the door handle as if I could magically unlock it, as if I could have driven the car home myself if it opened. Dad unlocked, and I thrust myself into the middle seat as everyone took their time getting settled. There was silence in the car on the drive home as I maniacally fidgeted. On arrival, I ran up to the front door, for which I was not allowed my own key yet. Fuck! I had to wait for Dad to open the door, and I pushed past him and into the basement to turn on our giant console color TV, wondering: had I missed the cool opening credits where the Bradys looked like bobblehead hostages caught in a tic-tac-toe board (or a modern-day Zoom conference call)? Did I miss the setup, the touching wrap-up, Mrs. Brady's fourth cup of coffee?

It didn't matter, because if I were so much as one minute late tuning in, it was like Woody Allen in *Annie Hall*, forgoing *The Sorrow and the Pity* because he had missed the opening credits. I didn't get up and dramatically leave the TV room, but the delay ruined all enjoyment, and for that I held my mother fully responsible. I'd go to bed without saying another word to her.

Today, when I hear the strains of *Brady Bunch* "lesson music" in my head, I realize Mommy knew what she was doing with the coffee routine. I used to think it was out of spite, but maybe, just maybe, she was trying to make a family moment last a bit longer before it once again got sucked up into the TV.

THE ME NOBODY KNOWS

When I reached puberty by age thirteen, on the days I had the house to myself, my visits to the full-length mirror became more intense. I'd take off my clothes and watch myself, wanking with as much adolescent carnal gusto as I could muster. The sheer freedom of being private with myself excited me, and the closer I got to the sensations of orgasm, the more the voices of shame faded away.

I would spend so much time in front of that mirror, pretending to be with whatever TV hunk I was into that day, not really knowing what I wanted sexually except the deep kissing I saw the boys do with their girlfriends and to touch those boys' shirtless bodies, and my penis responded to those fantasies. I enjoyed showing off like a male stripper for my private audience of one reflected back at me. Sometimes I'd put on the jockstrap from gym class because I covertly admired how beautifully they framed the other boys' butts.

It turned me on to imagine marching down Tripp Avenue in that jockstrap or a Speedo, showing off to my repressed suburban neighborhood and shocking the crap out of my family and their friends. But I knew I was too scared and ashamed to get past the bathroom door.

Sometimes I would go into my mom's panty drawer and slip on a pair of her nylon underwear. I didn't have a ladies' underwear fetish—it's just that I wished it were a bulge-inducing Speedo. They sold them at Mr. Eddie's, where I got the tank tops, but I was too embarrassed to even check them out, let alone actually wear one by the pool and give my sisters the opportunity to "woo-woo" me into a shame spiral. But those snug nylon panties gave me that superhero bulge, and I'd feel like the X-Men, the Avengers, and the boys I ogled at the pool.

I'd pull the waistband of the panties down and fervently masturbate, fantasizing that one day I'd have the courage to go out in public wearing a tiny bathing suit, drunk with abandon, shutting down the voices of disapproval in my head. And when that fantasy pushed me past that edge, I'd lie down on the cold bathroom tile and feel the waves flow through me, and then the unadulterated bliss of release.

Once I'd finished and my heart rate slowed, I'd feel that familiar intense remorse: that I was wearing my mother's underpants, that I was getting off to myself in the mirror, that I was doing the forbidden act of masturbation to completion, and that I would never be able to share this secret with anyone. It was as if hope left my body along with the jizz.

SONG AND DANCE

Like any good little blooming gay boy, I was a musical comedy whore who lived for Broadway show tunes. I discovered my folks' original cast albums when I was old enough to use the record player, and when no one was home, I'd go into the basement and crank up that burn-smell hi-fi stereo and sing into a microphone that was really an antique marble pestle.

I would emote the entire score of whatever musical we had at home or from the library: *Once Upon a Mattress*, *The Sound of Music*, and especially *Funny Girl*, because . . . well . . . Babs. I didn't really know how to sing properly, but I put my heart and soul into every note. My sister Janet once came down mid-concert, me flipping my head back, eyes closed, really feeling it. Seeing her on the stairs shocked me back to reality. I froze up as we glanced at each other. She just rolled her eyes and went back upstairs.

I turned off the stereo and sat motionless in the recliner, waiting to go up, hoping we would never speak of this. I'd be more careful in the future, checking often between numbers to see if anyone had come home. But as I got older, I got bolder. Mini-musical time . . .

*(Little David grabs a marble pestle and enthusiastically sings in his base-
ment to a song similar to any in the teenybopper oeuvre.)*

> *I gotta give it up to love.*
> *I'm sick of asking what if and why?*
> *I gotta give it up to love.*
> *I found myself a fabulous guy!*
> —from "I Gotta Give It Up to Love"

Pay attention! Attention must be paid. These thoughts forever
ran around in my brain and I finally got the nerve to go public. I had
started by singing commercial jingles at the top of my lungs in the
back seat of the car when I was five. My mom and dad seemed amused,
and I loved a captive audience. "Sing Ajax!" "Do Oscar Mayer!"
"Speecy Spicy Meatballs!"

(A sign drops that says Second Grade Talent Show! *David goes back to
center stage for the big finish. He sings . . . with choreography!)*

> *I gotta give it up to love.*
> *Put a pair of wings on and fly!*
> *I gotta give it up to love.*
> *I found myself a fabulous guy . . .*
> *uh . . . GIRL!*
> *I found myself a fabulous girl . . . uh . . . guy . . . girl.*
> *I found myself a fabulous Fabulous FABULOUS . . . !*
> —from "I Gotta Give It Up to Love"

From there, I began to write, direct, and choreograph little playlets
with mostly all-girl casts because the boys wouldn't be caught dead performing in them with me. I was such a little hambone. The teacher

would announce the onslaught of my forthcoming production and the class would start to rustle. I could hear stray little voices murmuring "Oh shit."

One of my greatest achievements was a musical based on the song "Windy." We sang about how she peeked out from under some stairway, smiling, tripping down the streets, and everybody knew it was Windy. I had no idea what the song meant or who and what Windy was, but I got a girl named Wendy to play her, so it all made sense. It was ten minutes of bracing and scintillating theater, turn cartwheels to the box office, complete with a finale of the actresses holding their arms out like airplanes, running in and out of the rows of the classroom and out the door, like skywriters leaving behind dust and ashes of drama on a mostly uninterested crowd of insensitive, uncultured, unappreciative little nine-year-olds.

I suppose the lukewarm reception I received as theater impresario and drama queen of the third grade should have halted my aspirations like a stop sign, but unlike being seen in a bathing suit, I couldn't be humiliated on the primary school stage, I had no fear of the scrutiny, I didn't give a shit whether they liked it or not—the teachers did. I was a tween fey David Merrick, a Show Boy who wouldn't say die!

But there was a cost . . .

(Lights change and David is now on a gym class baseball field. He recites . . .)

Standing here in right field,
twenty minutes to the bell.
That Nazi coach can call this "Gym,"
I just call it hell.

Baseball makes my skin crawl
and of course, they chose me last.

I'm useless as a player
so before this nightmare's passed . . .

(He sings . . .)

Take me out of the ballgame.
Take me out of this class.
Let me sing jingles and write my shows.
All I get is a punch in the nose
when I see line drives coming at me . . .
WHOOPS! They call me a fag.
So I'm one, two, three times embarrassed,
their punching bag!
—from "Take Me Out of the Ballgame"

In fifth grade, my classmates picked up a new vocabulary. *Fag. Faggot. Homo.* I didn't know what the words meant, but they meant ME according to the boys in school. I was just a smart little kid who liked to entertain and make the girls laugh. To the guys, I was breakfast . . .

They are natural athletes.
I'm a natural brain.
They're up to the plate and then, poof, a hit.
I cheer them on; but they treat me like shit . . .
—from "Take Me Out of the Ballgame"

. . . and the torture continued at recess. As on most days, I saw Gabe Kovinsky slowly approaching, eyes burning a hole through me. He was one of my many torturing nemeses, taking every opportunity to pick on me physically and verbally. Built like a powerful little fireplug he was, and I was no match in a one-on-one.

"Hey, faggot!"

"That's Mister Faggot!" I would have said if I knew then what I know now, but I hadn't an ounce of courage. I stood still, numb with fear, as he came face to face with me. He started poking at my chest with his fat little index finger. Maybe I seemed brave because I didn't run, but the truth is, my legs couldn't move . . .

. . . so I'd forge a note from my mother.
That worked until I was eight.
Stomach ache, headache, my aunt's sad fate.
Once, I said that my period's late.
There are no excuses for losing;
the boys just don't want to hear,
so it's one, two, three times I'm out and they call me queer!
—from "Take Me Out of the Ballgame"

The force from his prodding started pushing me backwards in jolts. I kept recovering only to be met with another push, and again and again, and I'd recover again and again until . . .

"Shit!"

Dale Lipschitz got on his hands and knees behind me and I fell over him like the ottoman in the opening credits of *The Dick Van Dyke Show*, only I couldn't see him and it wasn't fair. *Not fair! Not fair!* I thought as I tumbled backwards onto the frozen ground, landing hard on the small of my back.

So take me out of the ballgame.
Fine, I throw like a girl!
It's dirty, it's sweaty, I can't take the stress,
'cause next it's the showers and I'll have to undress
and I'll stand there fighting a boner

and all I'll win is more shame!
—from "Take Me Out of the Ballgame"

Ring! Recess was over. Dale and Gabe reacted to the bell like guard dogs and immediately forgot about me. Everyone ran past me as I just lay there, my little body in shock, grateful to be saved, yes, by the bell. No one paid attention, and I guess I was glad. My pants were ripped, my back ached, my face was red, and I was humiliated once again by the boys who knew I was a faggot even before I did. As always, I picked myself up, but I left some of my self-esteem in the dirt.

I stopped doing my shows.

So it's one, two, three times the anguish.
It's one, two, three times they hate me.
It's one, two, three times a SISSY!
The ol' ballgame!!!!
—from "Take Me Out of the Ballgame"

(Aaaand scene. Curtain.)

By fifth grade, gym class had seasonal cycles, each with a different sport: three weeks of baseball in the spring, four weeks of football in the fall, a plethora of ongoing horrors. Each cycle was varying degrees of Hades, and then it all moved indoors for the winter months: gymnastics, basketball, and the worst of all was wrestling. I was small and as noncompetitive as could be, and as much as I wanted to be a performer, I hated the spotlight on me doing anything sports related, one-on-one.

When it was time for wrestling, I wanted to die on a daily basis. I'd be paired up with some pubescent boy who threw me around the mat like a rag doll. The rest would cheer for him and jeer at me, and I could sense the unspoken "faggot" amidst the din. I fought back as best I could, but always ended up pinned, humiliated. I couldn't even enjoy the feeling of another boy on top of me because that would have opened another can of worms. I just wanted to get out of my match with some dignity intact, but I was a loser, literally, and the nasty boys never let me forget it.

The only kid I ever beat was a rail-thin Korean boy named Jin, and though I was relieved to finally win a match and hear the other boys cheering for me, I was sorry and ashamed that I wasn't kinder to him after winning. I fell into a drunken celebratory reverie when the gym teacher's hand slapped the mat after I pinned Jin, and said nothing in his defense when they threw their verbal brickbats at him, and I think I actually threw a few of my own.

But it was every man for himself, and in that rare moment of victory I lost my humanity and played the bully. At least as I remember it. School was a pecking order, and we scrawny boys were at the bottom, especially someone like me, a little gay boy under construction. I grabbed the chance to momentarily step up from the lowest rung of the ladder.

When Damien Gorgon (an archetypal teen film bully resembling a mini Danny Trejo) decided to lead "Let's Beat Up David" festivities on a daily basis in sixth grade, I took a karate class to learn to defend myself, but I never made it past white belt with a single orange stripe because I just did not want to fight. As "spiritual" as it was supposed to be, karate still felt like a group of boys in gym class watching me fail at sports. No thanks.

Gym class got worse in high school. We wore school-regulated Speedos for swimming class and I was despairingly self-conscious about The Bulge. I didn't know if my dick was supposed to curve down into the basket of the suit or straight up or to the side. I subversively looked at the other guys to see how they did it. Who knew there was a whole mélange of dick positions? I found curving it down helped alleviate the swelling I felt as we lined up to go into the pool area; just putting on a Speedo did that to me.

But the actual class was a big boner killer because I hated to swim. I thought I was going to perish every time I fluttered around in a pool (to this day my worst fear is to die by drowning). Beyond that misery, the jocks, who were starting to develop muscular, mature torsos, pulled out their bully best, mercilessly and gleefully chanting their own versions of "woo-woo" to us skeletons and big-boned boys standing awkwardly in our tiny briefs. Torturous.

And then came the showers after class, and I pretty much had to go into a comatose state, standing naked in line for a showerhead in the communal shower. Communal showers: injecting fear into little gay boys' hearts since, well, the dawn of communal showers.

> *Then like World War Two, we're forced to wait for the shower*
> *and I don't have the power to control my fucking glands.*
> *Thank god for my hands!*
> —from "Fight the Urge"

I stood there trembling, covering my "privates," praying to not give myself away so that the boys wouldn't know I was a faggot and beat me up and generally ruin my life the way they did in class, only now I was naked.

I'd think of ugly girls and body odor smells and my parents having sex and anything gnarly to stop myself from getting hard; breath control, cute puppies, show tunes, anything, begging the Lord to let me hold out until I got the towel handed to me like a trophy at the other end of the shower room so I could cover up.

> *So I'll never be normal and I won't have a wife.*
> *I can still have a life if I can get myself under control.*

That's the goal.
Don't think of a pole.
Or a hole.
—from "Fight the Urge"

And all the time, I'm telling myself I'm not normal, I'm a freak and a loser, and those perky show tunes running through my head would bleakly fade. That's how the whole thing felt—a slow, sad fade.

INTO THE WOODS

When I was thirteen, in 1972, I was forced to go to a four-week summer Jewish overnight camp in Michigan, although it might as well have been Dachau for how trapped I felt and how much I hated it. And funnily enough, they did indeed have "Concentration Camp Day." The counselors woke us in the middle of the night, made us get dressed, and, groggy and unsettled, we got in boats that took us across the river, where we waited, silently, until the sun came out. They then covertly floated us back across to find our cabins had become sanctuary ghettos, protected from the Nazis/counselors. After sneaking into our barracks, we had to go about doing chores such as finding food and water, and if we got caught by one of the counselors, we were taken hostage to a building next to the pool called the Bathhouse (for years that word had a terrible connotation until the first time I fucked a twink in a sling at the Unicorn in Chicago).

It was usually where we took our before- and after-swim class showers, but for this event it was "The Showers." My job was to get water, stealthily and carefully, and as I returned with two bucketsful, a Nazi-slash-counselor started running at me, so I dashed as fast as my little legs would take me, getting closer and closer to my cabin. I knew I could outrun him, but at twenty yards out I ran into a rope they had put up at neck level to contain us within the confines of our *shtetl*. I was practically decapitated due to my speed, but I slid underneath, safe, though I had a red, raw, bloody band across my throat for a week.

I survived the day, and in the evening, when the Jews were liberated from the Bathhouse (technically, they had died, but what can you do?), we all went to dinner, not knowing whether what we had just experienced was cool and educational or child abuse at its worst. (My nephew Ari, who's a rabbi, told me that a lot of Jewish overnight camps did this kind of event to illustrate how awful the Holocaust was, but they no longer do it. Smart move.) The camp was meant to duplicate the kibbutz experience, so besides sports and other typical camp activities, we would take Hebrew and Judaism classes and harvest vegetables for the meals on the working farm among the woodlands. You know, what every kid wants to do on their summer vacation.

I felt I had nothing in common with the rest of the boys, so being there was sheer torment. While everyone else was playing ball or hiking or kissing girls down by the lake, I was in the cabin reading *Dark Shadows* books. The only activity I was forced to take part in was swimming, which, if you'll recall, I just adored not at all. After, we would shower in the Bathhouse, but we stayed in our bathing suits, so I was safe.

The one bright spot was a camp counselor who had to be eighteen or so—tanned, taut body, long, sleek dark hair, stubbly beard. A dream. He doubled as the lifeguard, and always wore a tiny black Speedo, packed to the brim. When he showered, he loosened the drawstring so that the front would dip down and expose the top of his pubes. Oh, my god. I stared. I stared a lot, and I didn't really care who saw me, because I noticed the other boys staring too, we of the pubescent, unformed physicalities who all wanted to be him but had to wait five years or so, although I knew I would never look like that.

The water streamed down that gorgeously sculpted, shining body as if he were about to be photographed by Herb Ritts or Victor Skrebneski (who did those almost porn-like posters for the Chicago Film Festival), but my mind took the picture, etched in my brain to this very day. That's truly the first live erotic sex-symbol image I can remember, and I thank that beautiful boy for having the wherewithal to untie that drawstring in the shower. Perfect.

I spent the first two-plus weeks at camp agitated and unhappy, an outsider, with absolutely no enthusiasm for any camp activities. But something changed by the end of the third week, and I began to relax and enjoy myself as if I'd been replaced by a pod person, finding activities that hit a little more close to home, including arts and crafts, group singing, and handball, which my father played regularly and where I found I could hold my own if I played with other spazzes like myself. I even started a little flirtation with a girl named Naomi, which helped pass the time. My folks were shocked when they came to visit on the third Sunday, Parents Day, because I'd written a zillion "Hello Muddah, Hello Faddah" letters to them about how much I hated camp. I don't know how it happened, but the Kool-Aid was drunk. And the whole next year, I couldn't wait to go back to camp. I didn't shut up about it all year long.

However, that next summer, the instant I set foot on camp territory . . . boom. What was I thinking? I *hated* the fucking place. I didn't give a crap about any of the previous year's activities, I did not want to be around any of these people, any of those goddamn Jewish rituals, and I certainly didn't want to work in the fields or live with other boys in a cabin with the dirt and the bugs. And worst of all, the Boy in the Black Speedo didn't return. I despised all of it to the point where I was wondering if I was just plain anti-Semitic.

Total shutdown. I moped in the cabin for three weeks, until Parents Day. I packed my bag, fully intending to go home with my family even though there was a week to go. When my folks got there, my mom denied my request to leave, but I was resolute. Marilyn, the woman who ran the camp, was a friend and colleague of my mother's at the women's labor Zionist organization that they were active in, and offered to talk me down. She walked me up to The *Bayit* ("The House" in Hebrew, where the important people lived in luxury while we slummed in the crappy cabins) to chat and convince me to stay.

Ten minutes later, we strolled back to my parents with her arm around my shoulder, and she said, "Marcia. Take him home."

My mom's eyes bulged out and she got all huffy and said, "Why? Why should we take him home!?"

"Because he gave me an argument that I couldn't . . . I . . . I had nothin'."

"What did he say?"

She took a deep breath in and spoke, very deliberately. "He said, 'Camp is an outdoor place, and I am an indoor person.'"

Long pause. My mom glared at my dad with a sneer, shrugged her shoulders, gave me the stink-eye, and in a low growl said, "Get in the car."

I grabbed my bag, sauntered to our blue Toronado with a sly, subtle grin, and was liberated from the concentration camp. And I've never done any version of camping—except maybe a little bit of drag here and there—ever again.

THE PEOPLE IN THE PICTURE

In junior high, if you didn't have a girlfriend, you were either a loser or a fag. I made sure to have a different one each year. These relationships were less romantic and more brother and sister, but I was a funny, gentlemanly, gregarious boyfriend. I walked around with my arm draped around their shoulders and I think there were some make-out sessions. Honestly, I don't remember. It was more important that I showed everyone I was exactly like them, although the boys who called me "faggot" knew better than me what was really going on, because my attraction to the male body just confused me.

When the May 11, 1972, issue of *Rolling Stone* came out with the "nude" photo of David Cassidy from the TV show *The Partridge Family*, I wanted it. Bad. I was a passionate aficionado of that show, so the opportunity to see a sexualized Partridge thrilled me. I was actually more Camp Bobby Sherman because he was more mature and had a thick, sexy body. In 1968, Bobby Sherman made his mark on a show called *Here Come the Brides*, about mail-order brides in the Old West. It was pretty ridiculous, but Bobby and his TV brothers Robert Brown and David Soul were all tasty snacks. However, Bobby was the breakout teen idol from the show. I would grab the new issue of *16 Magazine* with my sweaty hands and sneak it into my stash of magazines and comic books. I loved the shirtless, benign photos of the young male stars, their innocent sexuality splayed out for young girls and homo boys to ogle and worship. *16* once did a photo spread of Bobby in which he did a handstand next to a pool in a Speedo. I couldn't believe they published it. Because of the backward curve of his body, his bulge popped out big as day as he smiled at the camera, probably thinking, "You're looking at my dick, aren't you?" Yup, Bobby, I certainly was.

Bobby Sherman never posed nude to my knowledge, but when David Cassidy's naked *Rolling Stone* pic came out, I told my eighth grade girlfriend Shirley about it, all "Isn't that weird that he would do that?" She was intrigued and I convinced her to buy a copy so that she could see—and, oh, bring it by 'cause I want to . . . umm . . . read the article. "Read the articles." She obviously hadn't heard that old saw in conjunction with *Playboy* magazine.

I remember Shirley bringing the magazine by my house. She always came to my place because I secretly didn't want to extend myself to be with her. She was a sweet girl and I liked her as a person, but there was no there there in terms of love. Though I tried to be the doting, affectionate boyfriend, there were times she kind of annoyed me because there was something else bubbling up in my soul that made me resent her advances. I was putting on a face and it was difficult to sustain. To get out of conversing too long on the phone, I'd eventually create a scenario and say, "Hold on. (*yelling*) What? Mom, what? What? Oh hey, Shirley, my mom needs me to take out the garbage. Bye!" Click. At the end of the day, I was fairly indifferent and unenthusiastic when it came to affection. I knew what I really was deep down and it was confounding as hell.

Shirley brought the *Rolling Stone*, and my dick was fully hard in anticipation. We opened the issue and turned to the centerfold (shot by

Annie Leibovitz), which depicted David, head thrown back with his eyes seducing the camera, wrapping his arms around his bare torso, revealing a thick thatch of pubes at the bottom. Kind of disappointing, but . . . pubes! Suggesting his cock, which I was imagining if the paper extended down another three, four, ten inches—who knows? We nervously laughed at it, tee-hee, pretty cool that he did it but maybe he shouldn't have, and hey, leave it here because I want to read it. She went on her way, and I took it into the bathroom and satisfied my teeny-bopper lust, which I did often to that picture and to handstand Bobby.

My friend Saul would buy *Playboy* monthly, and we read the magazines in his room, him focusing on the "hot chicks with big tits" and me subversively looking for whatever shirtless/naked man I could find next to the hot chicks with big tits. I especially liked when they would do the yearly roundup of Sex Stars, showing screen grabs of male nudity and seminudity in mainstream films, like Jan-Michael Vincent in *Buster and Billie*, Johnny Crawford (Chuck Connors' son on *The Rifleman*) in *The Naked Ape*, and Oliver Reed and Alan Bates in *Women in Love*. Saul's mom walked in on us one day, and I stood up like a lightning bolt, threw the magazine on the floor as if it didn't exist, stuttered a h-h-hi and g-g-gotta go, grabbed my coat, and ran out of that house, terrified. I didn't want anyone but Saul to know that I liked looking at nudity. If I'd been looking at women, I wouldn't have been so shaken. I'm sure I was on some page with some male movie star's dick hanging free, so being caught in the middle of that just flipped me the fuck out, and I felt depraved and disgusting. From then on, I started buying my own *Playboy*s whenever they had the annual Sex Stars feature because it was the only place I could look at lovely nude shots of famous men in private. But I was hungry to see more.

At sixteen years old, I discovered *After Dark* magazine. It was an arts-oriented periodical put out by the makers of *Dance Magazine*, and was about as homo-oriented as you could get without being porn. There were lots of pictures of male dancers in tights, actors without their shirts, sometimes in snug little '70s jean shorts, many of which were shot by the brilliant theater and dance photographer Kenn Duncan. Every issue was aimed at the gay male art/ballet/theater queen. Duncan's iconic photo of actor Maxwell Caulfield in a loincloth hanging on a rope is required viewing for every budding gay boy.

I later got a chance to know and work with Maxwell (he's a guest singer on my CD *Most Versatile*), and he and his wife Juliet Mills and daughter Melissa are the nicest folks around. I never told him about my crush, so he'll read it here. Hi, Max!

After Dark was harder to find in the burbs, but being a resourceful little 'mo, I was able to catch most issues at the only store near me that carried it, the Super X Drug Store. One copy was always relegated to the back of the rack, untouched and waiting for the one gay in town who had the courage to purchase it, and I heard it screaming at me, "Buy me! Take me home!" And I would.

I had a secret stash of *After Dark* and *Playboy* issues in an unmarked covered cardboard box that sat in the back of my closet along with my sexuality. I'd throw most other magazines and comic books into another box that was wide open on the floor of a wardrobe in my room where my mom kept extra linens and blankets. One day the summer before college, I was cleaning my room and I had the G-rated box out as I was going to prune down my magazines. My sister Janet came in and started riffing through the box and found the one *After Dark* I'd overlooked and neglected to hide—the issue with Ernest Thompson (at that time he was an actor, but later he wrote the stage play and film *On Golden Pond*) on the cover, wearing jeans, boots, and no shirt. Hawt. My sister picked it up and asked, "What's this magazine?"

"Heh heh heh, it's . . . um . . . it's a . . . thing . . . magazine . . . for the arts . . . kinda weird . . . but I like the theater reviews. Heh heh heh . . ."

Jesus.

As Janet paged through it, I tried to remember what level of nudity was in that issue. She put it down, uninterested, and I heaved an inner sigh of relief. I don't know if she was any the wiser, but I realized stealth was mandatory when it came to my media collection. Magazines like *After Dark*, *Playboy*, *GQ* (underwear ads in the back), and later the *International Male* catalog were the only access I had to images of male nudity and/or sexuality. I could have looked at art books at the library, but my aesthetic was a bit more lowbrow. I wasn't looking for abstract. I wanted the real thing: photographic depictions of naked men.

I don't remember exactly when I started looking at gay porn, but magazines like *Honcho*, *Mandate*, *Playguy*, *In Touch*, and *Stroke* both excited and disgusted me. I loved to see glamorized '70s and '80s porn bodies, men entangled, naked and erect, but I didn't like close-ups of hard cocks and spread assholes. That seemed kind of gross to me.

I was sensing that if I ever engaged in my true proclivity, I might have to get close to those bits in real life, and that mortified me. The idea that I would ever do anything sexual with another man just seemed so wrong, so punishable by death, that it was an emotional tug-of-war every time I opened a magazine. I love it, I hate it, I love it, I want it, I don't, I won't, I'll never, I need it—constant conflict. It was wrong and I was alone and I would never have the bond that my mom and dad had and I was going to spend my whole life having girlfriends like Shirley and no passion and no love and I told myself that was okay because I was going to be an actor, and there were no gay actors anyway, so I would be what I had to be and do what I had to do and it would have to be fine. That's what I told myself. Heady stuff for a sensitive, conflicted teenager.

THE BOYFRIEND

After not doing any kind of theater since the nasty boys shut me down in fifth grade, I got back on the horse during freshman year at Niles East High School and auditioned for the role of Prince Chulalongkorn in *The King and I*. I got cast and I was hooked. Doing theater became my reason for being. We had a prolific top-drawer program led by our terrific drama director/mentor, Jerry Proffit, and he always elevated us to be the best we could by choosing shows that no other high schools were doing, such as the rock musical *Two Gentlemen of Verona* and John Guare's *The House of Blue Leaves*. I was a proud member of the Thespians, a "theater jock." I even got used to changing costumes in the shared dressing room. The guys who beat me up in grade school became the hot jocks and sexy burnouts who hung out on Mulford Street, smoking cigarettes and acting tough, but I had found my circle and finally felt I fit in.

In my personal life, I was still confused. I dated a string of girls, but with every one I felt even more alone. I struggled with my attraction to male bodies, but there was so much about girls that I liked, as you would with any friends with whom you have so many things in common. My first journal is filled with my writings about wanting to be friends with other boys, talking "man to man," getting to know them better, but "not in a queeny way," covertly justifying this desire to get closer to guys without spelling out what that meant. There was lots of professing my attraction to girls in terms of their personalities but never their physical attributes.

The great "romance" of my high school days was Sheryl, a very sweet, pretty, incredibly smart young woman who had a wonderful, loving family who welcomed me with great warmth and inclusion. She was the epitome of the nice Jewish girl, so she paired perfectly with this nice Jewish boy. We dated for two years, until she went to college; she was a year ahead of me.

We were well matched in that we were both smart and not interested in sex; she made it clear that she was waiting for marriage. I think we really did love one another in our own way, but we were pretty much the safe choices for each other. I felt very protective toward her. One night I took her on a date to a drive-in to see a double bill of *Alice Doesn't Live Here Anymore* and *A Star Is Born* (Streisand/Kristofferson version). I had, of course, seen *A Star Is Born* twice already, and couldn't wait to share it with her (I might as well have worn a blinking sign YOUR WORST FEAR IS CONFIRMED). I sat with her in my orange Volkswagen station wagon that my sister Linda bought used and handed down to Janet, who then handed it down to me when she left for college. Linda had named it Adolf, not only based on it being a Volkswagen but as a dig at my mother, who was not a proponent of buying cars from Germany.

Adolf's heater was broken, and Sheryl and I sat together on this freezing cold night, shivering through both films, my bladder on the verge of explosion through the entire four hours because I chivalrously didn't want to leave her alone in the car. I did care about Sheryl, and I told myself I was romantically attracted, but it just wasn't there and I'd go home and whack off to *After Dark*.

During all that time together, I felt I should at least try for sex with Sheryl, but I wanted to respect her, so it was deep kissing and nothing else for two years. The night before she left for Harvard, nothing to lose, we were making out on her couch, and I let my hand wander to her breast and she politely moved it away. I tried three or four more times, but I knew it was not going to happen, and I was more than fine with that. I'd made my move, proving I was interested, so my secret was still safe. And we saw each other on her breaks from Harvard, but the "relationship" was over. Not the friendship, though—we are in touch to this day, and she's lovely.

I spent high school watching everyone else getting laid and having a fine old time while I was chewing my fingers off, getting ulcers over grades, and lying to girlfriends. No sex in high school, gay or otherwise—it was all masturbation all the time. *THE THEATAH* was my true mistress (my eyes rolled back in my head as a I wrote that, but it's the truth).

I did show after show, but beyond the plays we did, I absolutely revered musical theater. I felt my ambition swell to go to college and study acting, singing, and dance. The summer before my junior year of high school, my family and I traveled to London, England, and we went to see *Billy*, a musical based on *Billy Liar*, starring Michael Crawford. I was enthralled watching him (and a very young Elaine Paige) take charge of that stage the way I dreamed of doing. After that performance, I turned to my folks and said, that's it, that's what I want to do. (I would later sing Billy's "I Want" song, "Some Of Us Belong to the Stars," in *Reflections*, our high school talent show. I thought it couldn't be more appropriate.) I'd seen plenty of musicals, but this was the one that cemented my desire to actually do the showbiz.

My folks looked at me as though I were a unicorn because the only member of my family who was at all connected to show business was my uncle Leo, who was a jeweler but also a songwriter of dubious quality. More on him later. As much as I pressed to go to an arts college like Cincinnati Conservatory or Carnegie Mellon, both of which I got into, my parents insisted I go to the University of Michigan for a more well-rounded curriculum. Under protest, I gave in, and in the fall of 1977, I was off to Ann Arbor.

AIN'T MISBEHAVIN'

I spent my freshman year at U of M basically hating the place because it was a rah-rah kind of school and I was not a rah-rah kind of guy. Even the latrinal cakes in the men's room had big bright-yellow *M*s on them. My folks wanted me to diversify beyond just theater classes, nudging me toward a doctor/lawyer career, to have something to "fall back on." I now know they really wanted to spare me the heartbreak and struggle of being an actor and to go for a sensible profession first and foremost.

Besides my more mundane classes such as French, The Holocaust 101, and English Literature, I took acting and dance classes, and was able to land choice roles in a couple of extracurricular musicals: the lead role of Bill in *Applause* and one of the Jets, Baby John, in a fantastic production of *West Side Story*. There were other gay acting students in these shows, but I never brought up the G-word to anyone, even with a boy named Jason whom I followed around like a smitten puppy. He was blond, lanky, talented, and gay gay gay, but all the time we hung out, we never addressed the pink elephant in the room.

I spent the whole year dodging any consideration of my true sexuality, although I did have one last attempt at a girlfriend, a very sweet Michigan-born girl named Anne, but that fizzled pretty quickly.

My dorm roommate Nick had a girlfriend, and I was instructed to not come in if there was a plaid tie hanging on the doorknob. One night, after a long, exhausting rehearsal, I had had it with that game and, despite the tie, snuck in, lights out, total silence as they had finished shagging and were asleep. I went to bed and was awakened to the sound of him ramming into her with whispered "fuck me"s and "take my big cock, bitch," and I swore I'd never have sex with anyone, ever.

It was one long, lonely year in Ann Arbor (1977–78, the year Madonna was in the dance department—I was told she still owes my friend Lana fifty bucks), drowning in snow and sexual frustration and ignoring any class that didn't have to do with performance. I actually threw the finals in the non-theater classes; my answer to half the questions on the French exam was either *Je ne know pas* or *Je non care*. I convinced my folks how miserable I was and they finally let me major in theater and music. Reapplying and getting into Carnegie Mellon in Pittsburgh again allowed me to follow my heart.

My one year at Michigan in the closet was wretched and bleak, and I realized how desperately I wanted to break through the fear that was stopping me from indulging in my desires at school. You're supposed to be free to live your truth in college, but I just didn't have the nerve, and those shaming voices were screaming in my head whenever I got close to actually engaging.

I told my folks I was feeling depressed about generic "stuff" and asked if I could see a shrink the summer before I started at Carnegie. I didn't let on that I was hoping to deal with those voices and the angst and confusion about being gay, but once I started with the therapist, I was too scared to be forthcoming about my sexuality to him and we never discussed it. I would talk about school pressure or family dynamics, but after a while I went silent even on those issues.

Eventually, I got petulant and bored with him staring at me, saying, "What are you thinking?" and I would just stare back or say anything to cover up what was really going on, things like "I hate my sister" or "I'm worried about my career," which was bullshit because . . . what career? I never got down to the germ of why I was there, because I couldn't say the words "I'm gay" out loud, and the idea of sex in general gave me the heebie-jeebies. But fall was right around the corner, and I went to my new school in the same frightened headspace I was in before.

CRAZY FOR YOU

My first night in the dorm at Carnegie, a tall, willowy, gorgeous, and heavily inebriated girl from down the hall, whom I had met at orientation, knocked on my door in the middle of the night to see if I wanted to fuck. "David. David? You in there? Want me? Want me?" My roommate had not yet shown, so I was alone, and I lay in my bed trying to ignore her, eyes wide open with terror, shaking, praying she'd leave. Sex was obviously going to be a driving force at this place; actors + college + hormones is a pretty volatile combination. But I was locked in the closet and determined to live my life sexless, never to touch a man because of the courage it would take to come out, courage I didn't have. And that would have been all well and good had I not met Stan.

At orientation, I'd seen a boy who was the definition of my greatest attraction: Black Irish and all-American-looking, dark hair, thin but muscled, with dreamy eyes that seemed to bore right through my brain and down to my dick. Shades of my crush Brian Kelly. I was wildly attracted, but I felt in no way could he be interested in me. Stan was a serious Acting Major and I was a flighty Musical Theater boy. We spent a lot of time together in groups with the other theater majors, and I'd find myself staring at his perfect features, wondering what it would be like to kiss those lips. I almost couldn't breathe around him, and when he smiled at me, I got giggly and lost track of whatever I was saying. It sounds like a cliché, but what can I say? He was the reason clichés about love are created.

Stan was dating Sarah, a cute, witty, self-deprecating, and affable freshman actress. They were adorable together. Stan and I spent time away from the group and we'd talk and laugh a lot, and he was so smart and funny, but every so often he would drop the tiniest suggestion that there was something sexual going on between us, a lingering look or a slightly bawdy turn of phrase, which caused me to change the subject, cross the street, leave the conversation, anything to not have to deal with it. I had a sense he wanted something, but . . . Sarah.

The whole bisexual or experimentation thing never dawned on me. You were either "normal" or gay. I would sneak out to the off-campus magazine shops to look at gay porn, but it still turned me off to see the camera focusing on dicks going into holes, and close-ups of lube-y oversized penises filling the frame, as if that's what gay men are—giant penis racks and not much else. No love, no emotion. I was so scared of giving in to what I was feeling inside, not just because being gay felt like a life sentence of torture, but because if any boy touched my body, I was sure I'd go crazy with the shame of it.

Besides, I had a *nudnik* of a roommate, and though I had the bedroom and he slept in the living room, I couldn't even jerk off without feeling he was listening in.

I spent so much time dodging sexual overtures from Stan, ignoring comments filled with double entendre, that he finally got right to the point. We sat next to each other in the most boring class ever invented, History of Theater, and we'd scribble pithy comments in each other's notebooks for our mutual amusement, like "Lucy died and they played Babalu at her funeral!" We'd point at what we'd written, slyly look at each other, and giggle. One morning, as my mind was wandering, Stan snuck a couple of words into my book but didn't point them out. He just left them for me to find myself: "Fuck Me." I finally saw them, pretended not to see them, turned the page, and started absentmindedly taking notes, actual notes, from this snooze-a-palooza of a class. Nothing was said about those two words. But all I could think about was those two words.

Over Thanksgiving break, I went home and decided to have a session with the shrink. After a few niceties, I got right to it and admitted to him that I was indeed gay. There was a little stuttering, a little sweaty palmage, but it just came out fairly deliberately, almost clinically. I didn't have the big breakthrough moment because I wasn't revealing it to anyone I really cared that much about. I was able to tell him all about Stan, and to his credit he encouraged me to have sex with Stan, but added with a snooty Mr. Know-It-All sneer, "He probably looks just like you. All homosexuals are narcissists." I chuckled, because I didn't know what the hell that meant and didn't really care; I had gotten the okay to move forward with Stan and pursue. But something about the shrink's attitude perturbed me, so when I got home, I grabbed the dictionary, looked up *narcissist*, and was incensed. I thought, a) No, because I would never have sex with anyone who looked like me, yuck, and b) Fuck you, asshole.

However, when I got back to Carnegie after Thanksgiving, I was scared and apprehensive, but I was ready to engage.

I loved my classmates, and when we weren't in class or rehearsing scenes, we spent time in a group as often as possible. We got onto the subject of drinking liquor one day and I told them I'd never gotten drunk and that I hated the taste of alcohol, which was met with a lot of "Whaaaaat????" Afterwards, Stan pulled me aside and said I should try a 7&7. He said, "Friday night. Come to my dorm. I'll make you one. You're going to love it." It was going to be just him and me, and although

I had been in his dorm room to work on lines and talk theater, I had pushed any overtures away, any moment he moved a little closer as we spoke, and left when it felt a bit too real.

But that Friday night, December 1, 1978, I arrived at his place and he had a minibar set up: Seagram's Seven, 7UP, two glasses, ice. He gave me a taste of just the alcohol, which made me gag, but then created the concoction and I actually kind of liked it. We drank a little too fast, and it led to some loose lips, him telling me that he and Sarah had gone no further than making out, that it was over and they were just good friends, and that he thought he was really gay.

Hearing all this, I was a bit thunderstruck, but I kept nodding like a bobblehead, nonchalantly uttering, "Oh. Oh. Uh-huh. Oh." But the drink was making me woozy and shaky and sweaty from the heat in the room magnified by the extended Pittsburgh Indian summer and I couldn't stop looking at how his jeans were tugging at his crotch area and he looked even more beautiful to me in this newly altered state and my heart was bursting in my chest and I finally blurted out, "I think I'm gay too!"

I nearly fainted. Saying those words, out loud, to a boy that I liked . . . holy crap. I never thought the day would come. In the moment that closet door cracked open, yeah, I was a little drunk, but in the aftermath of vomiting out those words, I felt no shame or fear.

I think he was amused at the shocked look on my face, and he smiled at me with affection and empathy and it made my heart soar and I felt strong. We talked about our sexual histories. Mine was absolutely zero, his included fooling around with boys and girls, and though he had gone through some confusion, he was starting to acknowledge where his truth lay. Then he added that, of everyone, he'd found someone he really liked and wanted to get to know more—me. I kept going, "Heh heh heh," as if I thought he was joking, and I told him that I'd have to think about it and that I wasn't ready, and he said, "Well, I'm having a hard time holding back from kissing you."

Heh, heh, heh.

I left his room with those words hanging in my ears and an erection in my pants.

We had drinks in his room a few more times, and each time I loosened up enough, first to let him kiss me (I think I passed out for a second), then to make out—eventually with tongues—but he knew I wasn't ready to push things forward. Though I was insane with desire whenever our lips touched, I would resist his advances when it got too involved. What I put him through. Jesus.

About a week after my first 7&7 encounter with Stan, after I got particularly plowed (by the alcohol, not him), we took a walk into Schenley Park. It was a frozen evening and we were both bundled up in winter coats, sweaters, shirts, hats, scarves, layer upon layer. It was too cold for anyone to be out, but we found a spot to sit away from the wind, and as we talked, we inched closer and closer until our bodies were hugging, entwined—a mass of wooly layers and horny boys.

I felt his hand start to wander, and I sat, a bundle of tension, as he worked that hand in an almost comical journey through that mass, first unzipping my coat just enough to get his hand on my thick cable-knit sweater, which he lifted up so that he could get through to the button-down shirt, undoing three buttons to get through to the T-shirt underneath, which he gently tugged out of my pants, and the shock of his cold hand touching my naked flesh made me shake with a need I didn't even know I had, and I kept taking in little short bursts of air as if I was on a funhouse ride that I couldn't get off if I tried.

None of my skin was exposed to the elements. I was still buried in warm layers against the cold dryness of the evening and he just kept burrowing deeper and deeper and lower and lower, and I thought I was going to die, just die, as he began finagling open my belt so that he could undo the clasp of my pants to get to the zipper, lowering it with care, pushing away the sides of the open fly, gently rubbing his palm up and down the bulge of my Hanes until he pulled down the waist-band and let his index finger barely graze the tip of my rock-hard cock, and the instant he made contact . . . BOOM.

My body exploded from within and I shot and shot and shot and shot and shot and he held me close and I whimpered and cried and felt his hand pull away, slowly retracting back through the maze so that he could wrap his arms around me and just let me be in the ecstasy/emotion of the moment. When the storm passed, we barely said a word as I hitched up my pants and got myself presentable, and he took my hand and we walked back to our respective dorms in total silence. When I got back to my room, I looked for any signs that it had happened, but I could find no dried jizz, nothing from what felt like gallons of cum shooting out of me, on any of the layers of clothing. It was the Immaculate Ejaculation.

We continued to get together in his dorm room, and it always took a 7&7 or two to relax me into kissing because I was still in such a place of shame when it came to sex. We experimented with fucking and sucking, him being the seasoned pro and me the clumsy newbie, never getting past the pain of feeling his dick push into me. Eventually, I mostly just did it to him, but only when he requested it; it was like a special event. It also took me a while to get my head around giving head; the idea of a cock in my mouth was still kind of disgusting to me. All those porn magazine close-ups of drippy dicks made them seem so nasty and taboo, so I had to take Stan's lead when it came to cocksucking and just mimic it. His enthusiasm for my joint eventually rubbed off a little bit on me for his very pretty cock, but it was still not my favorite activity.

Being naked with Stan, kissing him, feeling closer than I'd ever felt to anyone—that was my favorite activity. Everything else, though it felt good, had some measure of shame attached. And because we both had roommates, we had to be tactical about when we had sex, and we never slept at each other's places. We never spent the whole night together and never got to have morning coffee while snuggling as the new day began. But I was gaga for him, and we were boyfriends, under the radar, on the down low, as neither of us was out to our friends. When we'd say goodbye to each other in public, we'd croak, really butch, "7&7," which was our code for "I love you."

Evan was one of my best friends at Carnegie, and though we talked about almost everything and were as close as could be, I did not let on that Stan and I were seeing each other. I wanted so badly to tell him, but that would have meant coming out, and though I was surrounded by a world of gaydom at this School of the Arts, it still felt impossible to be out and happy.

One day, Evan and I were going to meet for lunch at the student union cafeteria in Skibo Hall. I had gotten my food and was seated at a table, waiting for him. He showed up and seemed angry that I already had my lunch in front of me. He ran out of the building and I scurried after him to find out what was going on. He yelled that he had found out about Stan and me and why didn't I tell him?! I screamed back, "I was scared!" We went at it, two teenaged drama queens having meltdowns in the middle of the quad: "I wanted to tell you, but I couldn't!" and "I'm your friend and you couldn't trust me?!" and back and forth, and we're crying and yelling and making a gay ol' scene.

Eventually it all calmed down and we hugged, and it was good to be out, finally and fully. Stan and I were able to hold hands during group activities and I was blissful. Even Sarah was happy for us, and she and I became good friends (she recently told me that it was easy for her to accept Stan being gay because every guy she'd ever dated back then eventually came out of the closet). I went to Stan's home in Upstate New York over Christmas and met his family and helped with all the Christmas rituals, like schlepping the tree back to his house and decorating it, taking part in all the Christian family traditions

I had never experienced. I had asked my mom one year if we could get a Chanukah bush and she glared at me, bloody murder, and said, "There. Is. No. Such. Thing. As. A. Chanukah. Bush." Never brought it up again.

Stan and I had to sleep in separate bedrooms and I can't remember whether he or I thought it would be weird and distracting to have sex under his parents' roof, so we fucked in the family car. We then creeped back to our respective rooms. For the two months we were "official," I never really gave in to my animal impulses because I was the good boy, absolutely appropriate, even when naked and fucking.

By the end of the relationship, fucking was still fraught and difficult, regardless of whether I was topping or bottoming, which I never got the hang of. And though kissing Stan never got old, oral sex still repulsed me a bit. At that time in my life, I think I was great at love but lousy at sex. The effort to remain discreet and proper killed the feeling. As a result, I started to sense him pulling away. Stan never ignored me, but he began to treat me the way I treated Shirley, my eighth grade girlfriend, as if I were an annoyance. I felt as though he got what he wanted and needed more, so within a few weeks of our return from Christmas break we were spending less and less time together.

The sex was done and I had the feeling I would never find another boyfriend since he was over me. Stan moved on to other freshman guys whom he helped "come out" and I got through the year with a broken heart, vowing to never let myself open up like that again. Stan left Carnegie for New York City after our freshman year to start his acting career, and I was able to move on, but it was a while before I let myself get involved or even have sex—with anyone.

However, I put his name in an empty journal. His was the first in what was going to be my record of everyone I ever slept with in my entire life, my own "Book of Lust" . . .

See this massive volume?

It's my comprehensive listing

Of everyone from forty years of boyfriends, tricks, and trysting.

Each name brings back sweet memories,

from gentle hugs to fisting.

Excuse me as I try to keep my roving eye from misting.

It took a while to get the nerve to touch a naked man,

But once I did, the floodgates cracked . . .

Here's where it all began . . .

With Stan . . .

—from "The Book of Lust"

That solitary name was pretty lonely in there through most of college, because sex just flipped me out. But there was much more to come. Much much much more.

A CLASS ACT

These days I don't really care, but I used to be a bit of a clotheshorse. I always loved shopping for new school clothes, and was usually the only boy who actually thought about fashion. In 1967, I was the first in my school to rock a Nehru collar and huge peace sign pendant around my neck. In 1972, I wore a royal-blue polyester leisure suit with a heavy cream wool turtleneck underneath to my bar mitzvah party (I was stylish but sweaty). When *Saturday Night Fever* came out in 1977, I had the tight rayon pants and Qiana shirt that made me look like a beanpole in decorative plastic. I didn't always get to wear what I wanted. I bought my first flowered shirt in eighth grade, but my mom suggested I return it because it was too . . . you know . . . and I did. She was watching out for me, knowing my history of getting bullied, but I regret not giving that beautiful shirt a chance.

College was a great place to develop your style, with all the resale shops and boutiques like the ones in Shadyside, the trendy little college town next to Carnegie's campus where I shared an apartment after moving out of the dorms. The bright-orange linen pants I bought from Stylegate in 1979 were the talk of the town.

Clothes became a clear means of expression to me, and I didn't realize how important they were until freshman year at Carnegie. We were doing a simple sense memory exercise in acting class. I was recalling the time at recess when my gym buddies Gabe Kovinsky and Dale Lipschitz double-teamed me (not in a good way), Gabe pushing me over Dale, on his hands and knees, me falling to the ground, dirty, clothes ripped, humiliated.

I told the story in a calm, deliberate, and matter-of-fact way—very much the storyteller. We were supposed to relive the moment as we spoke, so my eyes were closed. I finished, satisfied that I had told the story as it happened. The teacher said, "That was fine." She paused for a moment and then asked, "What were you wearing?" I thought for a few seconds and then said with a gulp, "My brown . . . corduroy . . . co—" All at once I felt such a rage, emotion and tears started to build up from somewhere so deep I didn't even know it was there, and when I got to the word *coat* it was a primal gut punch that extended the word: . . . *cooooooooaaat!!!!* I had such over-the-top anger and anguish in my throat that it was almost absurd, like a banshee, and I ached, physically and emotionally.

I bawled my eyes out, choking and keening. I'd never dealt with that traumatic memory as an adult, but the detail of what I was wearing immediately took me back to the scenario and I experienced the stabbing pain and humiliation all over again for a live audience. Somehow, the teacher knew the detail about clothing was going to be the trigger.

These days, I don't pay as much attention to my attire as I used to. It's all top-notch resale for me. However, when I do a play, film, or TV show, the wardrobe really helps connect me to the inner workings of the character.

And I still get hard every time I put on a Speedo.

FALSETTOS

Carnegie taught not only drama and music, but self-preservation as well. The teachers believed every actor should be able to play every role, from Prince Chulalongkorn to King Lear. So, if you were a fey young man or an overweight girl, the faculty could be merciless, browbeating and threatening us that we would never work if we didn't butch it up or drop the weight.

I was just on the edge of effeminate, so they were able to whip me into "manhood," but others didn't adapt, either because they couldn't or, to their credit, wouldn't. They got kicked out of the program. Bagged. Some of us survived, but it was a constant burden on our sensitive hearts and fragile shoulders, always waiting for that shoe to drop.

And when we had to do things that were outside our abilities as artists—such as stage crew, freshman year—it became downright embarrassing. After building sets for the play *The Servant of Two Masters*, and mucking up everything I was handed to do, the surly crew head called us all together and said, "Okay, you all need to be here next Sunday to strike the set. And if you have an extra hammer, bring it along." Then he looked me smack-dab in the eyes. "You do know what a hammer is?"

I felt like I was back in gym class. Asshole.

I had a voice teacher named Miss Leech, a squat, brazen Texas woman with fiery, curly red hair and big round glasses—a cross between the actress Edie McClurg, musical theater legend Ethel Merman, and Little Orphan Annie. She hated any music written after 1945. I asked to sing a song from *Pippin*. "I hate that rock and roll!" she'd bark, and then forced me to sing big, booming classical art songs and "The Olive Tree" from *Kismet*, which I loathed. I understood I had to learn that kind of material from a technical perspective, but I didn't connect with it at all, and she never allowed me to do songs that really spoke to me. If any of us little musical comedy boys brought in a song made famous by a woman, she'd grab the music and shriek, "It's a girl's song, honey!" That not so subtle nugget of homophobia was lost on me at the time. I had come a long way from singing Barbra in our family basement, but that was the music I was most attracted to and wanted to include some in my repertoire. She was not having it. We just didn't get along, so senior year I was assigned a different voice teacher who allowed me to sing a little of what I wanted as long as I sang all of her designated music.

At the end of each school year, we had to perform individually in front of select music faculty so they could assess our progress in vocal technique and performance. At our senior year final juries, having traded in for that new voice teacher, I stood in front of the whole music department staff, Miss Leech sitting off to my right, all of them staring intently with huge expectations. First I sang my art song ("Beau Soir" from the album *Classical Barbra*), then my legit musical comedy song (some big baritone thing that I can't recall and felt no affinity for), and then the third piece was of our own choosing. I said, "And now I'm going to sing 'A Quiet Thing'"—I shifted my head and glared at Miss Leech squarely in the face—"as sung by Liza Minnelli."

Miss Leech picked up her knitting and ignored me.

HANDS ON A HARDBODY

In the remaining years at Carnegie, I could never just hook up for no-strings casual sex. It took eons of loosening up before I could get naked with someone, which, if it happened at all, pushed the actual act into the wee hours. On Saturday nights I frequented a bar in Pittsburgh called The Tender Trap, which had the lowest ceilings I'd ever experienced in a public place (until I went to the Monster in NYC). It was dark, sweaty, and musty, but full of energy and college boy sexuality. One night a young man in Jordache jeans and nothing else started to bump up against me on the dance floor (literally doing "the bump"). He was blond and all-American, with chiseled pecs and abs like a gymnast. The daily dance classes at school made my body lean and tight but hardly a muscle man like this guy, and I was still awkward at meeting and engaging with men in bars.

We danced for a bit, him rubbing his naked torso against me, and finally he gestured me off the floor and asked me to his apartment, and we left together. I couldn't believe this handsome god with a golden halo surrounding him wanted me, because guys like him didn't usually give the plain Jewish boy with the 'fro a second glance. But here we were.

When we got to his place, he excused himself to go into his bed-room. I sat on the flowery slipcovered couch among a large community of tastefully patterned pillows, nervous, inert, waiting. He came back in wearing a white, flowing caftan. "Oh!" I blurted as this puffy cloud floated toward me. I wasn't ready for that. He was so masculine in the bar and suddenly he was Auntie Mame making her grand entrance. It didn't make me want him less, but he did drop a few notches on my Brian Kelly masculinity scale, which was unfair and pretty awful, this self-imposed concept of what made a man a Man.

The Adonis stood me up and kissed me, and even though it was two in the morning, as was my way, I said that I would like to get to know him a little bit first, before we got down to business. With a shrug and a slightly irritated sigh, he sauntered over to his Barcalounger, plopped himself down, and said, with just enough snide bitchery, "Whaddaya wanna know?"

Somehow, hearing that question in that tone made me want to know absolutely nothing about him, but I had thrown down the gauntlet. I sat down and asked various stupid, non-probative ques-tions, and after a few of his pointed, cursory answers, I said, "Okay, I'm ready." He came over to the couch, lifted the caftan, pulled my face to his dick, and I sucked him off and later fucked him. Other than that, I remember nothing except that, after I came, I needed to get out of there. That's not just a limited recollection due to my present senil-ity. It was just dull. That's what sex was like in college after Stan. I had a few trysts, but nothing ever happened spontaneously. I needed to know the person better before I'd get naked, and some would play that game and some wouldn't.

Mostly, I was postponing that feeling I knew was going to wash over me once the jizz shot out of my body—the tortured guilt for what I had just done, just like after I ejaculated in front of that bathroom mirror as a boy. It's as if semen contained not only the potential to make new life but all my hope and self-worth, and when I would cum, both were all gone and I felt I would never find love or understanding, that I was a despondent, hideous, undeserving nobody.

SHOW BOAT

I tried to use my summers between semesters to work or study. The summer of 1980, between my sophomore and junior years at Carnegie, I was about to start a contract for a musical revue show at Busch Gardens Theme Park in Cincinnati. At the last minute I got an even better gig performing on the *Royal Viking Sky* cruise ship, which not only was going to be the best-paying job I'd ever had (my pre-college summer gigs had been caddying at a suburban golf course, scooping ice cream at Baskin-Robbins, and assistant at a school for special needs kids) but was going to allow me to travel and meet diverse people. I was so damn excited.

I didn't have my passport with me in Pittsburgh, so I had to make a side trip home to Skokie to pick it up, as well as things I needed for international summer travel. I had one night at my parents' house and then I'd get on a plane to New York, where I'd meet the ship and we'd start our Atlantic crossing. My sister Linda and newborn nephew Ari were staying with my folks while my brother-in-law was in Florida house hunting and starting his practice as an osteopath. When I got home, I found Ari sleeping in my room, which was a problem since I had to get in there to search for the passport and the other stuff I needed.

I was stressed about the journey, and had no idea what to expect from the job and all the travel, the first time I would ever be overseas without my family. I was pretty on edge. I'd gotten into town late, wiped out, and had an early flight the next day. When I told Linda I had to get into my bedroom, she said, "Too bad. Ari's asleep and he's going to sleep through the night. You can't disturb him." I replied in a panic, "No! No, I have to get in there! I don't have any time. You have to let me get in there. I won't wake him up. I just need to find my passport!" She said, "So-rry," like a royal bitch and walked away. I spent the next couple of hours watching TV, seething.

Linda was totally playing with me because, sure enough, the baby woke up and started crying and she and my mom went in to change him. The lights were on and I started searching. As my mom diapered Ari, I started to unload on my sister, that she knew I'd be able to go in, that it wouldn't take all night, that I was really nervous about the traveling and that she wasn't helping me at all, and as I anxiously rambled on, she started that mocking thing, mouthing every word I said as I said it, petulantly ridiculing me, as she often did. I usually just sat and took it and walked away with my tail between my legs.

Not this time. I was exhausted and angry, and all my defenses were down. Something in me snapped, and I charged over to her and violently raised my hand as if I was going to backhand her across the face. It was a reflex I'd never felt before, totally out of control. As much as I had gotten beaten up in school, my instinct was never to fight back physically, even after I took karate briefly, but something happened here. I had had enough.

I didn't follow through. I stopped myself after my hand flew up almost involuntarily to slap the crap out of my sister. She flinched and I saw real fear in her eyes. As I got control of myself, she nervously chuckled and said, "Ooooo," the way kids do if they're not impressed or afraid, but I could tell it unsettled her. She looked at my mother and said, "Hey, look what he just did. He was gonna hit me." And my mom just said, "Linda. Think about why he did that." Mom picked up Ari and took him out of the room. She stood up for me. That never happened, ever, when my sisters picked on me. And Linda kind of skulked out of there with *her* tail between her legs.

I ran into the bathroom and just started crying. I'd never felt like that before. The crazy, turbulent, unstable impulse frightened me, but something shifted inside in that moment, and once I got over the confusion and the trauma of it, I felt very solid and strong. And my sisters never picked on me again, because I wouldn't let them. I was starting to learn that when I was put down and made to feel like shit, it wasn't totally my nemeses' fault. It was me letting it happen, never fighting back. And in that moment with Linda, this became crystal clear.

The *Royal Viking Sky* was the Cadillac of cruise ships, smaller but more exclusive and ritzy. I performed in four different musical reviews, my own club act ("Let's welcome the Young and the Restless . . . David Pevsner!"), and a duo act with my friend Amy that made us the Donny and Marie of the high seas. We traveled through the fjords of Norway, to Russia, Poland, Greece, everywhere. It felt so glamorous, like an Aaron Spelling production, and we had our own versions of Julie, Gopher, Isaac, Captain Stubing, the whole crew.

I was able to split the six-month contract with another Carnegie actor who was not returning to school in September, so I made this my summer job and then returned to school in the fall while he took over for me on the ship.

I never slept with any passengers, although a very WASP-y family came on for the Atlantic crossing that I spent a great deal of time with: a brother and sister—twins—unbelievably beautiful people, and about my age, twenty or so, traveling with their parents. I was smitten with both of them. The girl, Harper, took a shine to me and we began a light flirtation, but it was her brother Yates—yes, *Yates*—that I thought of while I was having sex with a random waiter down in the servants' quarters.

Yates was an all-American ginger boy with blue eyes and a polo player body, and straight as a ruler. Both Harper and Yates were very sweet, and unaware of how gorgeous they were. Harper wore a stunning Missoni dress to the ship's opening night party and Amy mentioned how much she admired it. At the end of the cruise, Harper handed her a package—with the dress. I liked Harper so much, she was so smart and beautiful and classy and affectionate toward me, and I wrote about her in my journal, but it was Yates that I thought about constantly. Nothing physical happened between me and either of them, but I can see his face clear as day—a boy I could never get (straight wasn't so much the issue as that he seemed way above my league).

My big affair aboard the ship was with one of the French waiters who smoked like the Burning Bush and barely spoke English, but he had dark eyes and hair and a tight, compact, muscled body, and he wanted me. He was a troublemaker, so we had sex in places on the ship that were off limits to most staff. I kept thinking of Sally Kellerman in one of my favorite movies, *A Little Romance*, talking about the young man Diane Lane is in love with, referring to him as "that filthy French boy." That was this guy—filthy, with overwhelming smoker's breath, but so damn sexy. The affair lasted about a week.

The summer of 1981, before my senior year at Carnegie, I went to the American Dance Festival in Raleigh, North Carolina, to up my game as a triple threat musical performer. I needed to strengthen my dancing skills and I thought the immersive four-week training would be the perfect setting. It was there that I finally had sex with a woman—yay me—a gorgeous dancer from Louisville, Kentucky. Long, shimmering blond hair, big saucer eyes, sexy dancer body. We started as friends, but

I always found her staring at me with a suggestive little glint in those flirty eyes.

I put her off as much as I could by deflection and making jokes. She had been determined to get me into bed, so two nights before the end of the festival she got me drunk on Strawberry daiquiris—yup— and we did it in her dorm room. We kissed a bunch, she blew me, and then we did the deed. I remember how good it felt when I was inside her, and with my eyes closed it felt a little like Stan's butt—which, though I had my conflicts about fucking him, I remembered as being glorious.

It was a little weird that I was surrounded by horny male dancers and I slept with a woman, but I had a nice time. It was more being naked and hard in front of anyone that got me off. This was pre-AIDS, so we didn't use rubbers, and she said she was on the pill, but to this day I keep half an eye on my front door, expecting to hear *ding-dong* and open it to an earnest, needy fortysomething with a Southern accent: *"DADDY!!!"*

It could happen.

SCANDALOUS

Back at school and counting the days until graduation from Carnegie, most of us were setting our sights on moving to New York and starting our careers, so we had less patience for the dreck the teachers threw at us. They would truck in special guests to do workshops with us, one of whom was Richard Schechner, celebrated for creating performance techniques that mixed artistic disciplines with the academic and psychological. He made us do all kinds of weird-ass exercises that not only delved into our emotional lives but also became very personal, sometimes in a detrimental, invasive way.

In one session, the class sat in a circle, and after an exercise in which we had to tell something about someone *not* in the room, we were challenged to tell something about someone presently *in* the class. Most folks said benign things like he has a gerbil or she's a pro-quality bowler, but one of my classmates chose that moment to out my friend Jeremy—how Jeremy had privately showed him photos of his boyfriend who lived out of town. Jeremy had had various girlfriends through school, so after four years together we were astonished to find out that Jeremy was bisexual—privileged info for anyone who was still in the closet.

The silence was explosive as we all gawked at Jeremy, slumped down, pain and embarrassment written in red all over his body, not just as a result of the public outing, but also because his "deception" had been revealed when the rest of us were open books after four years together. No one said anything for what felt like a millennium, until Evan stood up, grabbed me by the hand, yanked me to my feet, and wailed, "This is BULLSHIT! We're going shopping!" He led me out the door, and we did, indeed, go shopping.

In the kitchen of the Shadyside apartment I shared with my room-mate Paul, a few of us (all fully out) gathered to break down the day's events. We silently skulked around, making drinks for ourselves, getting settled, until we were spread out like a *tableau vivant*, standing at the fridge, sitting on countertops, cross-legged on the floor. We all stared at each other until someone broke the ice: "Whoa." We were seasoned enough homos at this point to look at it as a good thing for Jeremy, but the agony in his face made my heart ache. Back then, even in an arts college populated by gay actors, dancers, and singers in an urban environment, shame was rampant. There's so much more to this story, but I'll let Jeremy tell it in *his* memoir.

NEW GIRL IN TOWN

I didn't really start my sexual exploration until I moved to New York City in 1982. I dropped my bags at my fellow Carnegie grad Kent Gash's place on 26th Street in Chelsea, where I was to couchsurf for months. I got an answering service called Standby (like "Susanswerphone" from the musical *Bells Are Ringing*), which you'd call at various times of the day to check in with a live operator for messages from agents and casting directors, as we didn't have phone answering machines back then. I was ready to take in whatever the city had to offer. I had spent the summer after senior year doing small roles in all the shows at Pittsburgh Civic Light Opera, which gave me my Actors' Equity card. I was raring to go.

I began auditioning for union musicals during the day, and Andy Baseman (my best friend from Carnegie) and I would spend practically every night in bars like Uncle Charlie's Downtown, cruising and comparing notes on all the denizens, giving them nicknames like the Pumpkin-Headed Boy (who just happened to have the roundest noggin we'd ever seen), Big Stupid Nipple Guy (football player type with gigantic areolae), or Flop (who had the biggest dick I'd ever seen—you could literally hear it go "flop" when he took it out of his pants to piss).

I'd sit in restaurants, stroll the streets, and, years later, when coffee-house culture became popular, nest at the Big Cup, the "Central Perk" of Chelsea, and just pine pine pine away at all the good-looking men and boys. Eventually, I found my own place, a studio apartment on 23rd Street at 7th Avenue across from the YMCA. From my apartment, you could peer right into the men's locker room, and on hot summer days the windows were wide open and you could see everything. Friends would come up to my place and as I opened the door, they'd push past me and beeline for my window without even saying hi to "hang out with all the boys."

I finally had my own bachelor pad, and though sex was rampant back then in NYC and I partook, I didn't give in to total sluttery. I was still the little boy romantic with the pillow, but it was much more complicated than kissin' cushions. In that great candy store called Manhattan, I only had eyes for the beautiful boys, ones who looked like TV stars, ones I couldn't have, ones who never looked at me, still, in my head, the skinny, ugly Jewish boy.

Funny coinkydink . . . well, not so funny. The first week I was in New York, I ran into a boy named Roger on the subway. I had met him the year before at a party while visiting the city. Roger and I had hit it off that night and found out we were both from the suburbs of Chicago. We decided to meet when we were home for Thanksgiving, so I picked him up in my dad's Cadillac and we went to see a show in downtown Chicago. Afterwards, I drove him home to Glenview, and just as we said our good nights, he leaned over and kissed me, and we proceeded to have awkward cocksucking sex in the back seat of my dad's car. It was actually fun and we promised to keep in touch, which of course we didn't since I was still in school and he was in NYC. So when I saw him on the subway a year later, I was thrilled and he was very sweet and said sure, let's get together. I thought, this is it, one week in New York and

I'm gonna be married! Sarah (the girl from Carnegie who used to date Stan) and I were best pals now after having bonded as his castaways, so I couldn't wait to tell her I had found someone. I gave her the whole history and she was all excited for me until I mentioned Roger's full name. Her face fell.

"What's wrong?" I asked.

She hesitated and then whispered, "He has a boyfriend."

It seemed so random that she knew who he was. I shrieked, "*What? No. How do you know?*"

She bit her lip, took a deep breath, and said, "I know. It's Stan."

"Stan? *My* Stan?"

"Our Stan. Yeah."

WAH-wah.

I met him on a college break back home in '79.
We had nowhere to do it, not at his folks' place or mine.
The first piece of advice I'd give to all young virgins is:
If you do it in your father's car,
Watch where you shoot your jizz!
—from "The Book of Lust"

To this day, I have a great talent for being in a bar, picking out two guys whom I'm attracted to, and watching them eventually meet and leave together.

PS: It's forty years later and Stan and Roger are still a couple. When it's meant to be, it's meant to be, and when it's not, I'm usually involved.

SOMETHING ROTTEN

One of my first friends in NY was the director/choreographer Jeff Calhoun. I met him back when he was an actor/dancer, a tall, blond, handsome, and laid-back Pittsburgh native whom I was absolutely taken with. I crushed really hard, but he was involved. I had to squelch the attraction in order to just enjoy his company, which I did. Unlike neurotic ol' me, he was easygoing and carefree, plus he introduced me to all his Broadway buddies and it was a blast to be included.

One night, we all got together to give his friend Ed a relaxing evening out because he was appearing in the troubled musical *Marilyn* on Broadway. It was a long-awaited production but stuck in a difficult and prolonged preview period, and they were working the cast to the bone. Ed was a dancer in the show and was exhausted, so Jeff thought a Boys' Night Out would be just the thing on his day off, with dinner and a movie.

Ed wanted to go see *Mr. Mom* with Michael Keaton, which had just opened, but I suggested a new film that had gotten amazing reviews called *Testament*. I guess I thought it was a horror film, which in a way it was, depicting the aftermath of a nuclear explosion. It's truly one of the greatest films ever about nuclear war: dramatic, emotional, personal, well acted. It's also dark, devastating, and absolutely the wrong thing to take a man's mind off his work, especially when he's in the mood for goddamn *Mr. Mom*. I don't know how I convinced them to go, but we did. Afterwards, despite Jeff trying to deflect by praising Jane Alexander's towering performance, everyone else wanted to kill me, especially Ed.

The Mexican food and margaritas afterwards helped to get me back in their good graces, but I noticed that one of their friends, Joe, had been coughing intermittently all night long. He mentioned that he had started swimming recently and that he thought he was having a reaction to the chlorine, and that he was going to his doctor over the next couple of days. Two weeks later, Jeff called to tell me that Joe had died. He was the first person I knew who died of "gay cancer." It was a slap of reality that it could come so close, and was the start of a parade of friends and acquaintances that passed away.

As we discovered more and more about how the disease was transmitted, it put the fear of God into me, into all of us, about sex. I still wonder how I made it through. We watched the world browbeat us and blame us for the epidemic, which was wrong on so many levels. Ronald Reagan couldn't even say the word AIDS, and New York mayor Ed Koch, that closet queen, was infamous for his deadly inaction, downplaying the virus until it became rampant and affected other communities besides gay men. They could have saved so many lives if not for their silence.

I went to ACT UP meetings and demonstrations, but I wasn't loud and angry like the rest because I was still in a bit of a sheltered dreamworld as an aspiring actor in NYC. Still, I saw firsthand the anguish and desperation that caused people to fight and I wanted to help as best I could. When the TV film of Larry Kramer's landmark play *The Normal Heart* came out a few years ago, I talked to so many young gay men who didn't believe the epidemic happened that way, and thought this was an overly dramatic depiction of history. That made me furious, because I thought the film got that period exactly right. It was an eye-opener to these young guys who only knew of protease inhibitors and PrEP. I would love to lose that angst I feel when I think of the word *bareback*, but I only see the faces of so many young men who are no longer here, friends and friends of friends who withered away in hospital beds back when there was no real treatment and just a stigma to shame them. I don't know if those feelings will ever fade.

My own New York reverie was shot to hell early in 1983 when I got kind of gay-bashed in the Village on the way to a party. I was with Kent, and as we walked, a heavyset drunk guy on the street asked if we were gay. We just ignored him. As we were buzzed into the building where the party was, the drunk guy was suddenly there and pushed Kent out of the way and slammed me into the entrance and backed me up against the door, shutting Kent outside. He started to throw punches at me, but since he was drunk, he barely landed any, just grazing my head a few times. When I finally got my wits about me, I pushed him away at arm's length and he shouted, "Are you a fucking faggot? *ARE YOU A FUCKING FAGGOT?*" And of course I wanted to say, "Yes, girl, what about it?" but in my best Clint Eastwood, I said, "No, man, I'm not." I hated to lie about it, but self-preservation kicked in. And he started to cry and said, "Oh, man, I'm sorry, I'm sorry, my kid's teacher molested him and I thought you were a faggot, and—" I cut him off and said, "Okay, gotcha, please let me go," and I opened the door and he went out into the night, and Kent and I went to the party, and NYC changed for me that day.

Suddenly, the struggle became real, to choose to be gay and out or not, and I vowed that I would never be closeted, in work or in life, and I stayed true to that. I stuck my toe into activism with ACT UP, and later did benefits for Broadway Cares and Equity Fights AIDS (they eventually merged), one year helping to organize their Gay Pride contingent. One of my favorite memories is the Broadway actor Howard McGillin marching with the Tony-winning twelve-year-old actress Daisy Eagan on his shoulders, who was wearing a "Support Vaginal Pride" button.

In the early '90s, my activism kicked in much more when I started volunteering for the Hetrick-Martin Institute on Astor Place on the Lower East Side, where the Harvey Milk High School was located. Hetrick-Martin is an LGBTQ youth organization that provides a safe haven for kids to reach their full potential, supporting homeless and abused kids, providing resources to help them survive in the city. I was part of their diversity training program, where I'd go with a staff member, great activist/speakers such as Ann Northrop and Andy Humm, into schools, corporations, anywhere that needed diversity awareness. We would do wonderful, eye-opening workshops that really affected our audiences, powerfully illustrating how much LGBTQ and straight folks have in common, and how we're not really so scary and different.

I truly felt that we expanded minds every time, from grade school kids to seniors. I was always amazed at how Ann and Andy could shut down bias with just a turn of phrase. For instance, when a participant would say something like, "Well, I don't think gay people should have kids because they'll make their kids gay," Ann would retort without missing a beat, "My parents were straight and I still turned out gay." Boom. Silence. And suddenly it was all clear as day. I continue to have so much respect for them, not only because they're still active activists, but because they taught me to be sharp and concise, and to put arguments into universal terms when gently but firmly shutting down a bigot.

BEAUTY AND THE BEAST

Columbia University used to hold gay dances in the early 1980s on the Upper West Side in their gymnasium. They were open to anyone, and at twenty-four I wasn't that far from the age of most of the gay college kids who showed up. It was the high school dance I never had, everyone joyously out and dancing and sweating and laughing. This was before dance music's only purpose was to enhance whatever drug you were on. It was all very clean-cut and sexy without being raunchy, and Andy Baseman and I went whenever we could. Though I was not one to take over a dance floor, it choked me up sometimes to see my people, my tribe, living out loud and having a gay ol' time.

I was standing on the sidelines one night, bouncing to the beat, when I felt a tap on my shoulder. I turned around and had to lift my head up to meet the eyes of the most beautiful man I'd ever seen face-to-face, with a genuine, warm smile that not only immediately captured my heart but made me instantly erect. Dark hair, tall, masculine—a *GQ* model had just summoned me into his world. I stuttered a hello and moved back so we could chat and watch the dancing together.

He was older than I was and seemed to be the most mature guy in the room, handsome, put together, and sure of himself—a real Man. Though we had to talk over the music, his soft-spoken quality came through and his relaxed allure brought out the nervous little Jewish boy in me who felt unworthy. But he laughed at my jokes and never did that glancing around thing, searching for something better. When he talked to me, he talked to *me*. We decided to take a walk around campus. I said goodbye to Andy, who looked at me as if I had just won The Big Deal of the Day, and my Dream Man and I left.

I remember how good it felt to be outside in the cool of the evening after the sweat and body odor of the youthful dancing gays. It turned out he was indeed older, thirty-five, and indeed a *GQ* model, a fairly well-known one—not as famous as Jeff Aquilon, Ed Fry, and Rick Edwards (yes, I knew all their names), but he had a great career, traveling, working, living the dream life I imagined whenever I saw the pretty people in magazines or walking down the street so self-assured. I wished I could be like that.

He was so charming and so interested in what I was doing as a young actor in NYC, and it shocked me that someone so good-looking would be concerned with my world, let alone even talk to me. We chatted and wandered for a half hour or so until he had to get home for an early call next morning. His name was Kalani Durdan, but when he gave me his business card, it said nothing but Kalani. It seemed odd that it had no phone number on it, and just his first name, but professionally he went by one name, like Madonna or Cher. I thought that was so continental and cool. I gave him both my home and service numbers and we hugged goodbye.

I was hoping for a magical kiss as we parted on 116th Street, but I felt he was being a gentleman, so I didn't push it. However, he held the hug longer than someone would have if they were not interested, so I took that and ran. He grabbed a cab, and after he got in and it pulled away, he did that final turn to wave that I love, the thing that cements the possibility that you'll hear from him again. There was no Internet at that time, so I couldn't go home and google the crap out of him. I got on the subway at 116th Street, the number 1 train downtown, starstruck and delirious with the way my heart felt. The possibilities. I fell in love up there at the Columbia Dance, the way I could fall so easily back then for a pretty face, and when I did—bang. Boom. Suddenly my world, no matter how dreary, became heaven-adjacent, and that night my pillow was Kalani. We cuddled and spooned, and I fell asleep about as happy as I could be.

I didn't stray from the phone all weekend and checked in with the service incessantly, and sure enough, he called me on Monday morning to have lunch. I met him at the Westside Diner in Midtown. In the light of day he was just as handsome and appealing, but I noted a heaviness to his demeanor, though he was just as engaging and laid-back sexy as the night we met.

I don't remember much about the conversation because he was so good-looking it was blinding, and I spent so much of the lunch trying to sound witty and important—to make him feel that dating me wouldn't be a step down. It was kind of pathetic and I think he knew what I was unwittingly doing. Kalani just sat, lanky and slightly hunched, smiling at every desperate absurdity that came out of my mouth, making jokes that never landed, roundabout stories about auditions and classes that wandered and simply led nowhere.

Though I blushed my way through lunch, I think Kalani thought it was sweet. He gave me his number on a piece of paper. I only had that card with his name on it, so I felt more secure when I actually had his phone number in my sweaty, shaking hand.

As overwhelming as my attraction to Kalani was, I was struck by what I believed was his own attraction to me. I felt in my heart that he wanted to sleep with me, and lord knows that's what I desired. But a couple of nights later I saw him for dinner, and as we said our good-byes, he held me close and we kissed good night, but I felt a wall had gone up and that the evening wouldn't end with romance and sex, which I so wanted, maybe too much. I'm sure Kalani sensed my need, my insecurity, my deep desire to feel love, to give love, gigantic full-throttle love that I had stored up for just this kind of man. It could have just been a fantasy, but there was something in his kiss that told me he wanted it too, and though I was not like the perfect men he was probably used to, just a regular guy with a big nose and a 'fro, maybe he was ready to slum it a little and go with someone who was vulnerable and loving and smitten.

In a way, I felt I'd be his charity case, but he seemed to really be touched by my naïveté and my unjaded new-to-New-York aura. He was leaving the country again for work and said we'd talk before he went.

I was still hoping we were going to sleep together, and that possibility teetered on the brink until he pulled it back, got in the cab, and did that wave again. I believed that Kalani wanted me, I knew it, I felt it in my weak, mushy bones, but there was something—something off. I didn't know what it was.

I was in my Kalani dreamworld for the entire week. I thought about nothing else, and though it was glorious, it was also distressing, not knowing where it was going, what could break through that wall to the next level of touching that beautiful body, of feeling as close to another human being as one could. I wanted him so badly. In the baddest way possible. More bad, baddy, baddest, badaboo than I have ever wanted anyone in my life.

Kalani never returned my phone calls. I knew he was leaving for Europe at some point, so I tried to call and say goodbye. I may have been overzealous in the number of calls I made, which multiplied as time went by, because my insecurity would not let me hold back, and if there was something stupid I could do or say, I would. But I knew he felt something. He *did*. I'm not making this up. No matter. I got left high and dry with my heart tatted on my sleeve, exposed to the elements, and it crushed me.

I gave up the phone calls after a month or so, and I never saw him again. I tried to chalk it up to experience and a wonderful memory. I never thought Kalani was an asshole or anything for not getting back to me. As I was to learn many, many times, you can't force love. And the person I'm going to be with is the one who loves me equally. I know that now. A relationship with Kalani was never meant to be, but I did love him, in my way. And, strangely, I still think he was falling for me a little bit.

Scott Kalani Durdan died on January 11, 1987, of AIDS. But here's where my memory gets murky. Did he tell me he had AIDS in one of our few moments together? I don't know if I dreamed that. And why did I feel he was protecting me from it by not sleeping with me? I sincerely believe that's the case, that he could not open himself to loving me because he was afraid of passing it on. Back then, we didn't know much about risk and exposure to the virus. But I don't remember if he told me that or if I found out when I tripped on his obituary. I saw his name in some magazine with a date of death, and then lost the use of my legs for a second.

Kalani was my embodiment of the perfect man: perfectly beautiful and a perfectly lovely person. I wanted him mostly in a superficial way, but I didn't know that back then. All I felt was love and hope and possibility—an innocence to it.

And as I write this, I'm getting a flash that maybe he did tell me, that he even said that was the reason we couldn't sleep together. Suddenly there was a pall over us, but I wanted to tell him I still loved him, that I appreciated how he was saving me, and frankly, I was so scared of the virus back then that I knew it was for the best. If all we did was kiss each other and hold each other naked and warm all night, that would have been enough for me, but that never happened. I don't remember it sounding like an excuse to not have sex. I really think he was trying to look out for me.

The memory of whether Kalani told me that or I dreamed it is being worked out as I write this. Andy (whose memory is better than mine) seems to remember that he did. And though I should go back and correct it if I figure it out, I won't. I'm shaking at the thought of what's come to me, and how sweet and noble he was, beyond his good looks. I have to stop now. I'm writing this at a Starbucks and I've started to cry.

GOLDEN BOY

When I was at Carnegie, I never said anything to my folks about my personal life. College was a bubble of discovery and they didn't need to know any of it and I didn't want to tell them. I wasn't ready and I didn't want to burst their notion of me being their perfect golden boy. But in 1983, having been in New York for a year and getting more comfortable with who I was, I was determined to come out to them on one of my visits back to Skokie. It was surprisingly easy. My sisters were no longer living at home, so it was just me and my mom and dad. I remember we had sat down to watch *Star Search* and as some Sam Harris wannabe (or was it Sam Harris?) was shrieking his lungs out, I took the remote and muted the TV. I turned to my folks and said, "I have something to tell you."

They listened as I revealed to them that I was gay and that I was out in New York and that though I did have attractions for girls early on, I had a boyfriend at college but was single now and was hoping they'd be supportive, blah blah blah, nothing particularly outstanding or different from the standard coming out monologue.

When I finished, there was silence. After a few seconds, Dad (who was a great father but had never been the most forthcoming in either emotions or commentary) said, "Do you need money?" And though I did, this did not seem the appropriate time, so I said no. My mom seemed fine until she got kind of devil's advocate-y, saying that I didn't sound totally sure about it and that it seemed like there might be a possibility it was a phase and that I should, essentially, keep my options open. I told her no, I don't think so, but it's something to think about.

That moment of hesitation on her part was really the only resistance I received, as they would always be great about me being gay, but I did have to educate them over the years about the politics of it all. However, it turned out that my mother's uncle, my beloved "longtime bachelor" Uncle Phil, who lived in Los Angeles, was also gay and in a long-term relationship of over thirty years, so it ran in the family (some of the relatives would refer to him as "the fagala," the Yiddish word for homosexual). Uncle Phil had come to New York City to visit and had dinner with Andy and me. Later, Andy told me that when I went to the restroom, Uncle Phil asked him to take care of me. He thought we were lovers. That's when I figured it out, and I confirmed it later by asking my mom. Who knew?

There were times when I visited home that I'd borrow the car to go to Boystown bars in Chicago—Sidetrack, Little Jim's, North End, Christopher Street (later the Manhole), and Roscoe's. Despite still not having a lot of self-confidence, being a new face in town made me more in demand and I often got lucky and would sometimes not return until the morning, worrying the crap out of my folks. I didn't know how to tell them that I had hooked up with some random guy at a bar, or that, after repeatedly circling the place but not entering, I finally got the nerve and spent hours at the Unicorn bathhouse (later Steamworks) walking around in nothing but a towel, having casual (safe) sex with multiple partners in the wonderful maze of a steam room.

Chicago was a great town for play, and back when you could park on the street with no permit, it was easy to drive in, hang out, get laid, and get home before dawn. Dad was an early riser, so he'd be waiting for me, silently, as I walked in looking like who-did-it-and-ran. I could tell my folks were pissed, but they never said anything, so I didn't either.

One time, as I was leaving to go back to NYC, I found a note in my backpack. It was from my mom in her perfect handwriting; she used a ruler to write in straight lines. My parents knew as much as anyone did about the AIDS crisis at the time (which wasn't much) and the note was just a way to tell me she was worried about my behavior. I don't remember everything it said, but I do remember this one line, every letter perfectly crafted, saying that if I didn't stop my recklessness, "you could get AIDS . . . OR WORSE."

At the time, I didn't think there was anything worse than AIDS, but I guess she meant that Casual Sex = Murdered In Your Sleep. Point was taken, and being the neurotic Jew I was . . . am . . . was . . . am . . . it took a while to get OR WORSE out of my brain every time I hooked up for sex.

We never talked about my relationships until they came to see me in a play in 1985 at the old Equity Library Theatre on the Upper West Side, an 1860s melodrama with music called *A Flash of Lightning*. My boyfriend (one of the many three-to-six-month relationships I engaged in—I was always looking for some other shiny new thing and barely ever committed past that time) was there that night, and I introduced him to my parents. His name was Blaine, and he was a dictionary-definition golden-haired WASP whom I'd met in acting class. This was the first time my parents ever met someone I was intimate with. They politely shook his hand and we didn't talk about it again until one day, on the phone, my mom said it was nice to meet Blaine but that she wasn't sure if she should be upset that I was dating a man or that he wasn't Jewish. We laughed and I thought, okay, if you can make jokes about it, you're going to be fine. And they always had been.

(PS: I broke up with Blaine after he commented on a scene in class, describing one of the characters doing business as "Jewing him down." Buh-bye.)

Years later, I asked my mom if she knew I was gay when I was a kid. She said she had ideas, but was pretty much sure when she saw *The David Kopay Story* on my bookshelf. David Kopay was the first NFL player to come out of the closet (after he left the game). His autobiography, written with Perry Deane Young, was a seminal book in my development and a must-read. I had left it at home during a break from college. As careful as I was to mask my true self, sometimes I subconsciously did things to let that mask drop.

GRIND

Back in high school, because I got good grades, was politically active, and did all the shows, I was voted "Most Versatile." Yup. Later on, not so much. It hurt too much to bottom, and I was vanilla everywhere else in my sex life—your basic kiss/suck/top. I wasn't into fetish or anything too adventurous.

More than anything, I wished my body were as muscular as the boys I sought out. I continued to go to the bars like Uncle Charlie's, but I couldn't look the really beautiful built boys in the eye because I didn't feel worthy. Except for the odd guy who could break down my walls of elitism and fear of engagement with a compliment or a good joke, I mostly left alone.

After most nights at the bars, I'd go home and turn on the TV, where they played three rerun episodes of *The Mary Tyler Moore Show* at 1:30 a.m. Pre-VCR, I would stay up and watch every episode, every night. It was just something everyone I knew did. Then I'd tune in to public access cable channels where you could see local sex-oriented shows on Gay Cable Network and Robin Byrd on Channel J.

Robin is an ex-stripper and NYC institution who had a low-rent talk show eponymously called *The Robin Byrd Show* on which she interviewed male and female porn stars and sex workers, who'd then dance for the camera and strip all the way down to full nudity, beaver and cock. There were ads for phone sex and Asian female hookers ("Geisha to Go!") and 970-PEEE: "the extra E is for extra pee!" At the end, all of the guests danced to Robin's signature theme song, "Baby Let Me Bang Your Box." It was all pretty crude, but very cheeky and fun, and as gay as TV got. Meanwhile, I longed to see those guys live.

In my late twenties, I finally had the guts to go to the Gaiety Theatre. It was a male burlesque house, an essential gay haunt over a Howard Johnson's in Midtown Manhattan, with strippers and erections and the renowned Mylar curtain. I went fairly often, sometimes with friends but mostly alone. Each stripper would come out clothed, from streetwear to costume, then dance, sometimes with great skill, sometimes awkward and tight, and after his song he'd exit the stage, leaving us in limbo with just the Mylar curtain to look at.

Suddenly the music would change and we'd see the silver strands of the curtain begin to sway, which meant the stripper was about to reenter, and there he was—naked, hard, bumpin' and grindin', and hungry for tips. This would happen with a shift of five or so guys on a weeknight and ten or twelve on the weekend. It fascinated me. I remember seeing the porn star Joey Stefano perform there, dancing laconically and in a haze, and later I watched as he fell asleep in the "social area," a room off the stage with carpeted platforms where you could meet and talk to the dancers for later, um, transactions.

When I was there, I imagined I was like Louise in *Gypsy*—I wanted to meet these guys and have them take me under their wing. Inside, I was still the good boy, but I wanted so badly to act out, to be like them, to do what they did. I loved the big bodybuilder guys, the cute blond boys with the great butts, and the hot rock-and-rollers, all long, dirty '80s hair and tattoos.

I fantasized about them giving me pointers on working out, stripping down, and showing off, and they'd be my hot best friends, and when I'd ask them, "What's the best part of stripping?" in my fantasy they'd reply . . . with a song! They'd tell me I gotta get a gimmick and show me stripper moves, how to pump my hips and shake my ass and flex my pecs—a more professional version of what I used to do in front of that full-length mirror when I was a boy. They'd bolster my confidence, and I'd think, I can do this! I'm MOST VERSATILE! A little Mazeppa, Tessie Tura, and Electra! (For those unschooled in musical comedy lore, those are the names of the strippers in the musical *Gypsy* who teach her what stripping is all about.)

> *I was poor and unemployed and hangin' out at the beach,*
> *when this guy said, "Hey, those tits are worth a million bucks each!"*
> *So I hit the clubs and hit the stage, and I made 'em dance.*
> *I'd have my bills and rent before I'd take off my pants!*
>
> *You want to make a fortune? Don't just be hot, be scorchin'!*
> *You need to bask in glory? Be kind of sweet, yet whore-y!*
> *You like the sin they're hatin'? So find your inner Satan,*
> *you'll see*
> *that the best part of strippin'?*
> *I feel free!*
> —from "The Best Part"

Of course, I never spoke to them and never acted on it—all just another fantasy unfulfilled. All my fantasies . . . unfulfilled. For now.

BIG FISH

My uncle had a good friend growing up named Michael Filerman, a tremendously successful TV producer who was best known for his work on the popular TV drama *Knots Landing* and, later, *Sisters*. I was visiting a friend in LA in 1985 and Michael agreed to meet with me. He had a huge desk in his home and I sat on the other side and thought, wow, this is Hollywood. We chatted about the business and the theater, which is really all I knew, but my dreams of being an actor and performing started with all the TV watching I did as a kid. Carnegie Mellon taught us absolutely nothing about TV and film acting. And when we graduated, we barely knew the difference between an agent, a casting director, and a manager. The school was a member of the League of Professional Theatre Training Programs, and at the end of senior year we did a big audition as a class in New York that allowed some of us to get agents and auditions for when we moved there.

Though I had an agent for theater, Michael wanted to help in any way he could and he said he would get me a general audition with the head of casting at CBS in LA. When I got back to NYC, they contacted me and said to bring in two monologues to CBS in New York; they would tape them and send them off. This was a huge deal, a wonderful opportunity that any young actor would have killed for, and I had stars in my eyes. However, I had never done TV and had no idea that acting for the camera was a whole different animal.

A week later, Michael called me. "David, we're not going to send that audition in," he said.

"Um . . . okay . . . why?" I replied, deflated.

"Well, you just come across really big. The camera is so intimate and it was like you were playing to the last row of a stadium. Plus your material. What was that Jewish monologue?"

"Um . . . that was from the book *Portnoy's Complaint*. Philip Roth."

"Yeah, no, it just came off as flat-out anti-Semitic. It's all Jews here. You can't do that kind of material."

"But it's classic literature."

"Doesn't matter. All Jews. Just a bad choice. Look, get yourself some more training, TV and film acting, and we can do this again down the line when you're ready," he concluded. "Really sorry, but this just isn't your time."

I was so incredibly disappointed. This could have given me a huge leg up, but years later I realized how great it was that it didn't go my way, for two reasons. First, I just wasn't prepared and I learned that you have to keep up your acting skills in all mediums because you never know what opportunity will be thrown at you from left field; acting on camera is a much more intimate endeavor, and I had a big ol' musical comedy face and attack. As my college pal Rob Marshall (the film director) said to me, paraphrasing his friend Liza Minnelli (have I dropped enough names here?), "Be ready when the luck happens."

The second thing is that if it had gone my way and I had started a successful TV career back then, I would be dead now. I had no self-esteem, was so enamored of Hollywood and celebrity and TV stardom that I probably would have done anything anyone asked of me—done any drug, kissed any ass, had sex with whoever dangled a carrot or a hard cock in front of me. And this was back when the AIDS crisis was just beginning, so I would not have put much thought into how I was being used. I just know I'd be dead. I truly believe that. Things happen when they're supposed to, and as Michael said, that was not my time. Sometimes, failure can be a good thing.

WORKING

All my life, I wished I were handsome enough to be a soap opera—or porn—star, but when it came to TV, I still had character guy looks. None of the jobs I took, acting or otherwise, depended on me being pretty.

Needing to get TV cred, I did extra work on a soap, *Another World*. I was the pool boy at the yacht club, only everyone at the club was about fourteen years old, so I was more like the pool zadie.

NEXT!

I graduated to small soap roles, under five lines. "Under fives" in the soap world. Here's my theory on under fives: They fall under two categories. Either The Servant—"Yes, ma'am." "No, sir." "Miss Kane, they need you." Or The Loser, who is there to make the other character look stronger, smarter, more heroic. These scenes always end up in some form of "Okay! Okay!" said with great fear as you raise your hands to defend yourself from an attack. The exchanges would go something like this:

Me: Sir, I'm afraid you can't go in there.
Him: Look, my wife is in there and no one can keep me out!

Me: But sir, I have my orders—

Him: I don't care about your orders! I'm going in!

Me: Okay! Okay!

(Arms up. Don't hit me!)

NEXT!

I did a bunch of regional theater gigs, and in between, to make a living, I waited tables. Waaay too many tables. My first gig was in a brand-new, noisy, bustling Upper West Side restaurant called Ernie's, the early reviews of which likened it to eating on the flight pad at Cape Canaveral. I was splitting a bowl of pasta for two drunken breeder boys who were loudly ogling "the tits on that chick." I picked up the two-foot-long pepper mill and offered:

"Would you like some fresh pepper?"

"No, but I'd like some fresh pussy."

Eeew. I lost 10 percent of my hearing working at that fucking place. I later waited tables at the Moondance Diner, where Kirsten Dunst worked in the first Spider-Man movie. I never got to service a super-hero, damn it. I moved from restaurant to restaurant.

I would also take on catering jobs and do everything from bartending at Jewish weddings (one of which had a puppet show as entertainment—*oy*) to serving at high end affairs at Sotheby's, which made me despise the rich—the X-ray women (so thin you could see their blood flowing) and their closeted homosexual husbands. All of this was done in an ill-fitting used tuxedo I bought at some vintage shop in the East Village. However, the abuse we waiters/bartenders/caterers received on a daily basis gradually ate me up inside. My motto became "Service with a Sneer."

NEXT!

THE GRAND TOUR

Finally, I hit the "big time." I left New York in 1987 to do my first national tour of a musical: *South Pacific* with Robert Goulet, Robert Goulet, My God, Robert Goulet.

The *South Pacific* tour was an amazing way to work, see the country, make some wonderful friends and colleagues, and explore my sexuality across America. I played The Professor, one of the Seabees (the male ensemble). More than half of us were gay, which was ironic since our big number was "There Is Nothing Like a Dame." I got along well with everyone, except one guy named Bart who was about ten years older than the rest of us and kind of jaded and bitter. The rest of us were so enthusiastic about every element of the show and tour, while he, having done a number of national tours, was pretty "meh" about the experience. It was just a job to him, so our obvious enthusiasm fell flat. I stayed away from Bart as much as I could because he intimidated the crap out of little idealistic me.

On a national tour, your only responsibility is to the show, and when you're woefully underutilized in the chorus, you have plenty of spare time in each city you visit. I began to think about spending that time working out. In NYC, I stayed in shape with dance classes, but as much as I fantasized about having a sexy, muscular build, the idea of going to the gym made me nervous. I thought my bones would snap if I tried to lift weights. Strangely, it was my mother who told me that if I got too muscular, I would never dance on Broadway; at the time, those guys were all lean and lanky. But with all the free time and the fact that some of the other cast members in the show were gym goers, I wanted to see what would happen if I went too.

I started my workout journey on the *South Pacific* tour because Ken Parks, one of the Seabees who went shirtless in the show, had an amazing body, so I asked his advice. Ken coached me on free weight techniques at each gym we went to across America, which—along with reading all the exercise magazines, such as *Men's Health, Muscle and Fitness*, and *Exercise for Men Only* (the last more to look at the half-naked fitness models than to learn their workout regimens)—gave me the foundation and motivation to build myself up.

It became my job in each city we played to find local gyms with which I could strike deals so we could work out either for free or cheaply (I also scoped out the gay bars). I'd spend three hours a day at the gym: huge spans of time weight lifting, going heavier and heavier as I realized that my arm bones weren't going to crack on the bench press; Nautilus machines, running, stair-climbers, aerobics, isometrics. I started popping protein shakes and the muscles began to grow, and I'd catch myself in the locker room mirrors and just marvel at what was happening to me, a far cry from the scrawny kid in my parents' bathroom.

I finally had muscles and I loved showing them off. Thanks to the *International Male* catalog and any gay clothing shop I could find, my gym wear became tight little shorts and teeny tiny string tank tops that barely covered my growing pecs, and I was rarely seen without my nipples to the wind and a prominent bulge at my crotch.

The gay guys in the cast would all hang out at bars and dance clubs after the show, and because of the confidence my new body was giving me, I was getting more and more admiration and had my share of hookups. Being on the road and in new towns every week made me throw sexual caution to the wind, knowing that any connection was only for the moment, and I fucked around a lot and loved it. No strings, just sex. I was always thrilled when there was a bathhouse (or two!) in whatever city we were in, because the sex there involved even less connection than at a bar, and it excited me to just reach out for what I wanted, take it, and move on.

Bathhouses in New York City went through a period of tremendous controversy when some were shut down in the mid-'80s due to the AIDS epidemic, but they soon became venues for encouraging safe sex, providing rubbers and educational materials to help stem HIV. Most bathhouses on the road fell in line with that. The subversiveness of it all was exciting to me: that behind an unmarked storefront in a suspect neighborhood I could get blow jobs in the steam room, or enter a guy's room, throw on a rubber, take his ass, and then move on, sit in the sauna, take a dip in the pool, and then go get laid again. I'd start up a conversation with a local guy in the TV room and then move to his little nook for a little nookie. They were my own little worlds to explore: hot, anonymous, casual sex, always safe but satisfying.

Some of the bathhouses were seedy and creepy while others were like spas. Some had outdoor decks where you could get fucked under the moonlight, some had full-size pools, every city had something different to offer, and I loved it, and I so enjoyed strutting around the hallways in nothing but a towel, knowing I was new meat in town and that my pecs, my arms, and the obvious tenting of that towel could turn heads. Sometimes I'd forgo the towel altogether and just wander the place in nothing but a metal cock ring, enjoying the random hands reaching out to touch my fluffed-up dick as I passed by. I didn't tell anyone back at the show about my bathhouse visits; in the real world, I was a bit embarrassed to say anything because I thought they would think less of me for being such a runaround, so I considered the venues my personal playgrounds and kept my carnal, exhibitionistic exploits to myself.

No one else seemed interested in going to the baths anyway, and I was fine with that. I gave myself the secret title of "Company Sleaze."

My favorite venue in all of America was the Club Baths in Cleveland. It had a maze of a steam room that seemed to go on forever, with lots of corners and crannies that encouraged solo and group groping, the steam bringing heat to all the sweaty, glowing bodies kissing, fucking, and sucking. The regular group sex rooms were too dark, but the steam room had really dramatic lighting, and we all know lighting is everything. It was an exhibitionist's and voyeur's dream. It was divine.

I ventured to Club Baths Cleveland a few times during the show's run there. One night after a performance, I paid my way in, got to the locker room, took off my clothes, wrapped the towel around my waist, and shut my locker door. As I turned the corner to exit the room, I ran smack-dab into . . . Bart. Boom. I sheepishly stuttered hi, there was an awkward silent moment, and then he broke into giggles. "You're as sleazy as me!" Blushing, we both had an uproarious laugh, and to this day he's one of my very best friends and I love him to death.

BULLETS OVER BROADWAY

When *South Pacific* closed in 1989, I was fortunate to get immediately cast in another national tour. I was to play Mendel the Rabbi's son and understudy Motel the Tailor in the Broadway-bound twenty-fifth-anniversary revival of *Fiddler on the Roof*, the ultimate Jewish musical (we called them Jewsicals; I was always the Jew-venile, and the young women were the inge-Jews). We went on the road for a good year and a half before we brought it to the Gershwin Theatre in New York. The show starred Topol, who had done the film version (which I loved), and I was thrilled to get my second national tour in a row.

The musical has such a rich tradition, and since it was one of the first stage shows I'd ever seen (in 1967, my folks took us to see Luther Adler as Tevye in the first national tour), I was proud to be a part of its legacy. The company was made up of a talented group of actors and some incredibly nice people. Touring can be a very bonding experience, especially when you're younger: you've got cash, you're in great cities, you just have to be there to do the show, then you have time to play. It really was a great life.

In each city, I continued to carry out my responsibility of finding gyms and gay bars. I remember doing the opening number, "Tradition," one night and singing the "Sons" portion ("*The so-ooooons! The sons! Tradition!*") and having an epiphany. I was at the upstage apex of the triangle of us dancing, and surveying the dancing sons in front of me, I thought, oh, they're all gay. Holy Anatevka! I loved touring.

For *Fiddler*, I had to grow a beard, and this confirmed something I'd learned about bar culture back then: thirty years ago, no one seemed to want to fuck men with facial hair (except maybe Colt models). Everything was clean and shaved—smooth torsos, smooth faces. According to a couple of gay historical websites, this trend was a bit of a backlash against what AIDS was doing to gay men's bodies; skinny frames and scruffy faces suggested sickness, so hairless, muscular bodies and clean-shaven faces were desired, looking "healthier."

But I was forced to have facial hair for my job. I'd go to the bars and this is how guys cruised me: they'd scan the bar, winking and nodding at each other, and when their eyes focused on me, their faces would contort as if they had seen a most vile, ugly, and disgusting troll monster, their tongues sticking out in distate.

Or sometimes I could see their glance just shoot over my head in order to avoid my eyes, because they could see the beard peripherally. Once, a guy came eye to eye with me and faux vomited in my face. Whatever the case, not much sex for David at that point, and I could feel my low self-esteem making its return engagement.

So, what's a hirsute boy to do? I discovered the leather bars! Finally, I got laid. There was a definite difference in the clientele at leather and Western-type places compared with the average gay dance clubs and bars; the leather guys were usually older and more diverse, with lots of body hair and physical types that went beyond the shiny muscle god.

I had started buying leather fetish magazines such as *Honcho* and *Drummer*, and I was so attracted to the hairy chests (Brian Kelly!)

and rough-hewn faces and the hypermasculinity of the leather and all the sexual depravity that came with it. Everything with initials: S&M, CBT, FF, WS.

Look 'em up.

Curious and open, I stuck my toe into pretty much everything (except fisting—back then, that freaked me out), and many of these leather-oriented men were happy to make me their student. Looking back, I was definitely in narcissist mode, because with my beard I was starting to be attracted to guys who looked like me.

For all my attraction to leather, I owned none of my own. The week we were in New Orleans with the show coincided with Halloween, so I decided I wanted to dress the part. It was our night off, and the whole cast was getting into costume and going down to Bourbon Street, but they were renting Beefeater costumes and Little Bo Peep. I found a great leather shop in the French Quarter owned by a master and his slave, and they gave me an education in all things kinky.

> *A metal armband, rubber jock, a pair of leather chaps.*
> *It gets a bit involved with all the zippers, ties, and snaps.*
> *And if you wear this harness to the Pride parade, my word!*
> *Use lots of 30 SPF, the tanline is absurd.*
>
> *These long thin metal pieces are called sounds, for your urethra.*
> *You stick 'em all the way inside to stretch the tube ya pee thra!*
> —from "Accoutrements"

They loved me and dressed me up like Leather Daddy Ken (much more butch than the actual Earring Magic Ken doll, which later became a gay must-have, much to Barbie's dismay). The money I was making on the road was great, and even though I was frugal and saving every penny I could, I spent hundreds of bucks that day on leather accoutrements because I loved how it felt, so ultra-manly, and I went back to my hotel room and duded myself up: tight leather tank top, slutty ripped jeans with holes at the knees, crotch, and butt, heavy motorcycle boots, thick leather belt, armbands, aviator glasses. When I was fully dressed, I checked myself out in the full-length mirror on the bathroom door, and after the initial shock, I just stared at my reflection. This is what I had always wanted to look like: masculine, muscular, sexual, dangerous, and really really hot. It sounds so weird to write that down in retrospect, but honestly, I would have fucked me in a second. Oh my god, that sounds horrible and I'm almost ashamed that I wrote that, but it's truthfully what I was feeling in the moment back then. Back *then*! Got it?

I got on the elevator shaking with anticipation, and when it reached the main floor, I stepped off and the entire hotel lobby stopped. I had the look and the attitude, and they were all staring at *me*. I'd never gotten that kind of instant attention (without walking around the dark hallways of a bathhouse naked with a cock ring) and I liked it. A leather man was born.

After that Halloween, I found every opportunity to gear up and go to bars that welcomed guys like me. I remember being in a Vancouver leather bar, having a drink, chatting with a big, burly, mustached guy, and this twink came over, got on his knees, licked our boots, unzipped both our jeans, pulled out our cocks, and sucked us both off, and as the whole crowd watched, we continued nonchalantly to sip our Scotch and sodas. My sexual portfolio grew, and I began to live out my deepest, darkest desires with men across the country who wanted more than vanilla sex and romance, sometimes one-on-one, sometimes in a group, always safe but definitely more out on a sexual limb than ever before.

The dreamy-eyed, insecure boy was becoming a man, and I enjoyed using and getting used, pushing the carnal envelope whenever and wherever I could.

When our production of *Fiddler* was in Los Angeles, I worked out at the popular all-male gay gym The Athletic Club. I pumped iron every day, not just to keep the pecs tight but because it was full of shiny LA-boy eye candy and possibilities, with a communal shower, a pool in the back surrounded by palm trees, and a private rooftop deck where one could go to sunbathe nude or play with a buddy.

One day during my workout, I was approached by a man who told me he was a photographer and asked if I might want to pose for him. He said his name was Tom Bianchi, that he specialized in male nudes, that I looked great and would be a wonderful model. I didn't know who he was and was tempted out of sheer curiosity, now that I had built my body up and put the skinny, ugly Jewish boy behind me (at least on the outside). However, I was having a Coco moment from *Fame*, suspicious that he was just handing me a line to get me to his place to strip me down and fuck me.

I told him I wasn't sure but that I would love to see his work. I was also feeling a huge ego boost that all those other gorgeous men were walking around half-naked and he chose me. He invited me to his place at Park La Brea Apartments in Hollywood, and when I got there, on my guard, I walked in and was floored. He had some blowups on his wall of some of his work, and the quality of his photos—they were beautiful and arty and erotic and pretty much not at all what I expected.

I thought I was going to see a lot of spread legs and blurry images, more like the porn I had started to look at in magazines such as *In Touch* and *Blueboy*. I loved what I saw, and I wanted so badly to pose, to be captured forever like these stunning black-and-white all-American gods. I couldn't believe he wanted me to be a part of this. But I was nervous I'd put my future TV career in danger if any nude photographs of me were discovered, so I said no. He told me, if I ever changed my mind, to let him know. He was a perfect gentleman.

Fiddler was a lot of fun, but the longer we ran, the more out of hand our star got—the least professional person I've ever worked with. I was told by cast members who had done many previous productions of the show that the role of Tevye lends itself to a kind of megalomania, as he pretty much is central through most of the show, and that various past Tevyes fell into that behavior; the role just seemed to breed that. As Topol was a veteran of the film and stage productions and knew the show inside out, he tended to prolong bits and ad-lib and do shtick and steal moments from other actors that made each performance run longer than any musical comedy evening should. Plus, his delivery became laconic. No urgency. He was funny and the audience loved him, but sometimes being in a scene with him was interminable, just waiting for him to get through his crap so we could continue to tell the story.

We could always tell when Topol was in a bad mood because he'd mock other actors' line deliveries during a performance or upstage them or change the rhythm of a scene to where it was impossible to make sense of it and connect with him. He seemed to like to pick one actor and terrorize them for a few days and then move on to someone else. It would have been fun and kind of exciting in terms of an acting challenge if he had been doing it as the character, but it was always a very personal thing, something Topol had up his butt that day that made the work go off the rails.

The audience couldn't tell, but we could and it made the job miserable. There was a moment at the end of what was called "the Butter-Milk-Cheese" scene where my character, Mendel, overhears all the bullshit that Tevye, on his rounds as a milkman, throws toward the activist student Perchik about the Bible. I came up with a bit after Tevye recites a particularly egregious misstatement of the Good Book in which I'd do a physical slow burn and then let my frustration bubble over on the line "Where does the Book say that?" It always got a nice hefty laugh and was a great way to button the scene.

Well, don't ever try to get a bigger laugh than the star, I learned. After a time Topol would start to move around while I prepped to say the line and it technically killed any of the anticipation, and the laugh would get smaller and smaller and the scene would just kind of fizzle out. On tour, we were playing theaters with huge stages and Topol had like twelve mics and eighty-five spotlights on him, so the slightest move he made would register and you'd feel the attention of the audience quickly shift back to him, even if all he was doing was rubbing his hands together or, I don't know, picking his nose.

Topol really had very little respect for his fellow actors and the rest of us all bonded more because of it. Backstage could get kind of gossipy, but I learned to just show up, do my job, read a book when I was off-stage, and then enjoy life in each city we traveled to.

One of the most exciting times for us was when Jerome Robbins came to see the show in Boston. If you're not familiar with him, he directed and choreographed the original production of *Fiddler* (as well as *Peter Pan*, *Gypsy*, and *West Side Story*), and he was Broadway roy-alty, with a reputation as a brilliant perfectionist taskmaster who could be a bit of a bully (some would say that's an understatement).

Robbins saw a Saturday night performance and then met with us to give notes before the Sunday matinee. We were all a bit anxious, but it was amazing to hear everything he had to say as he doled out individ-ual and group notes, dropping bits of insight that really helped put the show back on track. I loved him. One of the actresses challenged Robbins's notes a couple of times and he just laid into her. We learned to shut up and take what he said. Do. Not. Speak. I was fine with that, because this man knew the show better than anyone. It was his staging, his spirit that imbued the whole thing.

After he had a private session with Topol, we could tell that Robbins had rebooted him back to the soul of the show, editing down the shtick that was making it too long and painful. I was thrilled that I got my moments back and we all enjoyed the work again.

That lasted maybe a week. After that, Topol was back to his old tricks. It was enervating and depressing to act with someone who really tainted the whole spirit of this classic musical for me. Robbins helped out one more time, rehearsing us in a NY studio right before we opened on Broadway at the Gershwin Theatre. One of my proudest moments was doing that last bit of "Butter-Milk-Cheese" and hearing Robbins let out a guffaw. I was done. Making this legend belly-laugh was something I will never forget. We opened in great shape, but eventually our star got full of himself again and we were back to misery. I was always thankful that I made it to Broadway, but he really did screw up the experience for many of us.

Besides the toxicity of Topol, there was "The Cupcake Incident." Twelve of us came down with hepatitis due to some birthday cupcakes made by a cast member. He liked to bake for birthdays, which was sweet, but . . . somehow . . . the cupcakes got tainted. Eew. A mess. Our Motel, whom I understudied, was out, as was I, as was my understudy. We were dropping like flies, to the point that the producers were begging anyone who had ever done the show to step in. One friend said he was walking in Times Square and was breathlessly accosted with, "You've done *Fiddler*. You want to be on Broadway?" Coming back after two awful weeks, I checked in with the stage manager, who looked like death himself from the stress. I had not been told why this all happened, and when I asked if anyone knew, he said to me (à la Jack Lord in *Hawaii Five-O*), "It was those cupcakes. Those God. Damned. Cupcakes." Book 'im, Danno.

Though it was sometimes hell working with Topol (or, as I liked to call him, that crazy Smoker's Tooth Polish), I made it to Broadway and I got to work with Jerome Robbins and I'm grateful.

FOOTLOOSE

In late 1990, I was on Broadway and I was looking good, continuing my workouts at the all-gay Chelsea Gym on 17th Street. A guy there said I might make an interesting artist's model, and he arranged for me to pose naked for art classes at Columbia University for twenty-five dollars a class. I didn't really need the money, but I craved the experience. For a while it was exciting to be a naked object and I had to fight the urge to get hard in front of such a large group of students. (Eventually, you realize that they are not looking at you to appreciate you so much as to get the lines and lighting right.)

I was hitting bars, bathhouses, and sex clubs, and even with the beard I was getting to fuck around with the kind of guys I so desired when I was skinny and no one paid attention to me. That Book of Lust was getting a real workout, name after name entered and recorded for history . . .

Robby, Lance, Jamal, and Vince . . .
. . . boy, was he high maintenance.
William, Jerry, Sam, and Mick,

Rocky, Douglas, Dick . . .
. . . oh Dick . . . DICK!

He wasn't Richard. He was Dick.
That thing was big, and really thick.
He schlepped out what he had in store,
it hung six inches from the floor.
Erect, think of a baseball bat,
and then imagine three times that!

We spent our nights together trying hard to make it fit.
After our third date, I couldn't walk. I couldn't sit.
And then, misfortune ran amok . . .
a horrifying moment, a catastrophe,
the final straw . . .
he thrust and oops, he broke my jaw.

Larry, Barry, Gary, Dave . . .
all his pubic hair he'd shave.
Esai, Juan, and two Joses . . .
that was in my Latin phase.
Jordan, Colin, Dirk, and Huntz,
Sue (I had to try it once).
Famous movie heartthrob, who?
Sorry, but I can't tell you.

But . . .

The year he won his Golden Globe,
I met him backstage in his robe.
He shook my hand, without disguise

the terry cloth began to rise.
He licked his lips, the next thing . . . BOOM!
I'm on the couch in his dressing room.

He became my bottom boy, and I was his top gun.
It was risky, just impossible,
but really lots of fun!
I signed a contract to agree to confidentiality.
I say his name, I go to jail,
but I swear it's not an old cock tale!
—from "The Book of Lust"

Relax. Those last two stanzas are a fantasy. Don't go siccing the lawyers on me.

SMILE

I went to Fire Island for the first time when a friend invited me one weekend to the home he shared on the Pines. Fire Island is a gay mecca just off the south shore of Long Island, NY, and the Pines is the gayest of its communities. It's a hop, skip, and jump from Manhattan, a beautiful beach, a peppy gay social scene, opportunities for outdoor sex in the woods (the Meat Rack), but also a serene place to unwind. NYC gays galore would take summer shares and spend weekends away from the hot, sticky city, hanging with their friends, cooking meals together, going to Sunday Tea Dances, and hooking up. A lot.

I was walking on the beach in my Speedo and ran into a new pal named Tom McBride, a model and actor I'd met through a mutual friend. He always intrigued me and I crushed on him a little as he reminded me of Kalani. (We lost Tom a few years later to AIDS and he became the subject of a riveting and heartbreaking documentary directed by my friend and *Party* castmate Jay Corcoran called *Life and Death on the A-List*, chronicling the erosion of Tom's self-worth as his looks and body were tragically ravaged by the disease.)

I stopped to chat, and who was he with but the photographer I had met back in LA, Tom Bianchi. We looked at each other and he said, "I know you!" and realized it was from the year before. He told me I looked great and if I wanted to shoot, we could do it at his home there, which was the backdrop of many sessions he did during that period. I was still letting my fear hold me back until Tom McBride said, "David, if you were ever going to do a shoot like this, this is the guy to do it."

The next morning, I found myself posing naked all over Tom Bianchi's house. I was still a little nervous about it, concerned that I would get hard and have my erection photographed, but I made it clear that I was not ready to put fully erotic hard-core out there, and he was very respectful of that. At the time, it felt as though there was a huge leap between being photographed soft and hard. In my head, hard was porn, and I wanted to do art.

It went really well, and I left feeling pretty great, and the shot that he used from our work became the final nude image in his first book, *Out of the Studio*. I requested that the photo be headless because I still thought appearing nude could kill my acting career. However, I think it's a great shot, and I'm proud that it was included in the Tom of Finland archives as "All-American" (I'm posed in front of an American flag). The photo is cropped from my chin to my knees, so you can tell that I have a beard and my chest is hairy, and it all felt so . . . manly. Being approached, posing, seeing the final shot—the little boy in front of the full-length mirror was finally beginning to live his fantasy.

Side note: I walked into a gay-owned gift shop in Chicago sometime in 1991 or so with my sister. Browsing greeting cards, minding our own business, chatting away. I went to pay for a birthday card, and on the counter by the cash register was a little turnstile dotted with gay-oriented refrigerator magnets, lots of rainbow flags and oiled-up bodybuilders and drag queens with pithy quotes. I looked closer and focused in on one of the magnets that was full frontal, thinking, ooh, cock. Yay. My stomach suddenly dropped. It was me. The shot that closed Tom Bianchi's *Out of the Studio* book. On a refrigerator magnet.

I called my sister over and pointed it out. She sneered at me like, why are you making me look at some guy's dick? "Um . . . that's me." She looked confused. "That picture. It's me. From a nude photo shoot I did in Fire Island." I could tell she was embarrassed for me, and I had a moment of that myself, then immediately I said, "Oh my god, that is so cool."

When the cashier came over to take care of my purchase, I literally felt a tug in two directions between embarrassment and ownership, and I ultimately sided with the joy of it. I pointed at the magnet and blurted out, "THAT'S ME!" as if I was on the cover of *Time* magazine.

The cashier looked at my sister, who was still a bit taken aback, but when their eyes met, she started laughing, and then he started laughing and gave out a "Whoop!" He pulled the magnet off the display, grabbed my hand, placed the magnet in my palm, closed my hand over it, and exclaimed, "This belongs to YOU!" with a pronounced Southern drawl and open, generous, party hostess zeal. He threw up his right arm and declared, "On the *house!*"

I thanked him profusely and my sister and I walked out, and I felt different. This was the first time my proclivity toward exhibitionism had collided with my real life. And though I could feel the blush on my face, I also got kind of turned on. Aroused. But also proud. Less ashamed. Less secretive. Stronger. More . . . well . . . me.

STOP THE WORLD—I WANT TO GET OFF

After *Fiddler* closed on Broadway in June 1991, I found a fantastic one-bedroom apartment on 24th Street across from London Terrace, a gorgeous 1930s apartment complex that takes up an entire city block. Because of the beauty of that building and all the charming brownstone structures and the tree-lined curb that stretches from 9th to 10th Avenues, I thought I lived on the most fetching block in the city. I loved it. Great that I had a nice place to nest, though, because—as most artists do—I had bouts of unintended downtimes when well-paid work, love, or any fun at all just disappeared.

As you've seen, I've always struggled with self-esteem when it came to my body and looks, but I also had issues when it came to my talent and career. As driven as I could be, and for all the good work I'd done on and off Broadway, on tour, in lots of regional theater, as well as little bits on TV, the novelty of being a fresh-faced New York actor was fading. Though I had reached Broadway (my vow was that I would make it there before the age of thirty—I was off by two years, at thirty-two), now, at thirty-three, a part of me felt not good enough to succeed, a total hack, an imposter. I started rummaging through my history in my brain, which is sometimes a dangerous place to be.

Though I had made it through Carnegie Mellon, the faculty planted the seeds that not only made me insecure about my sexual orientation in the business but also undermined any belief in myself as an artist. I was constantly worried back then that I'd get kicked out of the program like so many others who couldn't make the grade. It wasn't about art, it was about survival. Those wounds ran deep.

In 1992, Dick Scanlan, a Tony-nominated playwright and lyricist who had been a musical theater major one year behind me, wrote a scathing article in *Theater Week* magazine about the Carnegie Mellon theater department. It addressed the school's merciless policies toward gay men and heavyset women and the practice of cutting actors from the program, giving the boot to students who didn't fit their criteria for what they thought actors should be. The article was called "Bloody Monday: 'Fats,' 'Fems,' and other casualties of Carnegie Mellon's cuts." It went in depth into the fear, devastation, and emotional violation these cuts caused not only to the ones who had to leave, having to explain to their parents the why and wherefore of their being expunged from the program (especially if they were not yet out), but to those of us who stayed, knowing that there was a target on our backs and that we had to hide any effeminacy onstage. This, of course, bled into real life. As one actor said in the article, "It basically comes down to 'You're gay and you should be straight.'" It was pretty fucking awful. And, being a mostly musical comedy performer at this point, I felt I was getting by on charm and force of personality alone, and that neither I nor the casting people looked at me as a serious actor, ready for "straight" roles (straight as in nonmusical). Beyond that, the ups and downs of the biz generally shook any foundation of confidence I might have had.

You need a thick skin to invest so much at an audition and then not get the role; it can be devastating. I hadn't yet learned to just do the deed and move on without expectation or pressure. Doubts were swirling in my head that maybe I should have gone the other route and become Dr. David, with a stable career, a family, a house with a backyard, a dog, all of it.

But I was never going to be that guy. I didn't want to be that guy. I was seeking a different kind of fulfillment, the kind that comes from being totally true to myself in every facet of my life: in work, in love, in my day-to-day existence. Growing up gay, closeted, and afraid retards the natural process of connection, not just to others but to yourself as well. We hold ourselves back from our truth out of fear—of being unloved, ridiculed, beaten up, held back from our heart's desires. It can drag you down. I was never suicidal over it, but my ego was delicate and my skin pretty thin. There were times I felt as if success was for other people; however my career was humming along—I made it to Broadway, for God's sake—I worried that I was never going to go any further as I let the demons in and my faith in myself waned.

I knew I had talent. I knew I had the ability to connect. But something was off. Relationships were inert, I got stuck in the actor/waiter lifestyle, I was in serious credit card debt, and getting out of bed was a chore. My best friend, Andy, was going through his own struggles as a set designer and decorator, and he called me one day, really low because he'd finished everything he had written down to do that day and now he was just twiddling his thumbs. "What did you write down?" I asked. He said, "Buy shoelaces." And sad as that sounded, we both had a good laugh (he's now an award-winning set decorator for TV and film). I focused too much on what was lacking in my life rather than the gifts I was given every day in health, friends, family, all that real stuff. It's hard to see the good sometimes when you're stranded in the mire. I started going to a therapist again, the first since the asshole back home in Chicago.

During these periods, I'd sit by the phone, hoping for that call that would change my life. You know, the one that never comes when you sit by the phone waiting for the call that will change your life? The one where you find out you got the job, or he asks you to dinner, or you won the *Reader's Digest* Sweepstakes? That one? It seemed that the only calls I got were hang-ups or crank calls, devoid of substance, hope, or potential.

I wasn't dating so much as hooking up for one-night stands, nothing lasting, and you tend to attract what you feel about yourself, so I was sleeping with hard-bodied, insecure, nervous wrecks.

I'd go to parties even though they can be difficult social situations when you're feeling crappy about yourself. However, I'd never miss an opportunity, no matter if it was thrown by my best friend or a friend of a friend of such and such, it didn't matter—I would always go in another attempt to find my future ex-husband.

And at these parties, the Drama Queen in me would come out full force as I let whatever music was playing in the background become the soundtrack to my search for Him, for my seduction. I'd move through the apartment or bar as if there was a pinspot on my face, a close-up à la film noir, looking to catch the eye of only the cute guys, ignoring everyone else, anyone I might have even had a sweet conversation with—that's not why I was there. I could feel the camera following my every move, gently, lushly working its way over my features as I looked for Danger! Sex! Glamour! Great romantic scenes from movies would play in my head and I'd let them lead me on, hoping that some hot guy would give me the cue, hoping the result would be the same as in the film. Boy gets boy (well, girl, as there were few gay films then, but you get the point).

And the music in my head inevitably halted with a record scratch. Of course, these parties were never like the movies, and when any of those boys made eye contact with me, I'd drop my head and check out the dirt on the rug because I was in low self-esteem-y mode, and the result was never the same as in the movies—boy did not get boy,

boy blew off boy, boy lost boy to boy with bigger tits. Here's the thing: since I kept going after only what I perceived to be the *crème de la crème* of gays, I couldn't connect. However, if I engaged with a regular guy, just someone really sweet and cute and, well, regular, I was funny, charming, sarcastic, cocksure. Two days later I'd hear from the host: "Remember that guy So-and-So at the party? He thought you were so wonderful." Of course he did, because I didn't give a shit.

But if you put someone in front of me who really intrigued me, with a handsome face and/or a built body—I would lose sight of myself; I would stare, listening intently, adoring eyes wide and hungry, and I would try to say everything I thought he wanted to hear, and when I'd go search for a pencil and paper to give him my phone number (a smartphone would have been oh so helpful then), Bachelor Number One would start chatting up Bachelor Number Two, who was the other guy at the party I liked, and they'd leave together (just call me Yente) and I'd be left to find Bachelor Number Three, who wasn't there anymore. Most parties, I was the first to arrive and the last to leave, a walking-bruised-ego deadened-libido frizzy-haired big-nosed ugly-Jew-boy party-food-eating fat pig.

And then I'd go fail at a bar.

In those wee hours of the morning, I would have been way better off lying in bed watching Mary Tyler Moore, Robin Byrd, and infomercials—Sy Sperling was starting to look pretty hot to me—but I'd force myself out of party mode and into the realm of bar games, standing with a drink in my hand and what I thought was a pleasant look on my face; sometimes I'd catch myself in a mirror and what felt like a smile was actually a scowl. I'd spend hours halfheartedly cruising only the sexiest (sexy being relative) ones, coming up empty, because inside I didn't even feel worthy of a hookup, and I wondered if it would always be like this.

At the end of the bar hop, I'd down the last of my Scotch and soda and walk outside into the crisp early morning, unsteadily making my way up 9th Avenue. And on that long walk home, I'd have no social gasoline left to even say hello to someone on the street and I so often went to sleep alone. It wasn't always like this, but more often than not the low self-esteem won.

One night, I ran into my friend Jason at The Lure, a pretty serious leather bar in the Meatpacking District, and as we were chatting, I noticed this older gentleman, sixty-something, sitting at the bar in a daddy cap, chaps, and harness, tits sagging, belly bulging, nursing a highball, hunched over, drunk, and looking absolutely miserable. I couldn't take my eyes off of him.

I subversively pointed the man out and whispered to Jason, "If you see me sitting there at that age looking that unhappy, shoot me or call me a cab." And he laughed and I laughed, but inside I felt a stab of serious recognition and depression. (PS: I later wrote a country song called "Shoot Me," inspired by the encounter.)

When jeans are too tight for a man my age,
no rings in my nipples, though they may be all the rage,
Lord, don't let me get to the stage
where I need to wear my harness . . . with a bra.

When you see me cruising in my little tank top,
let me know my sex appeal has started to drop,
and all attempts at hooking up are destined to flop
'cause you shouldn't use Lycra to wrap old meat.

Shoot me, or call me a cab.
If you see me out, don't let me start up a tab.
Too old for the joys of hanging out with the boys,
so just shoot me, or call me a cab.

Oh shoot me, or call me a cab.
Make me retire my wrinkles and flab.
They won't give a damn what a great guy I am,
so just shoot me, or call me a cab.
—from "Shoot Me"

In retrospect, I realize how terribly judgmental and awful that all is, because that fella at the bar might have just been having a bad moment. Contrary to the scenario I was writing about him in my head (and in lyrics), for all I knew, he was about to go home to his longtime movie star boyfriend and his duplex on the Upper East Side. However, I wrote the song as a cautionary tale that I think is kind of funny but I guess is pretty tone-deaf. I just knew that I didn't want to be lonely when I reached that age, or try to look younger and hotter out of desperation. And guess what? At sixty-two, I have great spells of loneliness, and I still wear a harness sometimes (and Lycra to the gym) because I like it. So apologies to the man at the bar. I still think he looked unhappy, but rather than judge him, I could have gone up and said hi. Would that have killed me?

I did work during this period, though. I'd get low-paying gigs playing in off- and off-off-Broadway musicals, in little theaters where you could hear every word and every crinkle of candy wrappers of the little old matinee ladies in the audience. I did tons of showcases and workshops, as we all did, to develop musicals for presentations, working hard for barely a dime, amid promises of "We're taking it to Broadway!" They ranged from earnest to horrifying and never saw the light of day once we finished working on them. We threw ourselves into the work as we actors do, feigning optimism that it would turn into something bigger, better, and higher-profile. I always worked with wonderful, funny actors who made the process worthwhile.

I did one where my big song was a duet with an African-American guy and I played the Jewish guy, duh, and we screamed at each other in song as to who had it worse. I got to sing . . . well, yell . . . the brilliant lyric:

"It's me! It's you! You're black! I'm Jew!"

Excellent. Another winner was a musical developed by Eric Blau of *Jacques Brel* fame, about the founding of modern Zionism—light summer entertainment—called *A Rag on a Stick and a Star*. We called it "Raggedy Shtick with No Stars." We had to make our own fun. I actually had a terrific experience playing opposite the wonderful Ann Crumb in the off-Broadway revival of the Stephen Schwartz–Charles Strouse–Joseph Stein Jewsical *Rags* at the American Jewish Theatre, a cramped space with view-blocking pillars underneath a Gristede's grocery store. I was finishing up an intense solo number, "Wanting," very emotional, and as I took my final breath to sing the last note, in the dramatic silence I heard a whisper behind me in the audience, very deliberate, very *Yiddishe* momme:

"Good Ecting."

Oy. Next.

I just wasn't progressing in my career, I barely met my bills, and I had no love in my life. As I tried and failed to yank the forefinger/thumb off my forehead, I'd get into conversations in my brain: "Ya ain't getting any younger and ya ain't really made it yet." And my other voice would get all defensive and start whipping off a list of my accomplishments: "Yes, but I've been on 'The Broadway!' I played leads off-Broadway! I've got a hot body! I'm naked in a book!" And I'd hear a snooty voice, "Well, you can justify it all you want" and I'd desperately think, yeah, I can justify it all I want! Okay! Okay! *(Don't hit me!)*

By 1993, theater work had dried up and I was waiting tables at a restaurant called Eighteenth and Eighth (surprisingly, at the corner of 18th and 8th), working catering gigs, posing for art classes for that same twenty-five bucks per session that I now needed, and selling sexy body-wear and bathing suits at Raymond Dragon, named after the designer and ex–Colt model, a shop that catered to what would now be called "the circuit crowd." I was literally all over the place and struggling. I felt as though the whole fucking world was succeeding but me. Considering my obsessions with sex and attention and "ecting," I started to wonder what would have been had I followed my true show business calling and deep-down desire to become a goddamn porn star.

But I couldn't get past the voices of my mother and rabbis and fear of what it would do to my career. I didn't have the balls, but it was always in the back of my brain. I did another Bianchi photo shoot in New York City, which gleaned a semi-anonymous shot in his next book, *Extraordinary Friends*, and it was a start, but I wanted . . . needed . . . more.

FOLLIES

I had resumed acting class because my confidence as an actor was shot. I didn't want to keep doing revivals of old musicals and under-cooked new ones. I really yearned to be a more proficient actor and challenge myself, but I wasn't feeling capable. After studying with a wonderful teacher named Suzanne Shepherd and receiving the tweaking I needed to get myself back on the right path, I got down to the final callbacks for the title role in the original off-Broadway produc-tion of Paul Rudnick's hilarious play *Jeffrey*. I didn't get that, but I was rewarded for my hard work by getting cast as Carl in Portland Stage's stunning production of Paula Vogel's *The Baltimore Waltz*, my first nonmusical since leaving college.

I loved the play, the cast, the whole experience. It's an amazing piece about a brother who takes his sister, dying from cancer, on an epic trip. But in the end, it's a fantasy and *he* is actually the one dying, of AIDS, a devastating switch at the end.

I couldn't wait for my folks to come to Maine to see my work and show them how I'd progressed as an actor. Afterwards, my mom was complimentary but not gushing the way I'd hoped, and my dad wasn't a gusher anyway. We went out for a meal after, taking my costar Pam with us, and I was surly and noncommunicative and let Pam deflect and charmingly make my folks feel welcome because I did not. I was pissed and needy. After my folks went back to their hotel, Pam and I were silently walking the hallway to our apartments when suddenly she grabbed me and threw me against the wall.

"What the fuck is your problem?!" she barked. "How could you be so nasty to your parents? They're fantastic."

"I don't give a shit," I replied defiantly. "They were so blasé about what we just did. Fuck them."

"David, do you realize that they just saw their son dying of AIDS? How did you expect them to respond to that?"

Man, that hit me like a thunderbolt. The next morning, as I drove my parents to the airport, I apologized and said I loved them and that the reason I was so hostile was that no one's opinion mattered more to me than theirs. And I started to cry and my mom said what I had hoped she'd say, that they were proud of me. Sometimes, you're not too old to need to hear that.

I finally got to play the lead in *Jeffrey* in a terrific Miami production (for which I was nominated as Best Actor at the Carbonell Awards, the Tonys of South Florida). It was a dream, except when the stage manager called to let me know that one of the other actors had been to see his doctor and discovered he had crabs, and as we all shared a bed in our underwear at the top of the show, he said I should check myself out.

Slutty as I was, I had never contracted an STD and had no idea what crabs even looked like. I went into the bathroom and picked around my pubic hair, thinking not me, never me, I would *never* have anything like *that*. My certainty was questioned when I saw a little dot on my skin amidst the forest. I picked it out and studied it, thinking it was lint. I put it down on the porcelain of the sink, moved in for closer examination, and suddenly, little bitsy legs extended and it started to amble down the sink. Perhaps you heard my shrieks where you live? Horrifying.

I started to rip through my pubes, finding a couple more, and I was mortified, angry, and just plain grossed out. I called my brother-in-law Mike, an osteopath in Hollywood, Florida, and he told me to pick up a prescription and get all the bedding washed. I was staying at one of the new art deco hotels on Ocean Drive, the Cavalier. The bed was the main design element in the room, so it had a zillion blankets, a billion duvet covers, and scads of pillows, and I had to tell housekeeping to clean the whole megillah.

I went down to the front desk and told the guy that the bedding needed to be laundered, and he haughtily asked, "Why?"

I whispered, "Please just do it."

"Why?"

"Just, please."

"Why?"

"BECAUSE I HAVE CRABS, OKAY? *OKAY????*"

His lips coiled up into a judgmental smirk and he said, "I'll take care of it."

Every time I saw him on my stay there, I averted my eyes from his, which were telling me what a slutty whore I was. Well, couldn't really argue that.

I went to the pharmacy to pick up the prescription. Waiting in line, my heart was palpitating and I just felt . . . dirty. When I got to the counter, the pharmacist, eighty years old if he was a day, asked the name on the prescription. I quietly told him my name and the doctor's name, and he said, "Huh? *HUH?*" as apparently there was a bit of deafness there, so I told him again, a bit louder, and he shuffled off to find it, literally shuffled like Tim Conway as The Oldest Man on *The Carol Burnett Show*. Years passed and he finally brought the bag up to me. He stared at it, then at me. Back to the bag, then to me. His eyebrows raised and suddenly he blurted out, loud as a foghorn, "WHAT DO YA GOT,

SCABIES?" I looked behind me at the line of smug, smiling customers who were actually listening as they didn't have cell phones back then to distract. I mumbled, "Yes. Yes. That's exactly what it is. Thank you."

I paid for the medicine, Kwell or whatever the fuck it was, went home, treated myself, got the laundry done, and wondered if it was Slutty David who contracted the bugs or the other guy in the show. I never found out.

The STD train did not stop there, and I later wrote a country song called "Pain in the Butt," which is my fave of all the songs I've written (in it, I never mention the actual words *anal warts*).

About ten years ago, I met a boy named Bo
in front of my apartment house and instantly, I fell.
So I invited him in.
He started with a rimmin'.
It felt real good until he gagged and let out with a yell . . .
"HEY!
You got little lumpy bumpies in your ass!
You got little lumpy bumpies in your ass!
Excuse me while I rinse my mouth.
I don't think I'll be goin' south
on you today. Nice meetin' ya. Goodbye!"
—from "Pain in the Butt"

I gave my butt doctor a CD of the song, and he called me to say that he laughed so hard he almost drove off the side of the road. Yay me.

THE WILD PARTY

In 1995, I auditioned for that off-Broadway play with nudity called *Party*, written and directed by David Dillon, which had had a long, successful run in Chicago and would receive a first-class production at the Douglas Fairbanks Theatre on Theatre Row, Midtown. The show was essentially a group of friends who get together to play a game of Truth or Dare and in the process learn more about each other until everyone is totally naked, physically and emotionally. I thought it was a funny script with a lot of heart, and I could tell it was going to be an entertaining ride. Three of the original Chicago cast members were going to play the roles that they originated, leaving four roles to be cast.

After reading multiple times for the role of Kevin, the host of the party, and doing that final callback in the nude to prove I would have no problem getting naked for an audience, I got cast in the role, and when I told some friends I got the show, there were two responses: either "I could never do that!" or "I can't believe you're doing that!"

Such judgment in the latter response, and though I didn't say it out loud, I thought, Fuck You. YOU have the cojones to do comedy naked. I couldn't believe the shade I was getting and the show hadn't even opened. They just expected it to be stupid and embarrassing and all about cock. None of that was the case. It was actually a very witty, sweet show with a fun-loving spirit to it, about how, as gay men, sometimes we have to make our friends our family.

We got a nice bit of validation when the *New York Times* gave us a very positive review. It was my first naked play, and although I only stripped in the last five minutes, I loved being a part of it. We were on the boards at the same time that the great playwright Terrence McNally's *Love! Valour! Compassion!* was on Broadway—another play with extended male nudity—but we were much lighter, and though hardly Shakespeare, *Party* was a delightful romp. I would periodically run into Terrence at the uptown bus stop, and we'd chat on the way to our respective Midtown theaters.

I was getting naked off-Broadway eight times a week, and we (cast and audience) were all having a fabulous time. The production did have its creepy moments backstage, though, because one of the producers was just gross. He'd come up to me at various times to tell me how juicy my cock looked onstage, or to make some highly inappropriate commentary about the other cast members' members. And butts. I'm a big boy (emotionally, I mean), so I could handle it and pretty much just laughed in his face and ignored it, but it cast a sleazy pall over the whole experience. Still it was a fun gig, high-profile and highly entertaining, and I was happy to be there.

IT SHOULDA BEEN YOU

Because of *Party*, I was starting to become a bit of an off-Broadway sex symbol, which I certainly took advantage of for trysts and hookups. However, when it came to men, I was still a bit of a body Nazi. My best girlfriend, Anne, said I would never find love if I continued to look only for the ideal, the perfect bodies, men who looked like TV stars. Fuck you, I thought, I don't want love, I want sex. But that little boy with the pillow—deep down, I knew she was right. I would never find love? I was determined to prove her wrong.

Country night at Boy Bar on the Lower East Side. I was waiting for the drag queen to start her show when I saw this cute little guy in big round glasses smiling at me. On some, those glasses would look silly. On him, cute. Not really my type, but he had a beautiful smile with these bright white teeth. I thought, here's my chance to prove Anne wrong, and I went right up to him to say hi. His name was Gus, and he wrote gay nonfiction books. He had a deep, manly voice and was smart, funny, and as possessed of a broad knowledge of pop culture minutiae as I was.

"Replacement Jan Brady?"

"Geri Reischl! Okay. *The Facts of Life* theme song was written by . . . ?"

"Hmmm . . . "

"You take the good, you take the bad . . . "

"Oh . . . uh . . . Gloria Loring and Alan Thicke!"

"Aha!"

As we bantered back and forth, we began chatting about more personal things, about our families and dating and work, moving into the world of truth telling, truth after truth after truth, opening up to each other in ways I hadn't in a very long time. The conversation jumped around. He went from the deep pain of his mother's death from cancer to—

"Have you ever been fisted?"

I recoiled with a giggle. "God, no."

"Have you ever wanted to? Come on. We only tell the truth here, remember?"

"Curious, so . . . yeah."

"Really?"

"How does one even approach that on a date?"

"Depends where you meet him. You can hire a specialist. Okay, truth: ever hired an escort?"

"No, um . . . I have never . . . hired an escort. You?"

"Yes."

"And?" I said with more than passing interest.

"And what?"

"Details. I want details."

"I called him. He came over. I fucked him. I paid him. He left."

"You're a writer?"

He laughed. "Well, it really was about as interesting as all that. Okay. First love?"

"Ah, that would be Stan."

"Tell me."

We went back to his place and sat on his couch and smoked Marlboros and drank Scotch and told each other everything. I hadn't had such a fantastic evening in forever. We started making out, and when it got hot and heavy, he took me into his bedroom. He lit a couple of candles, turned off the lights, and went into the bathroom. I sat on the edge of the bed; the room was beautiful, so romantic. I took off my shirt, stood up, took off my pants, sat down, stood up, took off my underwear. Nervous. Hard at the anticipation. It was so long since I'd gotten physical with someone I actually really liked.

The bathroom door opened. I saw the white of his towel, then the white of his teeth, and as he stepped into the candlelight, I saw the rest of him. He was . . . kinda paunchy. Slender and unshaped everywhere else. A little hairy. Well, a lot hairy. I should have known by the depth of his voice that the testosterone would make itself apparent in other ways. I assumed he would have a cute, toned body underneath. I didn't feel the need to sleep with huge bodybuilders—I'd at least gotten over that—but I liked a nice, lean, muscled body to play with in bed. It just turned me on, and I knew that my body could attract others of its ilk or better. That sounds terrible, because . . . it's terrible. But at the time, I figured it was no worse than someone who probably only wanted me for my body. But then, that assumption gave no credit to the other guy (or to myself) that he may indeed have wanted me for more than my shell. Since I had built myself up, I wasn't connecting with men on anything but a physical level, so that's what I always suspected was motivating others too.

He moved closer, melted into me, removed his towel, and whispered in my ear . . .

"Does my body disappoint you?"

Whoa. What? He knew. He could sense it. But I had to put him at ease, even though he'd nailed it. I gulped. "No. No. Uh-uh. No. No."

I saw a lie detector needle go PHWOOO! Shattering the glass, exploding with sparks . . . PHWOO! I shook the image off as I kissed him and we lay down on the bed and rolled around and did I-don't-know-what for I-don't-know-how-long. I wasn't present. I wanted so badly to get swept up in the moment and put everything we'd established that night into the sex, but I couldn't keep it hard. In this night of a gazillion truths, I had lied. I had to come clean.

"Hey, Gus . . . let's take a break?"

"Okay, mister," he said, sitting up with a goofy, contented smile.

I rolled onto my belly and watched his chest hair unravel and said, "I lied to you before."

He chuckled. "Oh no no no. We do not lie in this relationship. Hahaha."

"Um, I know, but . . . well . . . when you asked if your body disappointed me . . . well . . . I guess . . . it did a little."

Boom. I was being honest. But I knew as the words escaped me that it was a travesty. Oh, to take it back. I imagined brightly illustrated cartoon words tumbling out of my mouth and me sucking them back in before they were heard. "IT DID A LITTLE." Thwap! But nope. Heard. Loud and clear. I couldn't unsay it and he couldn't unhear it. Suddenly, lying seemed to be the moral choice.

"Really." He was immediately defensive. He looked straight ahead with a steely glare.

"Oh god, please understand that I'm so used to sleeping with these body boys, and I'm not used to someone who isn't into the gym."

"I go to the gym, thank you very much! It's just not my whole life."

"I know, I mean, I think this is a problem *I* have. I wish I wasn't so into this perky tits thing, but I am, and I'm afraid that if we start something, I won't be able to keep the commitment when the first pair of, you know . . . *legs* . . . walks up to me and . . . I don't know if I could control myself." Poor me. It's a good thing I never became a lawyer, because this argument sucked.

"Uh-huh."

"You are so wonderful and cute and everything I could possibly want."

Did I know I was being a total shit? That this diarrhea of the mouth was like ripping his skin off with a knife, that I was doling out the body shaming like a twelve-year-old in gym class, the way they did to me? Too late. I had dug the grave and thrown myself in headfirst. From the side, I could see his eyes start to well up, and I could feel his determination not to look at me. He said nothing.

"I had to be honest with you." No, I didn't, not in that moment, not at that point in our "relationship." Jesus. What the fuck was wrong with me? "Please understand this is something about myself that I hate. I wish I was over it, but it's there." Poor poor fucking idiot me.

What I wanted to do to save my skin was play the honesty card and say, "Well—you asked!" But for once, I shut up. He may have been hairy as a Fay Wray costar, but I was just a superficial asshole, no better than anyone who ever shamed me for being skinny, but this was worse because we were naked, in a bed, expressing affection for each other. It couldn't be a more vulnerable moment for him, and I pounced. I sincerely didn't have bad intentions and I didn't mean to be spiteful, to hurt him. I was never that guy, but in that moment . . . I was. In spades. I knew there was no way to clean up this mess, so I decided to just leave it on the floor. I slipped out of bed and put on my clothes to the most fraught and uncomfortable silence I had ever experienced. When I was finished . . .

"Bye?"

"Bye."

I left his apartment feeling like utter crap. I later convinced Gus to give me a second chance and we dated for a week, but it was doomed from those moments of "honesty" in his bed. It says a lot about him that he was willing to overlook our very rocky start, but we couldn't get over that rough night, and eventually we both lost interest. This lovely, sweet, adorable man. Heave-ho. Something had to change. I knew that. But nothing did.

I went on to more sexual conquests with barely any resonance, every so often falling into a month-long attempt to commit, but mostly there was no real intimacy to be had . . .

Cameron, Darryl . . . with a comma in between?
That was my first three-way, a frat boy hazing scene.
We role-played they were freshmen, and I was upper-class.
Cameron did my laundry, while Darryl ate my ass.
Oh!
Ricky, Karl, Mark, and Ben.
Lyndon, Sheldon, Marshall, Ken.
Ronald, Harold, Lowell, Don . . .
oy, the list goes on and on!
—from "The Book of Lust"

And as I continued to fill up that Book of Lust, I felt lonelier and lonelier. The list indeed went on and on and on and on . . .

NICE WORK IF YOU CAN GET IT

For all the high profile and success of *Party*, the salary was a third of what I'd made on Broadway and I still couldn't pay my bills, so I went to my screaming queen of an agent's office to discuss the direction of my so-called career. Sorry—it's another "actor complaining" portion of the book. Don't worry. It's short.

"So why can't I get seen for TV and film, Marcel?" I grumbled. I had been studying camera acting technique and was ready to go. "I can't afford my life just flashing my cock off-Broadway. You said you would—"

"Aha!" he said abruptly, cutting me off.

"What?"

"See? What you did?"

"What?"

He made a limp wrist gesture. "That."

"*What?*"

Another gesture. "That! Ya know, ya do a gay show and suddenly your behavior becomes all flamboyant, it's like it's it's it's . . ."

He was overemoting his rambling search for a word . . .

". . . *ingrained* in you! And you're not even aware of it."

"Marcel, where is this coming fro—"

"I am not going to send you into casting offices acting like a fucking faggot. They all know you're gay as it is, and they'll never see you for straight roles if you walk in the door like Charles Nelson Reilly!"

Jesus.

"Charles Nelson Reilly? Marcel, I know what to bring in the room and what to leave outside. I'm not going to stick my tongue down Oliver Stone's throat."

"Well, some of your feedback tells me otherwise."

What the fuck was he talking about?

"Really."

"Really."

I stared him down. Was he bullshitting me? He offered no examples and I didn't care to ask. Standstill. I stood up slowly, menacingly. I pointed at him in a butch and deliberate fashion as if I'd had a gun. I glared at him, bloody murder, and growled, "I'll work on it."

As I turned to leave, I was thrilled that this confrontation had brought a tinge of fear into his eyes, but I left there ultimately with no agent, and I was stuck in a little off-Broadway show making a dime. I couldn't wait another table. So . . .

I told an old acquaintance I was desperate for a job,
and oddly then he asked if I was anal or a slob.
He said, "I clean apartments, and I could use a hand.
But there's one stipulation. My customers demand . . .

Scrubbing toilets with my dick out.
Vacuum carpets in the buff.
Making sure my buttocks stick out
waiting for the sheets to fold and fluff.
Flash a lot of muscle

while dutifully I hustle
to make a hovel sparkle like the Taj Mahal . . ."

Hmmm. So I thought . . .

I'm obsessed with nudity,
Attention is like sex to me,
Cleaning is good therapy, and bonus, you get paid,
I think I found my calling . . .
—from "The Naked Maid"

. . . and I became a Naked Maid! I'd go to these sometimes messy, sometimes not houses, take my clothes off, and, weenie flopping, make benign chatter about Madonna or abortion rights, find the cleaning supplies, and begin.

Sometimes the guys would follow me around and we'd chat as I washed, waxed, and dusted—nothing too work intensive—or sometimes they'd just stay in their office and work or watch TV in the den. At first I thought it was a waste of the extra cash they were paying for a nude maid, but then I realized it was the thrill of suddenly having a naked guy in their room, nonchalantly cleaning while they went about their business. When I'd talk to clients, I'd turn on the charm and make jokes ("Polish your knob?") and sometimes the client would get naked, sometimes just to relax, sometimes to play with himself in hope I'd join in. I'd get on all fours to clean the floors, pushing my ass back as I "struggled" to get into all the crevices, reach past the client to dust shelves while letting my cock almost graze him, stand in the shower soaking wet while scrubbing the tub—anything to tease and put on a show. Good clean fun.

The job would end with either a clean house and nothing more or a request to jack off for them, which, after a couple of hours of teasing,

I was happy to do. It was a mini version of the Gaiety Theatre, and I always found it arousing and satisfying. The pay was pretty good, and usually, if I shot a load, there would be a generous tip. Sometimes, even though the business wasn't called "Mop and Blow" or "Spic and Spank," I'd engage sexually if I found the client attractive; I'd go off the clock and play, getting sucked off on the newly shiny-clean kitchen table or getting fucked in the bathtub while I was waiting for the Scrubbing Bubbles to melt the scum off the shower curtain.

The naked housecleaning helped financially, but I was still a little behind. See what I did there? Bah-dum-bum. Emphasis on the bum.

THE BODY BEAUTIFUL

When I told my folks I was going to be naked onstage in *Party*, they wished me well but told me they were going to take a pass on coming to NY to see it. My mom said she was fine that I was doing it but that it wasn't for them. I understood and was okay with that. However, one day a few months into the run, she called to tell me she was coming to NY for a conference for her women's Jewish organization, formerly Pioneer Women, now called Na'amat (I was the entertainment at one of their events, and my opening joke was "What's an *amat* and why don't you want to be one?").

My mother told me she was thinking of coming to the show. She had no problem watching other guys get naked; she just didn't want to **see** *me* naked. I told her I only had my clothes off in the last five minutes, so she agreed to come watch the show as long as she could escape when it was time for me to disrobe. I said sure, and arranged for my mom to sit by the exit door, and gave her the cue when I would be getting naked: right after we raise our glasses in a toast to friendship. When that happened, she could just slip out, having done her due diligence as a good mom watching her son do high-profile off-Broadway theater.

Except . . . no. She realized that if she opened that door, a large slice of light would pour in and draw attention to her, so she froze up when it was time. I didn't think it would be a big deal for her to sneak out early, but she did, and decided she had to stick it out for those last few minutes. So what would any good but squeamish mother do? She dropped her head and stared into her lap as I took off my clothes and continued on.

However, she looked to her left and noticed there was a reflection of the stage in the fire marshal notification that hangs by every theater entrance, a record of the marshals' visits under a Plexiglas sheet. It perfectly framed the very funny lead actor Ted Bales as he went about his final antics until the curtain came down. My mother watched in the Plexiglas, and when the lights came back on for our curtain calls, we were wearing robes and she could look at the stage again. Now *that's* commitment. Thank you, Mom. Even though I know *Party* was far from your favorite theatrical experience, you showed up. You kind of hated it, but you went. My mom was the best.

I was now full tilt into showing my body off wherever and however I could, onstage and behind closed doors. One of the prodigious perks in the NY theater community was being asked to appear in *Broadway Bares*, one of the great fundraising events of all time, for Broadway Cares/Equity Fights AIDS. The show was started by the director/choreographer Jerry Mitchell. It began as a strip show in a bar, and thirty years later it's the largest fundraising event of its kind, raising millions of dollars and providing a spectacular, memorable evening of entertainment unlike any other.

The first year I did the show was 1994. I appeared in a couple of musical numbers, including a takeoff of *My Fair Lady* in which I sat naked with another guy in a giant champagne glass. As publicity for the big show, we did a mini presentation at Splash, a hot gay bar in Chelsea that was known for its onstage shower performances.

A few guys from *Broadway Bares* did individual strips, and as I'm not really a dancer, I decided to filch a piece I'd seen in Vancouver when I was on tour, a cowboy strip to "Desperado" by the Eagles. Slow, moody, and the only strip that took it down to absolutely nothing (in Vancouver, the guy went fully nude, but you couldn't show cock in a NY bar), it was absolutely nerve-racking but exhilarating. I pulled out the sensuous, butch David as much as I could, and when I finished taking off everything and covered my dick with a cowboy hat, the place went nuts.

Afterwards, we raised a bunch of cash doing "The Rotation," in which we collected dollar bills in our G-strings as we moved along on top of the bar. It was so much fun and it felt strangely right. The ugly Jewish boy in me felt validated, my Gaiety Theatre fantasies were fulfilled, and the activist in me was gratified that we raised so much cash for a very good cause.

The following year, while I was in *Party*, the big show was at the iconic Palladium and they stripped me down to a G-string and turned me into an ice cream sundae to the song "Lick It." The dancers piled me up with fake ice cream, chocolate sauce, and whipped cream—messy but steamy. I've never heard an audience react like that, like at a rock concert, and once again we did "The Rotation," raising tons of cash. That's truly the best show I've ever been in, and it's one of the things I've missed since leaving NY.

The organization does a fantastic job and the show gets more spectacular and lucrative every year. Of course, we all hope that the day comes when the show is not a necessity and is strictly entertainment, but for now it's a phenomenal event in so many ways. And personally, a lot came together for me in those performances: my body, soul, and art all merged; stripping and getting naked on a stage in a beautiful theater piece could actually be a public service, could lend itself to a greater cause, a higher calling. It's the kind of legitimacy I was searching for, and I never turned back . . . for the good and the bad of it.

KISMET

I was waiting for the light to change on the corner of 23rd Street and 9th Avenue, on my way to the Chelsea Gym wearing my typically whorish tiny tight shorts with no underwear and cutaway tank top. The Chelsea was a male-only gay gym, and we all flopped around in the highly sex-charged wind on the gym floor, while the steam room downstairs by the sauna and showers was infamous for a lot of sweaty after-workout action. The late comedian Frank Maya coined it "The Low Self-Esteem Room." (Miss you, pal.) I did partake from time to time, getting and giving the occasional tug or blow job but not much more (the guy who infamously got double-penetrated and ripped his rectum in there kind of soured me on getting more adventurous).

On the corner across the street from me was an older man, hunched over with an intense look on his face, staring at me, bullets. It was a little unnerving as he looked like a Dr. Seuss villain. I looked down as I began to cross to avoid his eyes, but in my periphery I noticed him reach into his pocket and begin to futz. I thought he was playing with himself, but he pulled something out that I couldn't see and pressed it into his hand. As I was about to pass him in the crosswalk, I looked over at him, still staring at me, hard as nails, and he flipped his hand around and in his palm there was a folded twenty-dollar bill. I caught my breath. I got a) flustered, b) turned on, and c) a little offended. Twenty bucks? When I reached the curb, I nonchalantly turned around to see him standing stock-still, flashing that twenty-dollar bill. I turned to continue walking . . . and tripped. I'm sure his fantasy went to black, but mine went nuts. I got immediately hard, forcing the fabric of my blue-striped Dolfin shorts straight out into an obscene public bulge. I adjusted myself and continued on my way.

Inside the gym, I couldn't shake that incident or my erection. When I did my leg lifts, the constant rubbing against the nylon made me shoot in my shorts, right there, hanging from the high bar. As this was the Chelsea Gym, the queen working out next to me gave me a dead-pan look that said, "Oh. Her." I jumped down, covered myself, and slid into a corner. As I sat there waiting for the cum to dry, I couldn't let it go. Being a naked maid was one thing, but this—money for sex— would be quite another.

I never knew how far I'd go to make a buck, but I'd be lying if I told you that all of this happened just because I needed cash. There were so many things at work in my mind; it was just a matter of time before I gave in to the secret desires and fantasies that had been swimming around in my psyche for thirty-six years.

RENT

Two a.m. and I was sleeping soundly when the phone rang, shocking me to life. I flailed around, knocking over a half-filled cup of cold coffee. "Hello? Hello?"

It was Mo from "Maturity Escorts"—my boss, dispatcher, employer, pimp, madam, whatever. He apologized for calling me at home, as I had procrastinated on getting that beeper after my interview two nights before. He had a job for me, my first, if I wanted it. I couldn't think to say "no," so I gave him the go-ahead as I foraged, trembling, for a pencil and paper. He had gotten a request for one of his other guys who had similar coloring and body type to mine but was otherwise engaged. Would I go as him?

"Sure," I said. "What's my name?"

"Reno."

Reno. Okay.

My name was to be Reno and two guys would be there. One, Ben, would pay me to top him and the other, his friend, would watch. Mo gave me the address and wished me luck. I hung up. My heart was pumping madly. I grabbed a quick shower and dressed in my slutty, strategically ripped jeans and tank top. It was a little on the nose but sexy, so they wouldn't yell "Zadie Whore!" and slam the door in my face.

I hopped a cab to a nice apartment complex on West 34th Street and the doorman let me through with a shrug as if I was the thousandth guest at a party. In the elevator, I kept telling myself, "You're an actor. You can do this!" but my mother's voice was a lot louder. "Shame shaaaaaaame! A *shonda* for the neighbors!"

Shut up, I thought as the door opened to the tenth floor. The apartment was right across from the elevator—convenient, I thought, for my hasty, bloody escape. I went up and pressed my ear to the door. Music was playing: Cher singing, swear to god, "Gypsies, Tramps and Thieves." I pounded on the door and heard footsteps and giggling. I straightened up, flexed my chest, adjusted myself, and became Reno, body for hire, Italian porn stud inside a scared little Midwest Jewish boy-man.

The door opened, and my shorter, slighter doppelgänger (my age, with my nose and hairline) did a quick down/up with his eyes and broke into a wide, lascivious grin. Slurring like a lush, he said,

"Well, helloooo. I'm Ben."

"Reno. How ya doing?" I answered in my best De Niro.

We shook hands, he walked me past the door and shut it behind me. Game on.

Friendly disclaimer: this next section is for Mature Audiences only, and if any of it makes you a little uncomfortable, well . . . so was I.

"This is my pal Billy."

Here was the friend, Billy, in his green gym shorts and plain white T-shirt, eyeing me suspiciously. He would have been attractive had he not been so psychotic-looking, with a crooked mouth and intense brow overhanging squinty little eyes. His body was muscular yet malformed, like the figures in those picture books that allow you to put different body tops onto body bottoms with the turn of a page. His parts didn't match.

"Hey," I said, offering my hand.

He shook it and asked in a heavy redneck accent, "What'd you say yer name was?"

"David . . . uh . . . Reno." Damn it! Well, I was nervous. And besides, we all know even Reno's name wasn't Reno.

Drunk Ben slurred, "I like your body, just my type," and then led me to the dining room table, on which sat bags of white powder, rolled-up dollar bills, and dildos of various sizes and colors. He picked up a twenty-dollar money tube. "Blooow?" The word stretched out into three syllables; he sounded like Martin Short in an SCTV sketch. Knowing that I wouldn't be the most unhip person in the room relaxed me a little, and I said no, but asked for a cigarette. There was a pack of Marlboro Lights and a matchbook from the Candle, a sleazy Upper West Side bar, on the table. I took one, lit it, and began to puff. My nerves deflated me a little Down There, but the smoke gave me courage as I mentally fluffed.

Billy pulled off his T-shirt, and I took it as my cue to begin slowly stripping down. Ben quickly got naked, Billy stayed in his shorts, and I removed my clothes carefully so as not to fall on my face as I stepped out of my pants. When I was fully naked, nervous as I was, my cock jutted straight up the second the air touched it. Ben moved the accoutrements off the table and lay facedown on it, head hanging off the side, tongue out, waiting for me. I dipped my half-smoked cigarette into the dirty ashtray water as my signal that I was ready.

"Suck his dick," Billy growled to Ben, and motioned me into position with a flick of his head.

I hesitated for a moment, took a deep breath, and with exaggerated cockiness made my way to the table. The instant I was in reach of Ben's tongue, he began to lap at me, devouring it with a skill and a gentle suction that brought me too close too soon. I pulled out. "Easy. Easy!"

You don't get two hundred bucks for premature ejaculation.

When the sensation of impending orgasm subsided, I offered up my dick to him again and he began slower, savoring it as if it was the most succulent thing he'd ever put in his mouth. Billy began to play with Ben's ass, causing him to suck on me with more desperation, but I was now at the point where I could control myself without popping too soon, and I was totally intrigued by the intense devotion to my cock. I watched in wonder.

Billy interrupted my trance. "I want you to fuck him with these." He picked up two black dildos—one huge, the other *very* huge. Ben got all excited and walked himself on his hands and knees in a half circle before resting his belly on the table, legs dangling off the side, his ass at the perfect height and angle. I gingerly took the smaller of the two dildos (which was still gigundo). It was already greasy—I didn't ask— and I began to work it in slowly, slowly, slo—

Suddenly, there was a loud sucking sound as that big ol' dildo got hoovered inside him. Yikes. No foreplay here. I pulled it out and reached for the mega longer, thicker rubber tool and worked it in, meeting almost no resistance, until it was buried up to my fingers. Billy played with Ben's face, caressing it, slapping it, gently whispering to him, inaudible to me, as I worked this monumental toy in and out, in and out, in and out, in and out, in and out. It was mesmerizing.

After about five Zen-like minutes of that, I heard, "Fuck him with your dick."

"Oh," I said, as if I had just been interrupted while watching *Melrose Place*. I pulled the dildo out and looked for a place to put it, but the table was already covered with stuff, so I just laid it on the rug (it was Reno, not David, being so unsanitary). I found a condom among the cocaine and cigarettes, and I put it on and began to fuck Ben as Billy watched across the table. I flexed my chest and abs as I worked. I was living my fantasy, being paid for sex, being watched and desired and admired for my body and my sexual prowess. I couldn't get any further from my childhood, and it made me harder to think of how "bad" I was behaving. I lost sight of myself and began to fuck him the way I would for the cameras, as if this was going to be a porn fuck for the ages, a Gay Video Award–winning scene from the new hit film *Put Your Money on Reno!*

I plowed Ben so hard and for so long that I totally lost track of time, until he asked for a break to smoke. I pulled out and he went to the couch and lit a cigarette, but Billy ordered me to "Play with his ass!" As one who prides himself on taking direction well, and to show my creativity and range, I crossed stage right and brought my foot up and started teasing his ass with my big toe. Billy growled, "Yeah. Fuck him with your foot."

Shakily balancing on my left foot, I worked my big toe inside, and he began to gurgle and moan, so I pressed forward, finagling more toes inside until . . .

"Ow! Ow! Ow! Toenail! Toenail!"

Whoa! I pulled out, lost my balance, recovered, but . . . awkward. Instead of losing my composure, I suddenly channeled Shecky Greene and said, "Note to self: Next time, pedicure. Pedicure as well as douche. HaHaHa. HaHa. Ha." Eek.

Billy asked if I ever bottomed, and though I did from time to time, I had an image to uphold. I said, butch as could be, "No, strictly top." They looked at each other and laughed. I felt my fantasy slip a li'l bit.

Meanwhile, the hour was up and I assumed Ben wanted to cum, so I reached for his now-shriveled cock. He slapped my hand away. "Nooo. I want you to cum on me."

I said, "Okay," grabbed my impossibly hard stiffy, stroked it twice, and blew a huge load all over his face and chest and, oops, the couch. I usually cum a lot, but this whole episode had fed my little sperm makers so intensely that it was an almost endless creamy shower that knocked him backwards.

Silence for ten seconds as we looked at all the little puddles. Finally, Billy said, "Whoa."

I said, "Sorry about the couch."

Ben said, "That . . . was a Kodak moment."

Aaand g'night folks.

Billy went over to a messy antique desk, picked up a roll of cash, and pressed it into my left hand. I had jizz and nonoxynol in the right and a confused look on my face. Had I been excused?

There was a box of Kleenex on the table, so I grabbed a few and cleaned myself off. The room was loudly silent as I pulled on my clothes. Billy and Ben watched me, exchanging glances, and I pretended to be really into the act of dressing for an audience. With my clothes on, I still felt naked. As I sat down to put on my shoes, I figured this is the moment Billy pulls out a gun, calls me *"BITCH!"* and shoots me, so I nudged the scenario in another direction by randomly commenting on the weather and how I'd just seen a *fabulous* touring production of *A Chorus Line.* Ben picked up his cell phone, Billy pulled on his T-shirt, I grabbed my coat, and they waved and smiled, and I think Billy winked at me. Aw.

"Bye, guys!" was all I could manage as my heart pounded me out the door. I shut it behind me and leaned back on it with a sigh of relief. Did it! Made it! Liked it! Glad it was over! I counted the money: 20, 40, 60, 80, 100, 120, 140, 160, 180 . . . hmm . . . 20, 40, 60 . . . 180.

They stiffed me twenty bucks, and where was the proof? I weighed whether to go back in or chalk it up to experience. Fuck it, I thought, I worked hard for that cash. I pounded on the door. It opened. Billy, unsmiling. "Um, guys, um, hi . . . uh, there's only one eighty here."

They did a little faux negotiation. "Well, now, how's that possible? Did you fuck up?" "Noooo, it wasn't me, I didn't fuck up." I could tell the mistake wasn't meant to be caught. As a reward for my boldness, Billy grabbed the rolled-up twenty that had been up their noses and handed it to me. With a tinge of smug, he said, "Sorry . . . Reno."

"No problem. Byeee!" I was out of there and in that elevator that knew better than to make me wait. Trial by fire. Two guys! Drugs! Swindle! Deep down I was still a nice Jewish . . . eh. But I did it.

And that was the beginning of my double life.

I'd do *Party* and afterwards get paged for dates. Not every night, as I was still the oldest whore in NY, but enough to help me relax financially. It was good, but not without its uncomfortable moments.

One night, there was the guy who said, just as I was leaving his hotel room, "Can I . . . can I ask you something?" He then went to his suitcase and pulled out the *Playbill* from *Party*. He had seen it just that night and was floored when I walked in the door. The agency didn't have photos of me—this was pre-website, so Mo sold me by description only. The client wasn't going to say anything, but he really wanted my autograph. He was a nice guy, so I signed the program, which blew my hooker name—Darren—and when I asked if he could just not mention it to anyone, he said, deadpan, "I'm from Dubuque. Who would I tell?"

I accompanied my clients to dinner, made love to them, dressed up as TV repairmen and superheroes, got spanked, pissed on them, fisted a couple—no, literally, I fisted a *couple*—and did pretty much everything, safely. What can I say? Most Versatile.

But the through line of all this was, and you can believe me or don't: respect. Me, them. Them, me. This was actually the best job I ever had, outside of showbiz. I had great clients. They were always happy to see me, and I was always determined to give them a nice time. Even when I was just supposed to be a piece of meat, they never made me feel like a piece of meat. Some were lonely, some had wives or girlfriends, some were curious first-timers, some didn't want to waste time at the bars, some needed comfort in dire times, and almost all had something about them that made the hour go by pleasurably. And I was there to give them some fun . . . and a little connection.

I needed that too.

SEESAW

HX magazine had an ad for Carter's New York Prime, a monthly traveling sex party—organized orgies in various hotel suites and private homes for which you had to audition. They only allowed "prime meat": the best bodies, the handsomest men, the nicest cocks. I was told that, before each party, ten or so members of the club would sit in a half circle with clipboards. The hopefuls would enter one at a time and stand fully naked in front of the clothed interrogators so they could be interviewed.

The club sounded like a mix of fun/horrible, yet I was curious to see if I could make the cut, so I showed up one night, stood in front of the glitter gays, happily exposed (much like my *Party* audition), and answered questions like "Would you jump into a group sex scene or sit on the sidelines?" and "What kind of body turns you on?" and "Top or bottom?" I answered with chutzpah and charm, and since I was at my most muscular, I passed muster under the elite gay microscope and became a member and went into the backroom to join the fuckfest.

I was thrilled I had gotten in due to my body (the little boy in the mirror was proud), but I also hated that I had gotten in due to my body (the grown man knew there was something awful about the exclusivity). The qualifications made sense to me at first; the idea was that you would want to have sex with everyone there and it would feel like a brotherhood of sorts. However, being one of the "elite" did not excuse me from being ignored or sneered at because, being in my mid-thirties, I was one of the older guys there and some of the young 'uns could not get away from me fast enough and wanted nothing to do with me. What started as an ego boost would sometimes end up slapping me in the face. But I enjoyed public fucking and sucking, sometimes in a group, sometimes one-on-one, and I warranted enough attention that I kept going back.

Carter, the event's organizer, was always very welcoming, and on nights when I was feeling a little less desired, I would take a break and he and I would chat about other stuff beyond sex. We were closer in age than the rest of the guys, so we had a little more in common. One night he told me that a friend of his was coming to town from Los Angeles and that I was perfectly his type. Would I want to go out with him? He was a high-profile magazine editor and we would have a lot in common. I was up for it, and the star-fucker in me liked the fact that he was renowned and highly respected in a field that, as an avid reader of all things pop culture and political, was important to me.

One night after *Party*, I met The Editor at his room at the Paramount Hotel. When he opened the door, he greeted me with a wide, charming smile, and the first thing he said to me was "I like your nose." I blushed and smiled back, feeling good that there was a mutual immediate attraction. He was tall, swarthy, built, and handsome, and after chatting briefly, I found him soft-spoken, laconic, and incredibly smart and charismatic, all of which made him very sexy to me. We proceeded to have really good sweaty, athletic sex. He was the bottom of anyone's dreams and, unlike out of bed, was incredibly responsive and vocal to me being inside him.

Whenever The Editor came to NY, I'd meet him at the Paramount after my show and we'd have a whirlwind sexfest. Very rarely did we go out, but one time at lunch at the Broadway Diner he grabbed my hand under the table, and I was shocked. I found that very encouraging. I was the smitten kitten with him, but also a bit insecure. He was just such a good-looking, high-profile, successful guy, and deep deep down inside I began to criticize myself, some schlub in a silly off-Broadway show, selling my body on the side, unworthy of his attention. He was not very expressive about how he felt about me and it left me constantly wondering, so I was thrilled that he was reciprocating. It was going in a direction I hadn't been in a very long time, with me being wildly attracted to him both physically and as a person. I believed it was totally mutual.

I was leaving *Party* shortly and taking a break from escorting to play Marvin in *Falsettos* at the Skylight Opera in Milwaukee. When our three guys from the original Chicago *Party* cast moved to open the LA production, the NY producers hired replacements and immediately updated our ads with the screaming headline NEW CUTER CAST! It may seem hypocritical, because I was so exclusive about my own tastes in my private life, but I found that pretty offensive and disrespectful of the fine work we had established. I knew it was time to leave the show.

I was going to have one final evening with The Editor before I left town, so I wanted to make it really memorable, and I knew exactly where we were going to go. A couple of months earlier, the publicist for *Party* had gotten me one of those profiles in *Playbill* that says So-and-So Star eats at So-and-So Restaurant and then there's a whole piece about the place with the headshot of the Star right up top. I found out that, most times, the celebrity had never been to the restaurant, but in exchange for the photo and "recommendation," you'd get a free dinner for two. I always thought those profiles were real and so cool, and even though I didn't get to pick the restaurant, I was thrilled to be asked.

It was a Thai restaurant on 9th Avenue and 54th Street that I had never eaten in, but they had a blowup of the article in the window with my photo and I thought that was nifty. I wanted to impress The Editor with a nice dinner and my "notoriety," so I figured I would trade on my celebrity and take the restaurant up on that free dinner.

I stopped in the afternoon of our date to make a reservation and let them know that I was there to collect. The woman very sternly reprimanded me in a heavy Thai accent. "YOU ATE HERE ALREADY!" I told her no, I'd never set foot in the place. "YOU ATE HERE ALREADY!!" I gestured toward the window where my picture was still on display and said I never got my meal. "YOU ATE HERE ALREADY!!!!!!!!" Holy crap, she started shoving me out of there and began swearing at me in Thai (I assume it was swearing) as if I had just tried to rob the place. I hit the street and she slammed the door after me, and I felt like a bus depot hooker after a drug deal gone bad.

I ended up taking The Editor to a diner that night. He was a little weird and distant at dinner and said he wasn't feeling great when I brought him back to his room. I was leaving early the next morning for Milwaukee, so we just said our goodbyes, and my expectations were kind of dashed. I figured that the restaurant woman had put a curse on me for trying to claim what was rightfully mine, and let me just say—celebrity ain't what it's cracked up to be, especially if you're only a celebrity in your own mind and/or *Playbill* magazine.

I left town to do the show and periodically I'd call The Editor and hear nothing back, and it left me really distraught and enervated. Compounding that was the news that my college roommate Paul, whom I loved dearly, had died of AIDS complications while I was in Milwaukee. If you know *Falsettos*, I was rehearsing around a hospital bed, my character Marvin watching his lover Whizzer die of AIDS, and the actor playing opposite me was HIV-positive in real life. I wasn't feeling well myself, which was scaring me, so between Paul, the show, my health, and the Editor, I was a worn-out, crying mess. I could barely get it together to do the show, but they were the most raw and personal performances I ever gave.

I would do my show, go home to sleep, and then lie in bed all day. I ate practically nothing and just languished, watching *America's Funniest Home Videos*—not laughing, just staring.

Eventually, things started to work themselves out. The Editor finally sent a letter to say that the same time he met me, he'd met someone in LA, and because he didn't want a long-distance relationship, he'd decided to go with him. He just didn't know how to tell me that last night together. Whatever, I thought, and my heart hurt, but at least I had some closure. I got myself tested for HIV and I remained negative.

The show ended up being very cathartic, and though Paul was gone and I was grieving, I was able to focus more on the wonderful times we had together and just feel lucky that I knew him. I love you, mister.

When I returned to NY, I called Mo and continued my escorting. I also went back to Carter's parties, but I knew they weren't good for my head. After finally getting emotionally involved with someone, even briefly, and after having sex with men who may not have been as attractive to me physically but were welcoming and sweet and happy that I was there as an escort, something was changing in me. Being a member of such an exclusive club was a badge of honor for a while, until it wasn't—until it didn't feel honorable at all. It felt kind of empty. I went to a few more parties and then stopped.

I HAD A BALL

I credit David Sedaris with setting my whole world on a new trajectory. I used to be able to read books while walking the streets of New York, staying focused on what I was reading but still taking in everything in my peripheral vision so as not to get run over by a car or a fast-moving New Yorker juggling twelve cups of coffee and a briefcase. This was before cell phones took all of our walking manners away.

One day in 1996, I was reading Sedaris's first collection, *Barrel Fever*, while strolling down 8th Avenue on my way to the Chelsea Gym. Something in the book made me guffaw out loud, and out of the corner of my eye, I saw two guys who were walking past turn their heads in reaction to my hearty and resounding laugh. Three seconds later I heard, "David Pevsner?" and I turned to see them approach me. They introduced themselves as Phillip George and Keith Cromwell, and they explained that they knew me from an audition I had done a couple of years before for an off-Broadway musical called *Whoop-Dee-Doo!* They loved the audition and said I wasn't quite right for that show, but that they were associate directing and choreographing a new one, something I'd be perfect for, and that they were on their last day of auditioning, and would I come in later that afternoon? I said sure, they set me up to audition for the director/lyricist Mark Waldrop and the composer Dick Gallagher, and that's how I got cast in *Howard Crabtree's When Pigs Fly*, a fabulous show that we workshopped and then opened off-Broadway at the Douglas Fairbanks Theatre in August 1996 and ran two years.

I stayed the entire time. That show changed my life, not only because it was memorable, high-profile, and hysterically funny, but because it inspired me to write my own songs, which led to my very first material being included in the popular *Naked Boys Singing!* So, I owe David Sedaris a lot for making me laugh at the perfect moment, one that really set me in a whole new direction. Anyone else out there have that kind of life-changing single moment? Think about it.

Getting into *Pigs* affected my world in so many ways. Mark Waldrop hired me to be the beefcake guy who could also be funny, but since I was working with a cast of absolute comic geniuses, it was a master class in doing comedy. As the run progressed, I got even more into the wacky, campy, outrageous spirit of it. The show was a revue about young Howard Crabtree who, like so many of us little gay artist boys, wants to make fabulous musical comedy and entertain the masses, and against all odds, a slew of setbacks, and the evils of his dream-killing high school guidance counselor Miss Roundhole (me), he succeeds in creating a fantabulous over-the-top spectacular on a tiny budget.

Howard was the "straight man" character (comedically), but this was the gayest show around, so there was nothing straight about it (one of my favorite lyrics was "Just to be in it, you got to be out"). The show was hilarious, inspiring, smart, and even gently political in its own way. It was the most fun I'd ever had onstage. Over those two years, we developed so much goodwill and a devoted audience that still remembers how great it was. In fact, I went back to NY in 2016 along with the entire original cast to do two sold-out twenty-year reunion concerts for the show, and it charmed the audiences all over again.

The Howard Crabtree character, played by Michael West, was based on the real Howard Crabtree, the brilliant and innovative costume designer whose work inspired each of the songs in the show and was its reason for being. From vanity tables that turned into exquisite baroque gowns to a live purple centaur to a breathtaking take on Endora from *Bewitched* to an adorable pig that doesn't quite make it off the ground, Howard's creativity was truly one of a kind.

The rest of the company worked with Howard on one or both of his previous off-Broadway shows, *Whatnot* and *Whoop-Dee-Doo!*, but I was a newbie and hadn't met him. He had AIDS and became very ill during the development of the show and was never around. The only time I got to meet him was when we all went up to his farm outside New Hope, Pennsylvania, for the final costume fitting. I was brought into his room where he was lying in bed, frail and weak, but he reached up to me, pulled me into a warm hug, and said, "Welcome to the family." Each cast member proceeded to try on all these beautiful, hilarious costumes and parade for him as he lay back in bed, and he'd give notes on changes to his partner, Danny. That was my one interaction with Howard—he died before we opened. I'm so grateful to have met him even that once and to have been part of the legacy he left behind. He was a true genius.

Everyone in NY came to see that show: Bette Midler, Elaine Stritch, Liza Minnelli (twice!), Whoopi Goldberg, just a parade of fabulous entertainers and celebrities who would come backstage to sing our praises. Bette didn't stay after the performance she attended, which disappointed us no end, but we found out that she wasn't feeling well. However, the next day we found at each of our dressing tables the most beautiful, extravagant, and unique flower arrangements I'd ever seen, each with a lovely personal note attached from Bette.

When we found out Bette was going to do one of the songs from the show on her new album *Bathhouse Betty*, our company manager Bill Cannon was able to get an early copy of the cut. In our cramped and chaotic dressing room, fifteen minutes before the show, he popped the CD into a low-tech boom box and we sat, each of us in varying stages of makeup and costume readiness, and listened to this gorgeous, heartfelt, and very moving rendition of "Laughing Matters," the eleven o'clock number sung by Jay Rogers in the show. When it was done, we cried like babies. We were one very proud family. It is one of my most cherished memories.

The cast of *When Pigs Fly* was asked to be on the pilot for a new talk show hosted by Pat Bullard, a TV writer best known for his work on *Roseanne*. We were to perform the song "Wear Your Vanity with Pride," the aforementioned number in which Stanley Bojarski and Jay Rogers played heavily rouged baroque women sitting and preening at their vanity tables until the moment in the song when John Treacy Egan, Michael West, and myself, as their men-in-waiting, helped them mount the tables to their hips and pulled a cord, and like magic the tables became extravagantly decorated gowns, thus the double entendre of the title. It was an amazing and hilarious number, and though we hadn't heard of Bullard, we were thrilled to get a chance to perform it on TV and publicize the show.

When we arrived at the studio, we found that the other guests were former child star Kirk Cameron and Mrs. Fields, the cookie mogul. She was fantastic, so affable and sweet, and she loved our costumes, loved our number, and not only told us she would try to come to the show but later sent a big box of cookies backstage. Kirk Cameron was another matter. He wasn't mean or nasty but just couldn't look any of us in the eyes, especially when we were in our flamboyant costumes and makeup. As we all had pretty big personalities, I could tell he was in hell surrounded by our campy banter and enthusiasm. I remember passing him in the hallway as I was returning from having put on my makeup in the men's room, and his neck and head were so angled toward the floor that he looked deformed. He just could not look at me. At first I thought he was shy, but it was pretty clear after a while that he was just uncomfortable with all the gay shtick swirling around him.

At the time, I didn't know he was an evangelical, a Christian bible beater with a severe aversion to the gays, but I definitely got the sense that he wanted to be anywhere but around us. And sure enough, years later, he's one of the most homophobic celebrities out there. He's not shy about voicing his opinions, and neither am I. Kirk . . . fuck you. Fuck you for back then and fuck you for now. You're a piece of work and a piece of crap. Boom.

I continued escorting through the first part of the run of the show, and between *Pigs* and the side hustle, I was doing pretty well financially. But it ended up being an incredibly tumultuous two years of my life, and though everything onstage was lighthearted and happy, the real drama was developing offstage.

Side note: When *Barrel Fever* came out, I loved it so much that in my desire to communicate with David Sedaris (pre-Internet), I found his name in the NY phone book and called him. I did what Andy calls a "Hello, you don't know me, but . . ." and he was very kind and we had a nice discussion, not about his book but about cleaning products and utensils. He had been a housecleaner to make money— not naked, I assumed—so we went off on that for a bit. I love him as a writer and can tell you that he was a mensch to spend time on the phone with a fan, even if it was mostly to sing the praises of Lysol.

THE MUSIC MAN

You can be right or you can be happy.
You can go spending your life, defending your life,
instead of living it and letting go.
If you lose your way to bitter,
if your heart sounds like nothing but a metronome,
listen for the quiet voice inside,
and let it lead you from bitter and back to home.
—from "Right"

I come from a family of jewelers—my father was one, and his father and uncle as well. My father's uncle was named Leo, and as I mentioned earlier, besides the jewelry trade, he was also a songwriter. When I was a kid, I found some 45 and 33 rpm vinyl records of his songs in the storage compartment of the hi-fi that we had downstairs. I listened to them a couple of times as a boy, but as a teenager I became obsessed with them.

I thought the songs were kind of silly—well, bad. They were ditties, pop tunes, with simple melodies, benign lyrics, and generic singers crooning them. Some were recorded live in the '50s and '60s from a show that was broadcast nationally on ABC Radio called *Don McNeill's Breakfast Club*, and the audience would go wild after each performance. Others were done in a studio, and Leo sometimes sang them himself with his well-worn but above-adequate pipes. They were professionally done and sounded great technically for the time, but that made their lousiness stand out even more. I found aspects of them hysterical.

There was one song about being a school dropout, sung against a really hip '60s beat, and after each lyric was a very Beatles-like "Yeah Yeah!" It was about how, if you dropped out, you were a fool who should stay in school, that a good job was waitin' if you were graduatin', and on and on and on. One would think the title of that song would be "Don't Be a Dropout" or "Stay in School." Nope. It was called "Yeah Yeah."

There was another called "Gimme the Car," a novelty song in which a perky teenager tries to get his mother to, well, let him use her car. It's all very back-and-forth and broadly played and clunky, and the upshot is she'll let him use it if he does all his chores, puts gas in the car, and finishes his homework. The punch line of the song:

"Uh . . . I'll take the bus." Buh dum bum.

In college, Andy and I loved those songs. We would fire up the record player and listen to the album nonstop, and we'd belt out those tunes whenever we were somewhere and needed a chuckle. Our favorite was a ditty that was essentially a PSA for the charity the United Way. The early part of the song was literally singing the praises of the good work of the organization and how important it was to donate. However, the lyric went on about helpless old people, homeless orphans, the handicapped, and, yup, retarded children (the song's words, not mine). The first time I heard this tune, delivered with absolute deadpan delivery by a very earnest and tightly harmonizing white-bread quartet à la the Four Freshmen, I did a spit take. Andy and I thought it was hilarious.

The Broadway revue *Side by Side by Sondheim* was big with us, so we wanted to create a show called *Line by Line by Leo*. We never got around to it, but those songs remained a part of our shorthand, and we disparaged them for a laugh whenever we could.

When I moved to NY, I was so excited to finally get to use a Leo song at an audition for a Randy Newman revue. They wanted original comedy material, and since I hadn't started writing at this point, I decided to use "Give the United Way." I had to sing it a cappella in front of the casting director in a room the size of a bird's nest. However, in such close quarters and without the trappings of the cheeseball accompaniment and harmony, plus no explanation of what the song was originally for, there was no comedy to be had. When I sang the lyric about retarded children, in my periphery I could see the casting director silently put his hand over his mouth in horror. Back then I didn't even think about how incorrect and awful it was—I just thought it was funny. When I finished, there were crickets, and then a tight, whispered, "Thank you."

This is where I learned that context is everything.

My own legit songwriting began in 1996, a little after I began appearing in *When Pigs Fly*. Before *Pigs*, I had begun to write essays and stories about my life on a Radio Shack word processor, and I'd started to amuse myself composing parody lyrics to songs. *Pigs* was so inspiring to me because it was smart and funny and incredibly gay, and I thought, hey, I think like that, only dirtier, and I wanted to see if I could match the humor and intelligence and fun that Mark and Dick brought to their songs, only much bluer.

I upped my technical game when Bart, my *South Pacific* bath-house buddy, gave me his old 256 computer and monitor, and on this behemoth that couldn't even access the early-day Internet—it was just a somewhat higher-tech word processer than the one from Radio Shack—I started to pound out dirty poetry about such things as my fantasies of being a porn star, my life as a naked maid, and my angst over being nude in the showers in gym class. I had to save the documents every five seconds because the computer would constantly freeze up, and I'd lose chunks of material and just scream at the machine. I attached a melody to everything I'd written as I went along, which helped me to be really specific in my rhyming and storytelling, and the poems became lyrics for actual songs.

Once the songs were done, they just sat there until one day in mid-1997 when I was leaving a performance of *Pigs*, I ran into my friend Patrick Quinn (RIP, pal), who had come to see the show with his boyfriend, Marty Casella. Marty and I struck up a conversation and he asked if I was doing anything else besides the show. I didn't mention my escorting, but told him that I was writing those dirty little songs, which was fun and all but there was really nowhere to put them. Marty told me that a friend of his was mounting a show in Los Angeles and actively seeking material. I couldn't see my songs being done anywhere because they were so specific and kind of graphic and not very marketable. I asked what the theme of the show was.

"Nudity."

Holy shit. Perfect! Marty said that the Celebration Theatre, LA's only gay theater, was going under, and his friend, artistic director Bob Schrock, figured what do gay guys love? Musicals and cock! He was putting it all together for a show to save the theater, called *Naked Boys Singing!* I wanted in, so I hired a terrific pianist named Michael Lavine, who stepped in as a replacement musical director on *Pigs*, to help me lay down a simple cassette tape demo of my melodies and lyrics. I sent off two of the songs, "The Perky Little Porn Star" and "The Naked Maid." I also wanted to musicalize my poem "Fight the Urge," about three high school boys fighting erections in the gym class showers, but didn't feel equipped to write a trio with the harmony, counterpoints, etc.

I called Rayme Sciaroni, who composed the music for a show I did called *The Gym*. I loved his work on it. We recorded "Fight the Urge" together at his home studio, using the melody I came up with and both of us creating the arrangement. I'd had enough experience doing musicals to know that when the characters sang together, they each had to have a different rhythm to juxtapose on top of each other to create a counterpoint, but I really needed Rayme's abilities as a producer to pull it all together. We gave one guy a more staccato delivery and lyric, another more legato (sustained), and the third, more melodic. I wasn't sure they were going to work together, but I sang all three and let Rayme do his thing, mixing it and seeing what changes needed to be made.

I remember watching him listen to his final mix on the headphones and his eyes just popping out of his head. He said, "You're not going to believe this." I put the headphones on and he played the counterpoint section and everything worked perfectly, key words popping out when they needed to be heard, all the humor and emotion and character just exploding. It was melodious and funny and kind of moving. We didn't have to make a single tweak. We started hugging and jumping up and down and had such joy at giving birth to this musical baby.

Collaboration can be the most exciting thing in the world when it works, and we just basked in the sheer joy of creating art. Look, my songs are not Sondheim, I know that. But I think they're well crafted and witty and go into subject matter that wouldn't ordinarily be musicalized, and I'm as proud of those songs as anything I've ever done. We sent that song in along with the other two, and in the end Bob Schrock chose all three to be in the show, and I could not have been prouder or more thrilled.

I'm a perky little porn star from Skokie, Illinois.
My mother doesn't like my job at all.
If I have to go to work,

sexuality's a perk,
but she says it's just as far as I could fall.

See, I'm a Jewish boy inside,
but the nice part went and died
on the first day that I showed up on the set.
I could hear the rabbis screaming
'cause I did what I was dreaming
since the day I saw Tab Hunter soaking wet!
—from "The Perky Little Porn Star"

Once all the songs for the show were chosen, Bob had writer/ humorist Bruce Vilanch write some crossover sketches to bridge them, but in the end they realized they didn't need them and that it worked as just a straight gay revue (see what I did there?), and sure enough it played a year and a half in Los Angeles before moving to New York. In LA, "Fight the Urge" was choreographed by Kenny Ortega, who did the dances for *Dirty Dancing* and later made it huge as the director of the *High School Musical* films, among others.

When I went to the opening of the show in LA, I don't think I took a single breath through the entire thing. My shoulders were up to my ears with tension, but hearing the audience laugh at the lyrics I wrote was absolutely revelatory, and Bob, Kenny, and the other choreographers did a fantastic job. I remember thinking, "I wrote that!?!" I loved making people laugh in this very different way and I felt I had a real affinity for it. Later, after I moved to LA in 1998, *Naked Boys Singing!* won Best Musical at the LA Garland Awards, and I was given my plaque by Ken Werther, our publicity guy, as I sat in on auditions for the LA production of *When Pigs Fly* that I was going to do. I told Mark Waldrop, the writer/director of *Pigs*, that his lyrics got me started on this and I was able to thank him. *Naked Boys Singing!*

opened in New York in July 1999 and became a huge hit, and theaters all over the world began to license it for productions. I found it very encouraging (and lucrative).

When the original cast album CD of *NBS* came out, I brought it home to Chicago to show my folks. I was so proud that there was this physical proof that I had succeeded as a songwriter. I didn't anticipate that they would actually want to hear it, given the subject matter, the language, and their aversion to discussing sex. Way back when I used to sing commercial jingles in the car, one night I began singing a song from the new Broadway cast album I had bought: "Sodomy. Fellatio. Cunnilingus. Pederasty." I didn't know what the hell I was singing, but my dad practically drove the car into a ditch, and when we got home, they sat and listened to the original cast album of *Hair* with me in the basement, went upstairs in silence, and never talked about it again.

So one afternoon I was working at my brand-new Compaq laptop and my mom approached and asked to hear my songs. I thought, that's so sweet and supportive, and then I thought, oh dear god . . . she's going to hate them. They didn't have a CD player, but there was the CD-ROM on my computer, so I popped the disk in and skipped to my first song, "The Naked Maid." We sat and listened, staring at the computer as if it were a radio in the 1940s.

My mother had a pasted-on smile through that and "Fight the Urge" and I loved her for putting herself through the misery of hearing my rather blue stories. It seemed to me she was not deducing that I had actually been a naked maid or fought erections in the school shower. So far, so okay. Then came "The Perky Little Porn Star" with its references to my hometown of Skokie, Illinois, and suddenly the story became very immediate and I knew she was taking this one in differently. All at once it was like a documentary and she was hearing my real fantasy but probably thinking it was my reality: a gay porn star singing about how he needs to get the voices of his mother and the rabbis out of his head so that he can revel in his chosen profession.

"The Perky Little Porn Star" is probably the most explicit song in the show, and as she continued to listen, my mother's pasted-on grin was starting to harden. I thought, okay, okay, we'll get through this, so far it's not horrible and, oh, that's a good joke . . . we're good . . . and then I thought ahead to the lyric that was going to kill her . . .

> *If I shoot a film on Succos,*
> *dicks both in my mouth and tuchas,*
> *a sudden gust of family shame attacks.*
> *I continue giving head,*
> *and pretend that mom is dead,*
> *and my conscience and my sphincter can relax!*
> —from "The Perky Little Porn Star"

And the singer sang those lyrics, and I looked at her, and with that smile now spackled on, eyes glazed, not moving a muscle, my mother's body suddenly jerked slightly as she very quietly uttered from her gut, "Huh." I wanted to laugh, but my body was paralyzed with tension, and I was actually more mortified when I realized *Succos* and *tuchas* was a shoehorned rhyme that didn't really work, but we listened to the rest of the song together, and when it was done, she said nothing and I skulked to the bathroom and we never spoke of it.

My folks visited me just a few months after I moved to LA and, bless their hearts, said they wanted to support me and see the show. When I asked afterwards if they liked it, my mom shot back with a bad-cheese-smell face, "Oh no!" I knew that my material was never going to be their cup of tea, but that was what I wanted to write, and that was going to have to be fine. For now.

Depending on the ratio
of shtupping to fellatio,
and what I'll do and what he'll do to me,
I know I've really got 'em if I say I'll top or bottom.
Profit comes from versatility!
—from "The Perky Little Porn Star"

Some have criticized me for using profanity in my songs, suggesting that's a cheap way of getting a laugh and that there are more artful ways to express a character's thoughts. I don't agree. Yes, swearing and sexual themes can be gratuitous sometimes, but if a character talks that way, if it's justified, artfully done, and witty—sorry, I think it works. Most of the characters who sing songs in any of my shows are based on some version of me, and I write and craft their lyrics lovingly and thoughtfully. I swear and talk about sex all the time ("fuck me" is my favorite phrase when I stub my toe or can't find a parking place, and I freely interchange "asshole," "fuckjobs," and "shit fuckers" to describe, well, assholes), and nothing's better than a good fisting joke as far as I'm concerned.

I think sex is inherently amusing and sometimes hilarious, especially if you talk about it with a wink and pull the curtains back to reveal why our desires make people so nervous, turning fear of the flesh into humor. I know that my songs are not for everybody and I suppose you need an open mind to laugh at a three-minute show tune about anal warts, but I do believe my songs are kind of smart and, most importantly, funny. Not everyone agrees, but it took a particular experience for me to understand and come to grips with that.

In 2003, I began creating a show called *The Fancy Boys Follies*, which was more than just a revue of my songs. It was a burlesque/vaudeville show—I coined it "A Vaudelesque!" It was wall-to-wall fun, with a bunch of my risqué and very gay songs, as well as suggestive and provocative sketches and teasers. I envisioned it as a gay mini–Ziegfeld Follies, a small extravaganza much like *When Pigs Fly*, performed by genius comedic actor/singers who were also comfortable in various states of undress. I had done reading after reading of it in LA, and those audiences loved it, so I figured great, let's go for the big time.

Instead of mounting it in Los Angeles, I was hoping to have it produced in my old stomping grounds, NYC. I contacted a friend who is a very successful musical director and conductor, having served in that capacity for many Broadway shows of the last forty years. I love him as a person and have great respect for all he has accomplished, and since he'd been in the business for so long, and even though my show was way too small for him, I thought he might know someone who could help present it in New York. I sent him the script and a CD of the songs.

I was not prepared for the email I received.

He *HAAAAAAAAAATED* it, said that I was the devil for putting out smutty crap like this, and that he didn't know "where you think you're going to peddle this stuff." He said he despised *Naked Boys Singing!* (which had been playing in NY for a few years at that point) and anything like it, that it was all cheap and unfunny, and on and on (perhaps some of you agree about *NBS*, but to each his own).

I felt as though I'd been gut-punched. It just hurt too much to read that—so blunt, so uncensored, from someone I really respected. I took to my bed. For two whole days. I couldn't move. When I was able to somewhat function and get out of the house, a friend pointed out two things. One, my musical director friend was corporate Broadway, working only on very traditional and mainstream shows, and my stuff is so not the type of thing he would ever consider. And two . . . didn't I enjoy even a little bit getting such an emotional reaction to my work? It definitely struck a nerve, and I had to remember that it was the extremes of the material along with the humanity of it that many other folks appreciated and found funny.

This was my first experience with "you can't please everyone." Since then I have learned that I must be true to myself and my voice and have the courage to keep writing and putting it out there as long as I have something to say, in any way I can, in whatever medium that excites me. I guess I'm niche. I'm Niche. Nice to meet you.

One early morning in 2008, I woke up with a start and a spark of terror hit me. Was I a bad songwriter like my Uncle Leo? Had I become what I'd made fun of for years? I got up and read through some of my lyrics and listened to some recordings and thought, no, they're funny, I'm okay. But I'm sure someone or other out there thinks I'm a hack, and lord knows the critics are gunning for you when you write this kind of material if it's not done well—or even if it is, actually. I was so sensitive to criticism and had such thin skin that it took me a while to become comfortable with the old theory that one man's art is another man's United Way jingle.

While writing this book, I googled "Leo Pevsner The Breakfast Club." I had never thought to research him before and came upon an interview that I had never seen. It turns out he had written at least a thousand songs since 1933, continuing into his late eighties. He started by writing parodies of popular songs, as I did, like Al Jolson's "Sonny Boy" ("Climb down from my knee, Sonny Boy/You're almost twenty-three, Sonny Boy!"). His early songs ranged from political—a song he wrote à la "Brother, Can You Spare a Dime?" called "Next Year" got played at Franklin Delano Roosevelt campaign rallies—to fundraising and novelty songs that he sang for folks such as Harry Truman, Eleanor Roosevelt, and David Ben-Gurion. He wrote vaudeville tunes and gave them away for—you should excuse the expression—a song. Later in life, he contributed to NPR and *Morning Edition*; they looked at him as a kind of "folksy philosopher." Who knew?

This leads me to *thirtysomething*. Stay with me. *thirtysomething* is my favorite show of all time. In one episode, anal-retentive Hope throws a surprise birthday party for her husband Michael, the most hand-some TV Jew ever. It's a boring disaster until the roof literally falls in, a water pipe breaks, and suddenly the party takes on a whole new energy and it's great. And when the clairvoyant party planner (played by Renee Taylor) finds Hope lying in bed with the covers thrown over her head because she's so depressed that everything went "wrong," Renee tells her fortune: "You can be right or you can be happy." And that hit me, hard (it inspired me to write a song called "Right" that heads up this chapter).

As an artist, I was always trying to get it "right." To do it "right." But there is no right—you find your voice and put your work out into the world with love, no matter what the haters say. And boy, did my Uncle Leo know that.

> *. . . and I LOVE IT! And I've made it!*
> *Pretty soon I'll get a cut,*
> *when they start to sell the nifty rubber version of my butt!*
> *And when my posterior goes down for posterity,*
> *they can't say, "He's inferior because he chose to bare it!*
> *He's a perky little porn star from Skokie, Illinois!"*
> *Oy!*
> —from "The Perky Little Porn Star"

Andy and I had our opinions on Uncle Leo's songs, but he certainly had his audience and did his thing, and he loved it. And, like him, so do I. I sing my songs proudly with my well-worn but above-adequate pipes.

Generic baby photo, but . . . awww.

Always the good boy . . . back then.

12 years old. Class picture: No food in the braces. Don't touch the hair.

MOST VERSATILE

David Pevsner

High school senior survey pic. Who knew my class was a bunch of precogs?

Brian Kelly—"Flipper's Father"—my first TV crush at 6 years old. Can you blame me?

James Darren—TV crush #2, sans green *Time Tunnel* turtleneck. Again. . . can you blame me??

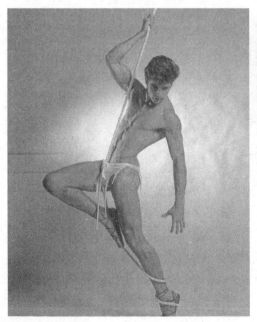

Maxwell Caulfield shot by Kenn Duncan for *After Dark* magazine. Etched into my little gay brain for the rest of my life.

Kalani—heartbreakingly beautiful to me.

My college roomie Paul Zappala and me at graduation from Carnegie Mellon. The first of my good, good friends to pass from AIDS. He always lit up a room and was one of the most genial, generous, and genuine people I've ever met. I miss him every day.

Knockin' 'em dead(ish) on the *Royal Viking Sky* cruise ship (with Amy Gluck). One can never wear too much gold lamé when performing in a musical revue.

The worst headshot in the history of headshots. Gilding the lily and a bridge too far when it came to the concept of "Character Actor."

Uncle Charlie's every night, and later . . .

Big Cup (my unofficial office in the '90s) every day.

Up the stairs and over the HoJo's to get to the naked men and the Mylar curtain. And after, perhaps the fried clams?

My bodybuilding obsession began on tour with *South Pacific* in 1987 (here in my typical daily attire, as little as possible).

My exploration of leather, 1997, shot by the wonderful Reed Massengill in NY. He told me he never published my nude shots because I was so restrictive: "no porn, art use only, no calendars, no club invitations." My, how things have changed.

Finally putting those pecs to good use in *Party*. The first of many times I appeared naked onstage, but it was way more than a nudie show. Funny, sweet, and an absolute ball, for the audience and us. Clockwise from top left: Ted Bales, Larry Alexander, Jay Corcoran, me, Kellum Lewis, Vince Gatton (not shown, Tom Stuart).

Backstage with my *When Pigs Fly* family. Total pros—talented, sweet, hilarious, and absolutely insane. Clockwise from top left: John Treacy Egan, me (as Miss Roundhole, the dream destroyer), Michael West as Howard Crabtree, Jay Rogers, and Stanley Bojarski. My favorite theater experience, ever.

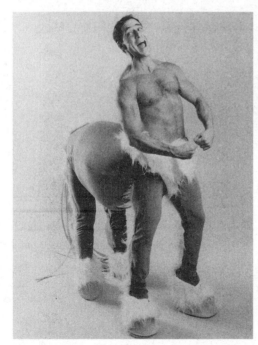

As a lovelorn, gym-going centaur in *When Pigs Fly*. "I got masculine charms to be reckoned with, so why do people look at me and say '*Oh, Myth!*'?" Poor Michael West was back there, praying that I wouldn't fart.

A ton of celebs saw *When Pigs Fly* in NY and LA, but none so Classic Hollywood as Ann Miller. Wow.

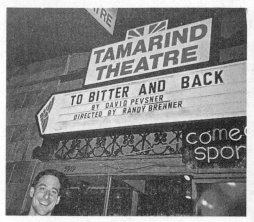

The pride and joy of performing my first autobiographical one-man musical in LA.

Living my Gaiety Theatre fantasies on stage (complete with Mylar curtain) in the first production of *Musical Comedy Whore* at the Desert Rose Playhouse in Rancho Mirage, CA.

Our original cast of *Corpus Christi*. I traveled for years with this play, and I cherish these people.

The *Old Dogs and New Tricks* gang. Me, Leon Acord, Curt Bonnem, Jeffrey Patrick Olson.

As Ben Scrooge in *Scrooge & Marley*, post-ghost visitations, spreading gay Christmas cheer.

As the Baker in *Into the Woods*, but also representative of how I looked in practically every Jewsical I ever did: standard immigrant garb.

My favorite photo of me and Andrew Baseman, my forever BFF. 40 years and counting.

MY ONE AND ONLY

I was in a successful off-Broadway production, writing songs, escorting, getting by, and all was fine . . . or at least I thought it was . . . until I fell in love . . .

> *I sit around and pray for love to fall from the sky,*
> *and when it hits me, I run away,*
> *but after years and years and years and years of nothing to show,*
> *it's time for me to finally say*
> *I gotta give it up to love.*
> —from "I Gotta Give It Up to Love"

Some friends came to see me in *Pigs* one night in November 1996, three months after we opened, and we went for drinks after and "ran into" Reid. I think it was a fix-up. He was a struggling film composer and singer—pale, thin, redheaded, and with a mystery about him I found very appealing. We actually had a lot in common as he was very up-and-coming in the indie music and film world like I was off-Broadway. We did a lot of witty back-and-forth and talked shop, but there was a subtle flirtation, made more obvious when we saw a hansom cab beautifully framed outside the café window. I mentioned that I'd **never** been on one. He said, "I'll take you sometime." Hmmm.

We exchanged numbers, and when I got home, instead of waiting the requisite two days, I decided to call him. I unfolded the paper and it said *Reid*, his number, and *I like your nose*. Once again, the schnozz that I always despised wins 'em over. I gave him a call and we talked for hours. Couldn't get enough. Had to do one of those hang-ups where you go "1, 2, 3, hang up." It was the start of a whirlwind . . .

He drove me kinda crazy, wasn't gorgeous or tall,
or half the things I had on my list,
but there was warmth in his eyes, and to my surprise,
he had me from the moment we kissed.
—from "I Gotta Give It Up to Love"

We met for dinner on my night off at the Hourglass Café on West 46th Street, where you could sit at an outdoor candlelit table amongst the happenings in Hell's Kitchen, which made it a most romantic place to rendezvous. After a long meal talking about his many relationships and my lack of such, we went to a patisserie and picked up dessert and brought it back to his place. Before we could unpack the chocolate cake, we were all over each other . . .

I gotta give it up to love.
No excuses, no alibi.
I gotta give it up to love,
I found myself a fabulous guy!
—from "I Gotta Give It Up to Love"

We spent the whole week together, every waking moment, except when I was at *When Pigs Fly*. He came to see the show—not really his thing, but he liked it. Afterwards, he whispered in my ear, "You were good. I was relieved." (I thought that was an odd thing to say after I had just put my all into a performance. Red flag?) Our bond was so strong, so fast. I turned down escorting gigs because he said he was the monogamous type, but a week away from making that extra side cash caused a strain on my bank account, so I decided to tell him about my other job.

Recently, I had gone on a first date with a guy and my pager went off in the restaurant, so I excused myself to call Mo. When I got back, he made a joke about a drug deal and I started stuttering an excuse, but I'm a terrible liar. I told him the truth, he listened, and when I was done, without missing a beat, he flagged down the waiter. "Check please."

I was anticipating it would be an issue with Reid, but I felt dishonest continuing to escort without him knowing the truth. I held on to hope that he would be, if not accepting, then at least understanding. Nervous and expecting the worst, I told him, but though he was taken aback, he was not totally nonplussed. I asked if he could date someone who escorted. He gave me a kiss and said he needed to think on it. I left it at that.

The next night, I went to the theater and there was a note at my dressing table.

After "Dear David," he got right to it, saying that although I called myself an escort, I was really a hustler, and probably hustling him. That it didn't even matter if I stopped doing it, just the fact that I was a whore (his word) made me untrustworthy to him, and therefore, undateable. He didn't want to think about me with other men, potentially picking up disease and bugs, and passing them on to him. Ultimately, he didn't want that kind of drama in his life. He wished me luck, cut off all contact, and ended with a very uncomplimentary complimentary close:

"With love. Without respect,
Reid."

Well, what did I expect? I ran to the backstage phone and called him. No answer. Every break during the show, I left message after message. After the performance, I waited outside his apartment building for two hours until he came home.

"Please, can we talk?"

"I don't think that's a good idea."

"Please . . . can I use your bathroom?"

He let his guard down for a second and brought me inside. When I came out of the bathroom . . .

"I can't date the kind of guy who escorts."

"That's so unfair. You know the kind of guy I am, and I didn't lie to you, and I won't lie to you. I'll quit."

"I don't want that responsibility."

"I'm not doing it for you, I'm doing it for me."

Then he got really close to me and, on the verge of tears, whispered, barely audible, "Why do you want to be with someone like me? Skinny. And I'm not very lovable."

I knew he was incredibly sensitive, but I didn't realize how insecure he was, and it gave him a vulnerability that made me want to take care of him. Unlovable? He was kind of judgmental, but I hadn't seen anything that suggested he was unlovable. This moment of raw intimacy made me love him even more. It was time to be a real boyfriend.

I've had enough of lonely; I'm over myself,
and needing my time and my space,
'cause now I get to think about how lucky I am
that I get to come home to his glorious face!
—from "I Gotta Give It Up to Love"

So I called Mo and I quit, started looking for catering gigs, and Reid and I began a relationship. I'd go to his apartment after *Pigs*, we'd hang out, have drinks, cuddle up. He cooked Thanksgiving dinner for me. I nursed him back to health when he got sick. It was really lovely, but he still had trust issues. I didn't blame him, but I was so committed to him—and us—that I gave him no reason to doubt me . . .

He's fine.
I love him so.
It feels so good to say
he's mine.
Don't blow it. Don't throw it away.
—from "I Gotta Give It Up to Love"

After three months together, he got a job scoring a film in LA for a few weeks, and I missed him terribly, so when I had a couple of days off from the show, I went to visit. A friend had given me a free weekend at the Loews Santa Monica Hotel. We had a nice calm day at the beach together, but there was a definite tension there. At six o'clock, in our room, I made Reid a gin and tonic, me, a Scotch and soda, and I said we had to talk. Reid told me that even after all this time, he just didn't trust me. My escorting made him believe that I was going behind his back, sleeping with other guys, and he hated that I had done it in the first place. He was bothered by the fact that I had never had a serious relationship, thinking I wasn't capable, despite my being totally devoted to him, honest to a fault, communicating with him along the way, feeling great about us except when the insecurity made him lash out at me periodically with a judgy comment or side eye that made me want to work even harder at the relationship, to finally make one succeed.

I kept assuring him that I had left the escorting behind when I said I did, that I was monogamous with him, that I loved him and us, but none of it was getting through. The whole conversation was as if I was pointing at something black and he was saying it was white. No, it's black, I would say. No, it's white. Black. White! Black! Fuck! I couldn't win and I couldn't convince him I was in it for the long haul. When we started the conversation, we were talking in really low, quiet voices, but as the evening progressed, we drank more and more and got louder and louder until we were screaming at each other, him telling me what a *WHORE I WAS!* Me having to *DEFEND MYSELF!* And blah blah blah blah blah . . . !!!!

It got so heated that Reid threw a glass out the window and just missed a passing car. He pushed the ironing board through the wall, leaving a three-inch hole. We had bought some snacks for the room and he took a bag of faux Lucky Charms and whipped it at the door, exploding toasted oats and marshmallow bits all over the carpet. The room looked as if a cyclone had hit it, and at ten o'clock the cops came. We promised to keep it down, but Reid had had enough. He called a friend in LA to pick him up, and we continued the drunken drama in the lobby.

"I loooove you! Don't go!"

"I loooove you tooooo, but we could never be together!" Reid stumbled out to his friend's car, and I went back up to the room, drunk as the proverbial skunk, threw up in the bathroom, fell asleep on the carpet amidst the carnage and magically delicious debris, woke up the next morning at 11:45, still drunk, still needing to vomit, but it was checkout time. Clean up, pack up, check out, move it, get out of there.

I went to stay with a friend in LA until it was time to head back to NY. I was done with Reid. I didn't need to keep defending myself when he knew I'd been a good boyfriend, whatever my experience was, whatever my history was. Done.

Then he paged me. I had continued to use my beeper, as most people did at the time, nothing to do with escorting, and he knew that. In fact, he paged me more than anyone. I went to his motel and listened to him apologize, saying if I got that emotional, I must really care. How did it go so fast from I'm the biggest shit in the universe to oh, how sweet? (Another red flag.) I gave in. I hadn't ever been anyone's boyfriend, and I really wanted this to work . . .

> *I'm lying there and thinking he's not ready for this,*
> *ready for something to last.*
> *But then I turn on the light and I hold him tight and whisper,*
> *"I know it's scary. We've both got a past."*
> *But I gotta give it up to love.*
> *Put a pair of wings on and fly!*
> *I gotta give it up to love, yeah,*
> *did you find yourself a fabulous guy or what?*
> —from "I Gotta Give It Up to Love"

When we settled back in NY, the next year—from early 1997 into spring 1998—was actually pretty good. We both struggled financially, but along with being happily ensconced onstage and drawing a salary in *Pigs*, I eventually started making good money from the songs I wrote for *Naked Boys Singing!* and for the most part we were happy. I even entertained the idea of living together for the first time with anyone, though I was hardly ready for that. It mostly seemed to be working, except for the odd sarcastic comment about my tight T-shirts or belittling the guys at my gym or ridiculing some of my song lyrics, which really cheesed me because those songs were helping me/us get by.

My favorite moment of all time: we were going to a screening of a film that Reid scored, and there was going to be a Q&A after, moderated by a much-loved mentor of his. I spent the whole dinner beforehand, just Reid and me, being told what a hack I was because I wrote these dirty songs and had been in that naked show *Party* that had us in our underwear on the poster. He superciliously said I was the devil for proliferating the whole gay naked theater thing. Charming. We got to the screening and Reid found his mentor in the lobby, ran up to him, gave him a hug, and then called me over, proudly introducing the mentor to me. The guy's face just lit up. "Ohmigod. You were in *Party*! I saw that five times! You were *FABULOUS!*"

The shocked look on Reid's face was . . . well . . . delicious. Nyaaah.

A few weeks later, I was picking Reid up to go to a party, but I was late. It was snowing and the subway was chaotic hell. I got read the riot act, with a lot of "Where were you? Were you having sex in the steam room at the gym? Are you on steroids?" Craziness. I had my typical tight T-shirt and jeans on and he told me that I looked like a whore and needed to dress better. We got to the party and his indie music and film friends were dressed like, well, indie music and film people— grungy and tattered.

I tried to make conversation, but since I wasn't in their realm and couldn't do anything for anyone's career, I got frozen out, except for one guy who blandly said, "Oh, you're the chorus boy." Reid was in his own little world with them, so I just sat in a corner and drank. As we were leaving, he was rattling on about how much fun he had and how much he loved his friends.

Three-quarters drunk, I said, "Your friends are so welcoming."

"You just don't 'get' us," he haughtily replied.

"What's to get? You go to a party, you're nice to people, you eat dip! What am I missing?"

"We're not that kind of—"

"What kind? Civil? 'Oh, you're Reid's boyfriend, nice to meet you, come join us!'"

"We're not into that whole 'theater people' thing, you're just 'on' all the time, Mr. Entertainer, Mr. People Pleaser."

"You mean Mr. Chorus Boy. Should've printed my résumé on my T-shirt."

"Yeah, your T-shirt. You look like a hustler, it's just embarrassing, you should think about how you present yourself to people. You have so much potential."

Squeeze me? He just went off . . .

"Why are you not more successful? Why am I your first relationship? Why did you escort? You need to look at those things!"

"And you think I'm not."

"To be honest, I don't think you have the depth to really . . . I'm trying to help!"

I covered my face with my hands, trying not to explode. "You know," I shot back, "I could've done, oh, any number of things on my night off from my *hit off-Broadway show*, but that party was as fun as a funeral and I don't need your advice. By the by, some of my best friends are chorus boys, but I'm an actor." I thrust my index finger right up into his face. "Don't shit on what I do!"

I needed to be alone, so I belligerently shook his hand and grabbed a cab. When I got home, there was a message on my answering machine, ultra ultra sweet and singsongy—"Good night, honey. I love you. Sleep well, sweetie. Talk to you tomorrow!"—as if nothing had happened, no apology, nothing. I felt horrible, so I nursed a Scotch, I nursed another, and then thought, fuck you, the rent's due.

I called Mo.

An hour later, I was at the Midtown apartment of sixty-five-year-old Rand, who met me at the door in the tiniest of pink chiffon bathrobes, drunk, but holding himself together. We said our niceties and he invited me in. As soon as the door shut, he grabbed me hard. A bit taken aback, I said, "Whoa. Easy." He coughed in my face, a big ol' gross hacking cough. I recoiled, disgusted.

He went into the bedroom and called out, "Hey, handsome, you like poppers?"

"No, thank you, I'm sure they're delicious."

This was a bad idea. I followed him into the bedroom. He was standing there, bathrobe wide open, snorting the poppers. "Come here, cutie." I got face-to-face with him and he went nuts, hugging me, grabbing me, squeezing me.

I pulled away. "Calm yourself or I'm outta here!"

He apologized and asked me to take off my shirt. As I did, he got on the bed on all fours, took another huge hit of poppers, and began to cough—violent, pneumatic, painful. Thick white snot came out of his nose, and he started to shake.

"Fuck me! Please, fuck me!" he gagged, coughing his lungs out.

I froze. He looked sick and I wanted to help, but mostly I wanted to leave.

"Are you all right?"

"I'm fine. Fill my hole! Come on! Fill my hole!" *(sniff sniff cough cough)*

"No, no hole filling right now. Maybe you should just lie down and get some sleep." I put my shirt back on.

"Don't leave me. Please don't leave me." *(cough cough hack hack)*

He looked as if he could drop dead at any moment. The caretaker came out in me.

"Look, I have to go, but . . . can I get something for you? Can I call someone?"

"I'm fine. Just go."

"Are you going to be—"

"GET OUT! GO!" (*COUGH SNIFF COUGH HACK COUGH . . .*)

His brutal tone came out of nowhere, and kind of freaked me out. I hurriedly left his apartment, stumbled down the stairs and out of the building, and went across 56th Street to a pay phone. I looked up and found his window, the only light on.

I called Mo, told him what happened, and asked him to check up on Rand and see if he was okay. I hung up and looked up at the window. No change. Mo called me back and said there was no answer, he was probably fine, and he'd check with him in the morning and get back to me.

I hung up. 2:13 a.m.

I stayed, eyes glued to that window, for hours, waiting for that light to change, fixated like a dog, and I couldn't breathe except to smoke.

5:14 a.m. I saw a shadow move, and the light switched off. The tension in my body finally released. I hailed a cab, went to Reid's apartment, and he buzzed me in. When I got inside, he was in bed, so I got undressed and quietly slipped in beside him. I spooned Reid until he slowly turned to me, and we looked at each other, a kind of silent truce. When we first went out, I couldn't stay over because I was such a light sleeper that I'd hug the edge of the bed all night and be wrecked the next day, so I'd have to go home. That pissed him off. Now it was natural and comforting to stay the night. He snuggled into my arms and we fell asleep.

The next morning, as Reid slept, I was getting dressed and I felt my beeper vibrate. I went to the phone and dialed Mo, but before he picked up, I heard Reid rustling in the next room. I hung up. He came in and we chatted about nothing—not about how he had talked to me, and certainly not about my unfortunate drunken fallback. I kissed him and ran to my matinee. After the show, I called Mo. He told me Rand had been fine, just fell asleep. He also had another job for me if I wanted it, but I told him I was done. He said it was a new client who liked older, Jewish-y guys with a nose.

I asked the address.

Reid's address.

I ran to his apartment and beat up on the doorbell. Ring ring ring ring. Finally, the door opened a crack.

"You're not such a shitty actor after all. Don't call me, don't come by."

He started to close the door, but I pushed it open. "How did you find out?"

"Redial!" Goddamn technology. "You never gave it up! You went right from me to some gross old man at the Royalton or the Paramount or the Ho-Jo's!"

"No. No! I was . . . you were just so shitty to me and I got a little drunk and I was pissed and it was all just a big mistake—"

"No, you are shit. You are shit and I can't believe I trusted you for a second! Tell me something—did any good come out of being a ho?"

That question caught me by surprise. Besides the cash, I hadn't really thought about it. I had to take a moment. I lowered my head to gather my thoughts, and when I was ready, I looked in his eyes and said as sincerely and deliberately as I could:

"I feel . . . I feel like I can see beyond men's bodies . . . their sweetness or warmth or humor or need for comfort. I just . . . I see men . . . differently."

"Lovely. So now you can be with a skinny little troll like me. It's a pretty fucked up way to make a living, letting men use your body, objectify you, putting yourself and your career in danger. You must really hate yourself!"

I couldn't give him that. That's not what it ended up being about for me. I didn't regret it and I didn't hate myself because of it. It . . . changed me.

"I love you, Reid."

"You don't know what love is, and as a boyfriend, you made a good trophy."

Look, I fucked up, but really, what did it matter? Reid had said he loved me, but he loved me when I was being who he wanted me to be, the perfect doting boyfriend, and he constantly spewed his judgment. Despite Reid's experience, his many relationships and my lack of such, I think I turned out to be the *good* boyfriend, and I think he would tell you that to this day. He never saw me as my friends saw me, as the good-natured, sensitive, loyal, funny guy I was. Nothing I could do seemed to please him, and everything seemed to lead to drama, and I was a lot of things, but I was not an epochal drama queen except around him.

Before Reid, I didn't have policemen coming to my hotel room, I didn't have drunken arguments in lobbies, I didn't make grand gestures like bashing on doors to get inside a lover's home. He said I didn't have a spiritual bone in my body, which I love since, in my experience, most people who claim to be "spiritual" are some of the most judgmental people in the world. There was not a moment that I would ever have described Reid as "spiritual." There were some shitty things he did that I could have thrown in his face to point out his hypocrisy, but I took the high road then and I'm taking it now.

I couldn't help but question why I stayed so long, but I was determined to finally have a relationship that worked, even if it was with someone who I thought was so bitter at his core and so waiting for me to fail. He always had to have things his way, he always had to be right, and he criticized me for the work I was doing when he was just trying to find any work at all. It was all classic projection, and he was an immovable object. Maybe he was right—maybe I didn't know what love was, but I thought what I was feeling was real, and it felt like love.

"I loved you, Reid. I really did, but this package is going back on the shelf for someone who really wants it."

With a sneer, he retorted, "Or can afford it."

I walked into that one. He went inside and came out with a handful of cash. I had lent him a hundred bucks the day before. "Here!" He threw the five twenty-dollar bills at me, and as they floated to the ground, he said, "Go buy yourself some integrity!" Slam.

At the end of the day, he never saw me as anything but a hooker and I never had a chance. Perhaps my escorting was too much baggage from the beginning. Props to him for even trying, I guess. The breakup was a mere fourteen months after we met, but the relationship felt as though it lasted eons. Reid was the last real relationship I've had even to this day. For the longest time, it soured me from ever wanting to let someone in like that again.

I've fucked around plenty since then. Remember my Book of Lust? Eventually, I stopped entering names into it, but I page through it from time to time, and what comes into my head is that sometimes I think I'm going to die alone and they'll find me when they smell me.

I never could get satisfied while I was sowing oats.
My friends said I'd be happy screwing cows and blowing goats.
I've spent a lifetime running round, and yes, I've been a whore,
but a true romantic lives inside, and I want something more than . . .
Ray and Kevin, Drew, and Ike,
and Stanley, Johann, Scott, and Mike, and . . .

Reid.
—from "The Book of Lust"

That name on that page always stops me in my tracks. I think I did love Reid in my way, but when I think of us now, the word *failure* comes to mind. Yeah, he was a shit to me, but beyond that, one thing I know is that no relationship can succeed without trust. Truth is, as much as Reid didn't trust me, I don't think I trusted him either, because as open as I tried to be, he could always sneak in sideways and hurt me.

My days and nights with him were filled with trying to be worthy of his love or whatever the fuck he claimed to be love, what he was used to. I didn't know that I actually knew more about love and devotion than Reid ever would, because it seemed to me that for him, our relationship was all about holding me in line, to mold me into what served him and his desires. He liked that I was somewhat high-profile in my job as an off-Broadway actor, because Reid always went after the shiny thing. I saw it with his choice of friends—musicians, actors, and filmmakers who were either very successful or on the cusp, and that's who he thought I was when we met. And then Reid learned about my escorting and then about my dirty gay songs, and I think I dropped in his esteem, but I also know he liked my body. If you'll recall, he said I made a good trophy, and I think Reid loved having a built boyfriend. I'm not great shakes in the looks department, but he liked my tits and I think, for him, that was enough to balance out the rest.

I actually enjoyed being monogamous with Reid, having never done it before, and there were times I felt the kind of closeness and intimacy I thought boyfriends should have, and I reveled in it. I believe I became the boyfriend anyone would want because I would have done anything for Reid, but I also spent a lot of time trying to climb my way up the very steep ladder that Reid kept shoving in front of me. I discovered the hard way that I was never going to be enough for him, and when I sensed the foundation of the relationship really cracking, I knew it was over, and that's when I drunkenly felt the need to get back at him with Rand.

Part of me always wanted the kind of relationship I'd seen so many couples have. In my heart, I was, and always have been, a teenaged girl with my head in the clouds about love and romance. To this day I still cuddle up to my pillow, and sometimes, yeah, that pillow may be some TV star I've been crushing on, and I'm fucking sixty-two years old. I just haven't had much of it in real life, so I create it in my head. I don't even know if I'm capable of an equally committed serious relationship, monogamous or not. Those are untested waters for me. I'll have to cross that bridge should it happen to come up.

What I do believe is that a couple should want the same things. If one wants monogamy and the other wants to fuck around, then that relationship isn't going to last very long no matter how much love is there, is it? And I've seen plenty of relationships break up over small bullshit sexual proclivities that have different importance levels for the two partners. "But he kissed you!" "Yeah, he kissed me, but I didn't kiss back." "It's over!" Reid told me once that if I ever did sleep around, he just didn't want to know about it. I told him I wasn't going to, that I didn't want to, and I meant it. And then he said, well, just don't tell me about it. I wasn't gonna win that one, was I?

After Reid, it's been hard for me to let people in, to let them get close. I think one of the reasons I don't is that it is so fucking painful if a relationship goes wrong. They say it's better to have loved and lost blah blah blah. So far, I have no indication that that's true. I'm not saying I regret feeling love for Reid. It was good that I finally let someone in and that I stuck around. But when you keep getting abused mentally and that person brings out all your insecurities and yet you keep coming back like a big dumb dog, something isn't right. I stayed with Reid because I loved him, I'm not a quitter, and I felt the relationship was a puzzle I could solve.

Now I notice how friends in long-term relationships speak to each other, and for all the couples who retain the love and respect in how they intermingle, I've seen some communicate with each other with nothing but sarcasm and bile, or with absolutely no concern for each other's feelings. I would think to myself, if you ever spoke to me that way, I'd be out the fucking door so fast it would make your big fat head spin. Well, back then, twenty-something years ago, I didn't make it out the door as fast as I should have. One day I hope to find someone who's willing to see past my history, because I can't change that. Reid certainly wasn't the one.

I'd been in therapy the whole time, but beyond trying to work this out with a shrink, I needed a more creative way to make sense of the emotional whirlwind I had just been through. I wrote a script, a screenplay, a roman à clef that included my escorting and my relationship with Reid. As an artist, I felt there was something in my story that needed to be told and that folks could identify with, that maybe they'd be kinder to themselves after seeing it.

I had no experience writing a film script, so a screenwriter friend talked me through the structure, and a film editor pal helped me shape and develop the story to be more cinematic. I did my best with their guidance and we thought it had real possibilities. I called the screenplay *Puppy Love* because, along with the escorting and relationship storylines, there was a subplot about the lead character Doug wanting a dog and not being able to commit even to that.

That was the truth, because I've wanted a dog my whole life (see the Chanukah dog story), but I've also had dreams where I forget to feed my dog for weeks at a time, and I wake up crying, thinking I've killed it. As much as I love animals, it still scares me to be responsible for the life of another being—dog, cat, human. I've never really done it, never felt that bond of emotion and total trust that any loving relationship demands to be successful.

And to digress a moment, I'm such a fan of *The X-Files*, not because I like sci-fi, but because Mulder and Scully's relationship was beyond love, beyond trust. Any fan of the show knows what I mean. I'm looking for my Scully . . . well, Mulder. Either one would be great. Here's my head in the TV romance clouds once again.

I was getting incredible feedback on the screenplay I had written, even tying for second place in the 1999 Outfest Screenwriting Competition, the biggest gay film festival in the country (the script I tied with was *All Over the Guy* by Dan Bucatinsky, which did get made). I was hoping to get some high-profile NYC indie producers and directors involved, because *Puppy Love* could be shot in the city as an ultra-low-budget feature.

When Reid found out I had written our story, he was furious. One of the industry guys I had met through him mentioned to Reid that I had pitched a script, and when Reid asked what it was about, the guy explained the plot and Reid declared it was about him. I never told anyone I shopped the script to that it was about us, but I felt no obligation to hold it back because of how poorly he treated me. Plus, there was a pretty small pool of gay-oriented producers who could possibly help get the project made and everybody knows everybody. What the hell was I supposed to do?

In a letter to me, Reid claimed I had no sense of honor pitching the project to people I met through him, and he threatened not only to blackball me with his connections but also to call my parents and tell them everything about me, the escorting, everything. I know I wrote a movie about it, but putting a slightly fictionalized story on the big screen and telling loved ones the hard truth about my life are two totally different things.

As a result, I wrote a letter to my parents, explaining everything about me. They had met Reid very early in our relationship when they came to New York to see *When Pigs Fly*, but they had no idea of the tumult we were causing each other . . .

I feel we have had our distances over the years, and we are as close as a family can be that believes only the best about each other. Mom, you said to a friend once that I am the finest person you have ever known, and that stuck me like a dagger in my heart. The person that I am is that person, what I have done though may very well blow that away . . .

I wrote further about the escorting and why I did it, and then I talked about Reid and our relationship, the screenplay and why I wrote it, just everything I could to let them know the truth about me. I ended with this:

> I knew I was going to have to face up to all of this whether I wrote a screenplay or not, whether I ever had sex for money or not, whether I ever loved a man who thought I was a piece of crap or not. Maybe this is all something you never wanted to hear, needed to hear . . . I'm sorry. This is my life. Somehow I want to come out of this on the other side that I've heard about where people are happy and working and feel the love of friends and family and give it all back. I don't know why, but I have never felt part of that world. I have tried, but the chewed fingers and the sadness and the pressure and the hopelessness that I have always felt have been more indicative of how I've lived my life than anything else. Maybe now I can move on. I pray you understand and remain as loving a presence in my life as you have been. Or maybe I'm just asking for a miracle. I love you.

Reid never made good on his threat. The movie never got made. And I never sent the letter.

(Curtain. End Act One.)

CITY OF ANGELS

In October 1998, after Reid, two years in *When Pigs Fly*, and just needing a change after sixteen years in NYC, it was time for something new. Finishing *Puppy Love* was the impetus to go to LA and see what the market might be for it there, as well as to look into TV and film work as an actor. I was intending to check it out for three months to see what was what, but I quickly knew it was where I wanted to be. I was told most folks go to LA to reinvent themselves, but after getting the lay of the land and beginning to audition for TV and film, I began to fall into the same routine as my last couple of years in NY.

A few weeks before I left, I began flirting in an AOL chat room with a guy named Ian Praiser, a TV writer/producer from LA who actually knew me from seeing *When Pigs Fly* on a trip to NYC. The first night I was in LA, he took me for dinner and mentioned that he was interested in producing *Pigs* there. I put him in touch with the NY producers, and soon enough the show was ready to go and I was going to be in it. It was a terrific cast, including the wonderful and incredibly funny Jim J. Bullock, and it was a dream to do it in Hollywood. But again, not enough money to live on, so in addition to getting speaking roles on TV shows (a bare-assed leather bartender on *NYPD Blue* and a homeless person in the Disney TV film *Annie* directed by Rob Marshall), I started escorting again, on and off over the next five years or so. I just found it an easy way to make quick money, much more so than any other job outside of showbiz that I might have been qualified for, and it was better than waiting tables or catering.

Perhaps that's what played into Reid's insecurities about me, that he felt it was inevitable that I'd go back to it—if so, it turns out he was right—but when I was with him, escorting was absolutely done and gone, and I never intended to start again until that one fateful night when the relationship was imploding.

I'm sure some of you are going to psychoanalyze me to see what kind of delusion I'm under, but really, I've thought it through a zillion times alone and in therapy: "What kind of man am I that thought I could sell my body for cash and enjoy it? Is there such a thing as a 'hooker mentality,' and do I have it?" Have at it if you will, but for me, I am so glad I was able to live out that fantasy and find out that it was not at all what I expected and more than I had hoped.

Even though money was involved—and that was a huge part of my motivation—what kept it interesting and fulfilling was that connection between me and my clients. And though it was temporary, I don't think I could have sustained being an escort all that time without some sense of emotional connection with them. I hoped that our interactions were fun and healing and sexy. I always did my best. I'm not denying that the bad boy, sex pig aspect of the job was enjoyable and truly part of who I am, but it was always more complicated than that. Escorting played into a lot of different aspects of my personality and instincts.

Did doing that work get in the way of having a relationship? Probably. After Reid, I didn't really want to have to explain or defend my choices to anyone, so I pretty much didn't date at all because it was just easier not to. However, I never felt guilty about escorting unless, as I said earlier, I imagined my folks finding out. That would have disappointed them no end, because as urban, liberal, and cool as they could be, sex was never something they wanted to address, let alone the idea of taking money for it. There was also the little fact that it was illegal and my folks were as straitlaced as could be when it came to the law (as, usually, am I). It was also kind of different back then—I rarely ran into clients who did drugs (at least in front of me) and most were level-headed and in the moment. I took pleasure from it, I felt I did it well, and the flexible hours freed me up to work on my acting, singing, and performing career, and I started to accrue more TV roles.

In LA, rather than an escort service to meet clients, I used AOL chat rooms and was able to talk directly to them online. If their spelling was way off or their tone was a little eerie, I was able to sift them out. My handle was *Mld2Wldscort*, i.e., Mild to Wild Escort. At the time, "mild to wild" meant I was willing to go from vanilla to kink, but by the tail end of my time in this work I found that, with that name, guys expected me to either do or bring drugs and have no limits sexually, including barebacking. None of that was my thing and I stayed away from it.

I'd log in and just hang by my computer, writing until someone instant-messaged me. We'd chat about what they wanted, I'd send pictures, we'd talk business, and then I'd either go or not. It was a fairly easy way to hook up. I had one regular client where we spent most of the hour drinking cocktails and chatting about his day. He wanted to feel there was someone to come home to, to talk about everything from his job to the news to his dating life, and sometimes it led to sex and sometimes it didn't.

I did enjoy it when it was just show up, fuck, and leave; those jobs were actually easier and usually didn't even last the hour. I especially liked it when they requested massage. I was not a certified massage therapist, but I did give a mean body rub, using my entire oiled-up body on top of theirs, and I always found it arousing and intimate, having so much skin-to-skin contact totally under my control. It usually served as foreplay to whatever else they requested.

I didn't escort on a daily basis. It was a welcome addition when things were slow in the other areas where I was making money: showbiz, bartending at catering gigs, and, once again, cleaning houses. I worked with a company in LA that did housecleaning, sometimes naked, sometimes not. I signed on with them for occasional jobs that, when naked, paid fifty bucks an hour, minimum three hours. A third of that went to my "pimp," a quirky guy named Chuck who was sweet but always stressed that his business was not bringing in what he needed. Just a guy trying to make a buck.

Chuck also provided bartenders and waiters for parties, both nude and non-nude. I did a few naked party service jobs for him, but I would only go shirtless for more elite ones where important biz people might attend. You never knew who you'd run into at an event, and I figured serving some major film director a cosmo with my dick hanging out wouldn't be the best career move.

I did some private parties as a naked waiter, usually just for couples—small anniversary dinners or intimate birthday celebrations—and that was actually a lot of fun, serving appetizers while just letting my cock graze their hand or letting them cop a quick feel of my ass as I poured wine, very subversively flirty, amping up the sexuality for what would happen after dinner between them, and sometimes I was included in the festivities afterwards for a very generous tip.

I always enjoyed the combination of cleaning, service, role play, teasing, and outright sex. I was a good housecleaner (naked and not) and a good escort. I never did drugs except occasional poppers, not even pot. I always kept clear so that I could be in control should anything go awry, plus the last thing I needed was to get stopped by a cop at two in the morning on my way to or from a client.

I had a couple of run-ins with guys I was acquainted with who unknowingly booked me off the Internet. My pictures were slightly veiled for discretion's sake when I worked on my own, but I showed up a couple of times to men I knew from some other aspect of life. There was the TV writer who ran in some of the same gay industry circles that I did, and when I showed up, we were both taken aback. I asked if it was okay or did he want me to leave, no obligation. I stuck around and we had a great time. I respected discretion, always, nothing was ever said, and we remain friendly to this day.

Another time, I showed up . . . and my dentist answered the door. He was tall, blond, and, I believed, very straight. After deciding it would be fine and not weird, I proceeded to fulfill his request: to fist him. I fisted my dentist. I thought it wouldn't matter, but the next week, when I had my checkup, it was just too weird thinking of my hand up his ass while his hand was in my mouth. I sought dental care elsewhere.

I think back most fondly on my return clients, knowing that, when they contacted me, there was no sifting process and we already had that connection. I just got dressed and made my way over to them. Although I was there for financial reasons, I did feel very warmly toward them and the feeling was mutual.

One repeat guy lived in Torrance, California, which was quite a schlep from West Hollywood at two in the morning when his AOL message would pop up after his work shift. Sometimes I'd be too wiped out to travel, but for the most part a quick shower and a cup of coffee would get me awake and I'd be on my way. He was a sweet, soft-spoken African-American gentleman who had a roommate, so I would have to skulk in, but once we were alone in his room, it was all very sensuous and fun, and his dick was *huge*. I won't lie—I do enjoy a big cock, but it's definitely not required, though I am amazed at just how large some guys' penises are. I noted how their confidence grew when they went from clothed to naked, especially if they were overweight or skinny, taking great pride in the size of their cocks.

I had one client in New York, a businessman, whose erection was so long and girthy that all I could do was masturbate him and lick it a lot all over because I did not have a hole on my body that could have stretched open enough to take even an inch of it; it would have split me apart.

Whatever their dick size, I enjoyed being with all kinds of guys as long as they were not assholes, and I found that a big part of the job was playing toward what made them confident and sexy, never judging or disdaining. I was paid to be positive, arousing, and exciting, and the actor in me always rose to the occasion (as did my dick).

The Torrance guy was so appreciative of my showing up at that late hour. He was semi-closeted and worked arduous shifts, so I was his one real sexual outlet in a very busy life. He paid well, but I did always feel a strong connection to him—not love, but true affection. He was just so dear, a gentle giant. I felt terrible when he called me by my hooker name, Darren, and I never let on what my true name and occupation were. I'm sure there were guys who clicked on the TV and saw me doing some guest spot on a television show and thought, "Didn't I just pay him to fuck me last night?"

I always tried to be available when Torrance Guy contacted me, and I was usually fine driving there. It was motoring back at 4 a.m. after an hour of sex that was difficult. More than once, I almost fell asleep behind the wheel. In order to avoid an accident on the road, I learned to do three things (take note, anyone who has to drive home in the wee hours after sex): 1) I wouldn't cum. That shuts my body down and I'm ready for a nap. Torrance Guy understood about me holding that back, and it never mattered as I always focused on his orgasm; 2) If I did feel sleepy, I would turn on the radio, find my jam, and sing at the top of my lungs as long as I could; and 3) I'd pull out my cock and masturbate. I'd often jerked off from one city to the other in my car when I felt like The Drowsy Chaperone, and focusing on my dick made the time go by and kept me awake. Except for the odd truck driver, no one noticed.

JAGGED LITTLE PILL

Mostly, I was asked to top, but I did occasionally bottom, although that was fraught with more anxiety as HIV was still the phantom hovering over our sex lives. I was ultracareful. I topped one guy and came in the rubber, but he asked me to immediately put my cock back inside him, and after a few minutes I felt that intense skin-to-skin contact that I hadn't experienced in a long while. I discovered that the rubber had broken, and my cum was now swimming around inside him. I told him and he wasn't the least bit unnerved. He said he was positive but undetectable. I was shaken, though. I always just went about my sexual practices as if everyone was positive, and had safe sex. I was aghast at the broken rubber even though I was the top and barely—if at all—at risk. I didn't know back then that if someone was undetectable, he couldn't pass on the virus, so I still found myself neurotically checking rubbers a zillion times when I was the bottom.

HIV was always a present concern for me (this was pre-PrEP). I did everything I could to protect myself, some would say to irratio-nal levels, but here's the thing: it's very easy to say hey, relax, stay safe and you're fine, but when you were having as much casual sex as I was, you tended to be more reflective about the experience. And in the light of day, the next morning after a regular hookup or after I left a client, I was stuck with myself and my thoughts, and bad news scenarios running around in my brain, and as I've said before, my brain can be a hazardous place to hang out. But after what we all went through in the '80s and '90s, seeing so many friends disappear, struck down in their prime in the most painful of ways—those are not battle scars that will fade with time. Honestly, I don't know if they'll ever go away, even after years of therapy.

That's why, these days, when a younger guy wants to plow inside me with his unwrapped cock, telling me it's fine, he's negative on PrEP, the answer is always no, not without a rubber. And sometimes they look at me as if I'm nuts. I don't go into the whole history of AIDS and other bugs with them, because it can be an erection executioner, but if they're not respectful or they disdain my wishes, I'm out of there.

I don't like to talk about "breeding." I know it's gotten more and more in the mainstream of gay sexual behavior, but it's just not for me. I get so many messages on the dating/sex sites—"Breed me, daddy"— and I always answer back no, not even in fantasy, and if it's a deal breaker, so be it. So to this day, if someone tells me I'm too careful or too wrapped up (literally and figuratively) in prevention, well . . . sorry. You're not me and you don't live in my skin. I do what I need to do to function, even though to some my caution seems a bit extreme. Would I love to be more stress free and able to fuck any which way I can with no mind games? Sure. Besides the fact that PrEP (which I've started taking as of this writing as an extra precaution to ease my mind) does not protect against other STIs that are on the upswing, who knows what the next big thing is that could be passed on . . . OR WORSE? Very Jewish mother, I know, but I don't want the next generation to go through what we went through (and, by the way, the AIDS crisis is far from over as the HIV medications don't work for everyone).

I've gone this long staying negative, I'm not about to change my practices until there's a total cure and a 100 percent way of protecting ourselves beyond rubbers. I don't judge those who choose to go bare, but I just can't do it.

When I was with Reid, he wanted to throw rubbers away after we'd been together a year, and as the relationship was troubled, I wanted to save it by giving that to him. We had both been tested over the year, so I complied, with the agreement that he would still not cum inside me, which he thought was paranoid crazy, but that was my one request. Yes, I know, pre-cum was still getting in there, but whatever—the agreement made me shakily comfortable with raw fucking.

Actually, I didn't love going bare inside him as I am so sensitive that I'd want to shoot the instant I entered him; it took a lot of concentration to not explode when I started to fuck him. He loved it, though, taking my rather copious loads of cum, but I was uncomfortable every time, and also found it kind of manipulative. We were monogamous, but once he started traveling for work, he gave me permission to fuck around as long as he didn't know. I had no desire to do that (until I knew the relationship was absolutely over), but if I had strayed, I'd have had to tell him in case some STI came up, and I think that was part of his plan in throwing away the rubbers—to keep me in line.

One day, I was eating lunch with a friend who, much like Reid, was definitely a monogamous type of guy, preferring men who agreed with him on everything and whom he could fully trust. He seemed particularly distant and distracted, and I asked what was up. He told me he'd found out his much younger, supposedly monogamous boyfriend was having unprotected sex as a bottom in bathhouses. As they were not using rubbers, it was freaking him out. This was pre-PrEP. I just listened and felt horrible for him. It's all well and good to trust your partner, but men can be men, and it just seemed easier and more secure to be safe.

Of course, I've never been in a relationship with that level of com-mitment, trust, and time, so I'm not one to speak. But I felt so badly for him—that someone not only betrayed that trust but also put his life and health in danger. He was highly distressed and I would be too, so I just don't change my practices, PrEP or no PrEP . . . for now. And because I have such a vivid mind-set about sex, perhaps my caution helps to rein in desires and fantasies that might get me in trouble if I tried to live them out (like being the bottom in a twenty-man gang bang then getting pissed on by every one of them—who knows what I'd pick up? See?). Maybe that'll change down the line. I don't know. Still working through it. Maybe I always will be.

ALL ABOUT ME

Getting a screenplay produced is a herculean task, so I was making the business rounds in LA with *Dog Days* (the new title of *Puppy Love*), but I needed to stay creative beyond performing *When Pigs Fly* six times a week and the supporting TV roles I was getting. Since the success of *Naked Boys Singing!* I was enjoying taking risqué gay subject matter, personalizing it, and putting it to music. I had brought those essays and lyrics I'd written years before to LA and, after all that time, found myself intrigued by them, as if someone else had written them.

I thought my storytelling had sensitivity, humor, and humanity that anyone could relate to, so I decided to incorporate the narratives and songs into a show. *To Bitter and Back* started out as a one-man revue, but I wanted it to have more emotional heft than just a hodge-podge of tales and lyrics. I also needed a pianist to play the show and help me shape the musical aspects of it.

One day, I walked into the rehearsal room at the Coronet Theatre where we were doing *Pigs* to hear Jamie, an intern at the theater, playing piano like a prodigy. He told me he had been a musical director in Houston, but while in LA he took whatever jobs he could (these days, he is an in-demand composer for TV and film). I asked if he would help me out with my show, and that was the beginning of not only finishing a bunch of songs I had written (I can't play piano) but also having someone to stick by me as I developed the show musically and incorporated those songs into the stories.

When the LA production of *When Pigs Fly* closed in October 1999, the producers kindly allowed me to use one of their theater spaces to work on my show. Jamie and I would do mini readings of it, and at each of those I'd invite two or three folks to watch, listen, and give their input. Early on, most said they loved the material but it was still playing like a revue and they wished everything was more integrated.

And then it hit me: I had unwittingly given myself a through line in almost all the material. I wrote so much about wanting things and not getting them—jobs, boyfriends, money, love, all pretty relatable stuff— and I knew I had a show if I could just pull it together. I remembered that time Andy called me in despair because the only thing he had written in his book to do that day was to buy shoelaces, and the laugh we had over the depression of it inspired me to write a song called "A Shoelace Kind of Day." I knew that needed to be my opening number—a guy who can't get out of bed in the morning because his life has come to a halt. And why? Because he keeps wanting things and not getting them. Anyone can identify: How do you get out of bed when you just can't?

In the end, through telling all these stories, the character realizes he focuses too much on what he doesn't have rather than what he does— family, friends, roof over his head, brains, talent—and when he shifts his thinking, he's able to get out of bed and onto the streets of NY, even if it's only to buy some shoelaces. Like that episode where Mary Tyler Moore cleans her apartment—start with emptying an ashtray and then see where it goes.

Can't turn on the TV.
The remote's too far from me,
and I just can't stomach Regis or that goddamn Kathie Lee.
Maybe coffee'd get me up,
but I'd have to wash a cup,
and I'd rather wet the bed than go and pee.

Buy shoelaces. Buy shoelaces for shoes with broken soles.
Those old black Kenneth Coles have big fat gaping holes.
Buy shoelaces. Buy shoelaces. I used to have a life,
but nothing happens now, so tell me, where's the knife?
—from "A Shoelace Kind of Day"

During my development of the show, I visited NY to see Andy, and while waiting for him at the Big Cup coffeehouse in Chelsea (where I used to spend hour upon hour writing and cruising—it was my "office"), a young man, maybe twenty, with a ton of energy and verve, plopped down at the long table I was sitting at and greeted his friends. He dumped a pile of paper in front of them that sloped upward in one corner. "I got the flyers for my one-man show! They're here!" His friends each grabbed one and busily chattered about how exciting it all was and how they couldn't wait to see it. I looked over at the flyers. They were professionally reproduced, but instead of a photo being printed on the paper, every sheet had a Polaroid of him in various flamboyant positions stapled to the corner. He looked like Lucille Ball in the film version of *Mame*, jumping up on tables and yelling, "Listen everybody!" (I do love a *Mame* reference.) And then I saw the title of the show: *It's About ME!* The flyer made the show look pretty sincere and earnest. There was no irony there, no satire on one-man shows, just—it's about me.

I had a moment of terror. Had I written *It's About ME!*? Was that what *my* show was? My belief in it began to flag a bit, until I got back to

LA and continued the workshops. I think that young man did me a favor by making me hyperaware of the importance of emphasizing the elements of my story that an audience could identify with: my struggles to find love, success, and self-esteem, and eventually getting past the limitations and obstacles to finding happiness and hope.

Sure enough, finally, folks were reacting emotionally to what I had written. We were ready, and after a lot of fundraising and theater searching, I was able to get the first production of *To Bitter and Back* up in February 2001 at the Tamarind Theatre in Hollywood, directed by my pal Randy Brenner. We'd been friends for years and I love him to death. He's also an actor and had tons of Jewsical experience. Back in our regional theater days in NYC we would often see each other at auditions for the Jewish immigrant role in productions of the musical *Tintypes*, which he'd get until he started turning it down and then I'd be cast. We had an excellent working relationship because he really "got" my material.

The show was so much fun to perform, and I had a healthy and successful six-week run, and later was nominated for the LA Weekly Best Solo Performance award. I wanted to take *To Bitter and Back* to NY, but after the tragedy of 9/11 it was going to be near impossible to mount a small, independent show there. However, I went to see a production of *Naked Boys Singing!* at the Bailiwick Theatre in Chicago when I was home visiting my family, and David Zak, the artistic director, asked if I wanted to split the week with *NBS* and do *Bitter* there. He didn't have to ask me twice.

I took a break from escorting and auditioning to do a month in Chicago, and thanks to my mom's Rolodex and a lovely article in the *Daily News*, anyone who ever saw me in a diaper showed up in the audience at some point. I was certainly a tad anxious about presenting such a personal and intimate theater piece in my hometown in front of so many folks from my past, but it was a wonderful time, performing this show that was born out of blood, sweat, and tears. It really seemed to touch the people who saw it and made them laugh.

There was the added bonus of never knowing who was going to show up. I was talking in the lobby after my performance one day about a friend from high school named Paula Sugarman. The box office person overheard and yelled out, "She's coming Wednesday night!"

When I found out that Joe, the object of my tank top seduction as a kid, was coming to see it, I was a little agitated as I had included that story in the show. However, I thought there was no way he would recognize himself as my crush that I wanted to entice because I truly believed he had been oblivious to how I felt (although I could have changed his name—that might have helped. Duh). My folks happened to be at the show that night. Not only did they remember Joe from back in the day, but he was also the owner of their favorite Italian restaurant, so they saw him pretty regularly. Wouldn't you know it, right before the performance, my mom pulled him aside and said, "Joe, did you know you're a character in the show?" Dear god. Thanks, Mom. Joe actually invited me to his house on my day off and I met his wife and kids, and when we were alone, we chatted about the show. He was very flattered, didn't remember things the way I did, and was very good-humored about being included. Phew.

My folks came to see *Bitter* a bunch of times, and even though there are moments where my mom does not come off great—I included the Chanukah dog and the Normie's Delicatessen coffee bits—she loved it and understood that these stories were funny and honest. She knew I was not trying to disrespect her or get back at her by telling them.

However, after she saw the show the first time, she told me that my memory was off about the Chanukah dog story: the piece of canine furniture was meant for my dad, who had had a bulldog as a kid, not for me, something I believed (and resented) for over thirty years. Mom told the *Daily News* in an interview that she was okay that she came off as a horrible person in the show because it was funny and it was my memory of the incident. She "got" it, so I'm grateful.

Marcia is no longer with us. We lost my mom in 2017. At the end of her life, I found out she preferred Mommy to Mom, even though we were adults, so as I write this, I'm looking up and saying thanks, Mommy. I may have made her a nemesis in my show, but she took it in good humor, even bringing all her friends to see it, and up until her last days they couldn't watch her drink a cup of coffee without breaking into giggles.

CABARET

During my one year at the University of Michigan in 1977–78, I did shows with a group of acting students who had all gone to New Trier High School in the Chicago suburbs (Ann-Margret and Charlton Heston were two of its famous alumni), and just like my high school thespian friends, they were very tight and very driven. In the summer of '78, back in Chicago, one of them invited me to perform with some of his high school classmates in *The Showtoppers Revue*, which had us doing show tunes loaded with choreography, full-out musical comedy, at various venues in the city. Though I was later to have my own club act on the *Royal Viking Sky* cruise ship, I wasn't one to embrace the cabaret life, singing into a microphone while the audience nursed their dirty martinis, but one of our first gigs was at a gay bar called Gentry.

I was nineteen years old and not yet out to anyone, and had never been inside a gay bar, let alone performed in one. I was a wreck. There we were in our matching vests and button-down shirts, looking very Up with People, ready to strut our stuff for a bunch of show tune–loving queens. Always the supportive ones, my folks came to see the performance, which added to my nerves.

For my solo, I chose "She Touched Me" from the Broadway musical *Drat! The Cat!* It was originally sung by Elliott Gould, but I knew the song from his ex-wife's recording "He Touched Me" (Barbra, it's a boy's song, honey). I sat on the stool, leaned into the mic, and began singing, softly and sensitively, "Sheeee touched me." As one, the boys in the audience went, "Ooooooooo," as if to say, "Get *her!*"

Suddenly, I felt flushed and shaky and scared, and it was all I could do to keep singing, to get through it, and having my folks watch me get gay-shamed for singing a love song to a woman when I was obviously as queer as anyone in the club—mortifying. I don't remember much afterwards except that, in the "Oooo" moment, I felt as helpless as I had when Gabe Kovinsky beat me up at recess, when I failed at sports in gym class, when my sister found that copy of *After Dark*. I also remember not being able to look my parents in the eyes after, and they may have said "Good job," but in the end what was supposed to be a fun, exciting evening was just a loserly blur.

One thing I did come away with: pick appropriate material for the room. Lesson learned.

Years later, while doing *To Bitter and Back* in Chicago, I was asked to sing "The Perky Little Porn Star" at the Grabbys, the gay porn awards at the Circuit nightclub in Boystown. I knew I couldn't pass that up; it would be weird as hell and quite the experience, but I also knew it would be a tough crowd. The song couldn't be more appropriate, though, and I was performing it in *Bitter*, so I was ready. But did they really want some musical comedy guy from LA singing them a show tune?

I was told I'd open the second act, that after intermission they would make sure everyone was in their seats, the lights would go down, I'd get an offstage intro, enter, get to the mic, a spotlight would hit me, and then I'd start.

Not quite how it went.

The crowd did not want to sit back down for more show, so there was a lot of hubbub as the announcer droned in the droniest of drone voices, "Have a seat, everyone. Please sit down. Time for Act Two. Have a seat. Everyone. Please sit down. Everyone . . ."

Bueller? Bueller?

"Okay. Here's David *Pervsner*."

I walked out, the spotlight hit and blinded me, and absolutely no one was listening. I had a little bit of patter that got a laugh or two, but the chatter drowned it out, except for the guy who yelled out, "Take off your pants!" Massive laugh for him. Audience heckler: one; David: zero. There was that flushed feeling of impending humiliation starting to well up, but I just began the song with as much charisma as I could muster.

The first quarter of it was pretty rough, but as it went on, they paid more and more attention, there was more laughing, and by the time I ripped my shirt off for the final verse, they were cheering, and in the end they gave me a roaring ovation. I was proud I got through it. As I was leaving the venue, I felt a slap on my back. It was Matthew Rush, then one of the biggest porn stars out there. I turned and he said, "Hey, you were funny." I blushed and said thank you. "The Perky Little Porn Star," porn star approved. I'd come a long way from Gentry.

WONDERFUL TOWN

I loved performing *To Bitter and Back* for that month in Chicago. I stayed with my friend Melissa, whom I'd known since kindergarten and who lived close to the theater; I saw my folks and my sister Janet often; and every performance brought someone from my past to chat and reminisce with after. I was so proud of the show, and any fear I had of sharing such intimacy with my audiences faded to nothing. I felt absolutely at ease with myself, my family, my friends, and my work.

On top of that, I got a membership at Steamworks bathhouse (formerly the Unicorn), which had a gym on its third floor. I worked out every day nude or in just a jockstrap, which made me push myself harder, and I got myself into the best shape I'd ever been in. Plus, I was able to alleviate any sexual tension immediately with the businessmen on their lunch hours, and then, happy and depleted, I could go back, eat a meal, take a nap, and be refreshed for the show that night. Being in Chicago was an entirely satisfying experience.

Beyond all that goodness, doing *To Bitter and Back* in Chicago gave me my first inkling of why *Naked Boys Singing!* was still running in NY and all over the world. In splitting the stage time, I was scheduled to do a late show of *Bitter* on Fridays after a 7 p.m. *NBS*. The first Friday, I was waiting in the lobby for their show to end and I was hearing a lot of high-pitched laughter and shrieking, which had to be coming from women—the vocal timbre was definitely alto/soprano. Sure enough, the doors opened and out walked streams of ladies, hardly a man in the bunch, excitedly and energetically dancing and singing their way to the street, covering their eyes and doing that thing where they hold their two hands a certain distance apart to indicate penis size, and just having a grand old time. Some were wearing tiaras or feather boas. Holy shit. That's how the show ran for twenty years in various productions—bachelorette parties and ladies' nights. To this day, that's the lifeblood of the show. Still running somewhere in the world twenty-plus years later.

One of those weekends in Chicago, the annual International Male Leather competition was taking place. I'd heard about it for years, and it was a welcome coincidence that I was in town doing my show. I couldn't go to the actual competition because I had a performance, but I figured I'd spend Sunday morning at the host hotel (the Hyatt Regency Chicago), check out the leather marketplace set up in the basement, and then hang around and watch the leather people parade until it was time to do my matinee.

The whole place was taken over by the leather men, and it was certainly a scene—guys with codpieces and assless chaps and harnesses wandering and cruising hallways, the lobby, elevators. It was quite the spectacle. I ran into a friend who had just gotten fucked in a makeshift sling in one hotel room and was on his way to another to fist a guy he'd met at the baths the night before. These guys were not kidding around.

I would have loved to have been more involved as I roved the hotel, wishing I had brought my leather garb from LA—which, by the way, was a combination of the pieces I bought in New Orleans during *Fiddler* and gear that was given to me by an escorting client whose friend had passed away and bequeathed him all his leather. He didn't want it and passed it on to me. Yup, I had a dead man's leather.

I still enjoyed getting duded up from time to time and hitting the Faultline or the Gauntlet, leather bars in LA, and I was much more well-versed in all things leather and fetish by this point as a part of my sexual oeuvre and portfolio. However, since I was not about to spend a fortune at the leather market for just a couple of hours, and because I not only had the matinee but was going to perform at the Grabbys right after, I chose to just watch and not partake.

I stood in the mezzanine overlooking the lobby as the spectacle unfolded, and at one point I turned my attention to the café, which was wide open to the atrium, crowded and bustling. There was a large table with a slew of colorful balloons as the centerpiece, and then I noticed who was sitting at the table: ten kids, each maybe eight years old, having a birthday party, eating cake and ice cream, blowing into noisemakers whose sound mingled with the din of the lobby. Those kids were going about their business as if nothing was happening around them.

I wanted so badly to approach the woman in the glittery party hat overseeing the festivities to find out how the hell that booking happened. Did she know? Did they tell her? Did she care? The kids seemed fine, so I guess no harm, no foul. I'm sure if I had been the birthday boy, I would have been maybe a little distracted. Or a lot. Happy birthday to me!

FADE OUT FADE IN

I think I've been clear that there has always been a part of me that wanted to be in gay porn. "The Perky Little Porn Star" was my fantasy, but the angst that character had to get over about sex was very much alive inside me. My whole life had become a journey to find out who I was sexually, to explore who I wanted to be with no apologies, no self-judgment. The covert desire to be in gay porn was there before I built up my body, but once I did, there was the notion that I could actually do it, even though in my head I was still a big-nose ugly Jew trying to find validation in the superficial.

When I realized that I could express myself sexually through my work, I wanted to do it with more substance, with an aesthetic and creative point of view. I wasn't looking to do regular porn. Around 2004, I heard that John Cameron Mitchell, the creator and star of *Hedwig and the Angry Inch*, was writing and directing a film called *Shortbus* that would have full-out penetrative graphic sex. I wanted in. I had loved Mitchell's work ever since I saw *Hedwig* at a little club on the West Side Highway in New York before it became a big deal. The producers were taking video audition submissions in which you could do anything you wanted, from talking about yourself to jerking off to fucking to whatever.

There was no mention of a plot or characters; they were going to develop the film in a workshop, and wanted people who were fearless. I'm your guy, I thought, but I also heard that once you submitted your tape, they could use the auditions for the DVD extras portion. I was still holding back in my desire to be utterly shameless because of my TV career, and if I didn't get into the actual film, I didn't want some anonymous video of me shooting a load as a throwaway on the DVD. So rather than copulating, jacking off, or performing fellatio in my audition tape, I decided to tell a story about my sex life. Then, being absolutely true to myself, I wrote a song that I sang a cappella to the camera, about how:

> *I'll get fucked on camera for the sake of my art,*
> *film hand, rim, and blow jobs, if I get this part.*
> *Since I so agree sex should be cinematic,*
> *I'll do anything . . . pretty much . . . except scat. Ick!*
>
> *If it helps make the plot and relationships hum,*
> *Then you shoot the scene, John, and I'll shoot the cum.*
> *And my reputation? Fuck! I have no fears.*
> *There's enough dirt in my life to kill twelve careers!*
> —from "For the Sake of My Art"

I did not get cast, but I got an email from Howard Gertler, one of the producers, who said they enjoyed the song but "we're looking for 23." I didn't know that. Oh well. I saw the film and loved it, it was right up my alley, and I knew that someday I would figure out a way to be in something that was artistic, character driven, and as brazenly honest about sexuality as that film.

9 TO 5

In 2007, while continuing to build my TV résumé on shows such as *Desperate Housewives*, *Criminal Minds*, and *Las Vegas*, I had begun doing odd jobs for my friend Nic Arnzen, who not only was a member of the original Chicago cast of *Party*, but also directed me in various theater ventures. David Dillon, the director/writer of *Party*, suggested I look Nic up when I got to LA, and we hit it off and became fast friends. Nic was the house assistant to a fairly wealthy and eccentric entertainment executive, and I would help hang pictures, arrange party details, cater business meetings, anything that Nic either needed a second hand for or didn't have the time to take on.

The executive collected everything from Fiestaware to Disneyana to bobbleheads and a shit ton more, and when he took possession of his new house, the movers kind of just dumped a bunch of bins and loose knickknacks and tchotchkes into the garage. Nic had his hands full with other aspects of the move and asked me to see what I could do to organize the stuff.

I entered the garage and something took over. I was like a beast who made this messy, discombobulated garage look like a department store.

I didn't even remember doing it. It was as though I was possessed. Truth is, I come by those anal tendencies honestly, because my mother was the most organized person in the world, and suddenly I found it came naturally to *me* too.

I did some organizing for another of Nic's clients, and then began to tell people that I was doing it as a business, and so I built a clientele through word of mouth for Address the Mess, my makeshift LLC. It was, and continues to be, fun, creative, and physically and mentally rigorous. Not only can I make my clients' surroundings more efficient and livable, but getting rid of the clutter seems to alleviate so much of the stress that can arise from a messy, chaotic environment. I also found I was using a great deal of armchair psychology to help my clients change their habits and get real about where they lived, played, and worked. And for myself, I found that I became a much more positive person about everything, because each time I started a new organizing gig, I wasn't there to commiserate on how lousy things were; I was there to say, yup, we're gonna turn that around and you're going to love it.

The longer I did it, the more I developed clever and resourceful techniques to help folks rearrange their space and repurpose what they already had to keep their expenses down.

Organizing is like a big ol' game of Tetris (the only video game I ever played) and it uses a part of my brain that I didn't even know I had. I love it. It began to replace escorting as my way to make money outside showbiz. Even though I still enjoyed escorting, the game was starting to change—with more requests to do drugs and unsafe sex—and I was becoming more germ-phobic than I used to be. Plus, as much as daddies are in demand now, back then I felt that the market was shrinking for a man in his mid-forties. I never lied about my age, and sometimes the connection was cut after I was asked, "how old are you?"

I'll never regret the time I spent escorting. But it was time to move on.

TITANIC

Our songs will range from classy to uncouth,
delivered with great pluck as in our youth.
If it's odd to call us "Boys," 'cause we're too long in the tooth,
WHO CARES?!
We're Fancy Boys!
And don't forget it!
We're Fancy-Shmancy Boys!
—from "Fancy Boys"

My screenplay *Dog Days* generated a lot of interest over the years, from producers who were able to help get it close to production but could never quite run it over the finish line for one reason or another (usually money). I'd heard the stories of films that took twenty years to get produced, so I knew I had to just keep soldiering on. I changed the title again to the more on-the-nose *Musical Comedy Whore*, because *Dog Days* seemed too generic and remote from the subject matter.

In the screenplay, Doug is in a long-running off-Broadway musical called *Fancy Boys* (inspired by *When Pigs Fly*). I'd intended to use some numbers from *Pigs* in *Fancy Boys*, for texture. However, over the years, I wrote more and more songs on my own, and eventually I decided to take the musical within the screenplay and create an actual live stage show out of it. *The Fancy Boys Follies* was developed between 2003 and 2007, and was intended to be a mix of vaudeville and burlesque. Although my musical director friend had hated the songs I sent him years earlier, I thought the material had merit. After workshopping it in Los Angeles, I had the opportunity to present an actual production of it at the New York Musical Theatre Festival (NYMF) in 2008.

I had such hopes for the show. That festival was very exclusive; only twenty-four shows were accepted, as compared with the hundreds that get into most other festivals. NYMF was the birthplace of the hit shows *Altar Boyz* and *[title of show]*, the festival's main claims to fame.

The director of *The Fancy Boys Follies* was Randy Brenner, who had also directed *To Bitter and Back*. We had a hard time casting the show because it was the gayest show in the festival, with a lot of risqué material, but between LA and NY actors we were able to put a cast together and start exploring. We were thrilled to have my pal Jim J. Bullock along for the ride. He is one of the dearest, funniest, most talented people I know. Once we were in rehearsal, though, there was a lot of turmoil behind the scenes as the actors were not comfortable with the style of the show: broad lowbrow humor with material that was very blue, including songs about leather and fetish, straight guys having gay sex, and of course "Pain in the Butt" (my infamous anal warts song), as well as sketches with language and sexual entendres that were very funny but had to be handled correctly to make them work.

The actors needed to be bold and fearless, and that was not what we were getting. Randy told me that my presence in rehearsal as writer and coproducer made some of the actors self-conscious, and they told him they felt as if I was staring over their shoulders as they worked on the more explicit material. I understood, so I stayed out of the room to let them explore.

However, there was some friction in the room that I ended up not knowing about. One actor half joked to Randy that since he was only getting paid five hundred dollars for the entire weeks-long commitment (festivals are on a special limited Actors' Equity contract), he didn't feel he had to extend himself as much as on a normal contract. My theory is a "joke" like that comes out of some element of truth. Randy and I were of the same mind that it doesn't matter whether you're getting five bucks or five million bucks, it's the same amount of work, and it's your ass out there, and if you want to give the five-buck performance, you kind of suck. On top of that, some of the guys were struggling with totally committing to the material, thinking it was too racy. Thus, the friction.

My choreographer got pissed at me because he'd spent so much time creating and rehearsing the opening number and it wasn't working (the song was too muddled and all over the place—my fault, not his), so I, as the writer, came in and slashed some of the musical material, cutting not only a whole bridge to the song but his choreography as well. That's the way it goes when you develop a show: you kill your babies and everyone else's as well. What matters is the show, the story you want to tell, the clarity, and it is not personal. At all.

Beyond issues on the performance end, I began ignoring our budget. Not only did I extend spending on publicity, we had fantastic designers with so much talent and enthusiasm that, rather than limit them, I kept passing bucks over to whoever asked. I wanted our show to look as good as it played. I'd done a commercial that year that paid crazy well. (Despite the fact that it was 2008 and the rest of the country was in a financial tailspin, I had to zip my lips when someone would bemoan their fiscal situation, because that was the best year I ever had.) With that and the fundraising we did, I had the cash on hand.

That was a mistake. Once you start kicking in, you don't stop. Money always seems to be the way to solve production problems, but it isn't. A strong hand and decisiveness are what does it, and I did not have either. I wasn't sure we were going to get where we needed to be by opening. It was an incredibly stressful production period.

For publicity, we were asked to present a number at a Midtown bar called Therapy that was helping to promote the festival, and as we were one of the later shows to open, we only had a couple of numbers learned and staged. So Jim was to sing one of his solos, "Pain in the Butt"—graphic, but funny. He was worried that the audience was going to hate him, the song, everything. I'd learned a long time ago that you can't do such material with any kind of fear. I just told him that you have to play the character (a drag queen at a country bar), and that character talks that way, has that story to tell, and it must be played fully, no holding back. He promised to just go out there and lay it on the line, and he did. And the audience roared with delight and I was so proud of him. After, he said, "I get it!" I thought we were on our way.

The night before we opened, despite all the difficulties, we had a show. We did an invited final rehearsal in the studio for about ten people, and we had to keep stopping, they were laughing so hard. The guys were starting to understand how this "Vaudelesque" was going to work, and they were eager to get it in front of a paying audience. Meanwhile, the whole production team and I had tears in our eyes after the run-through because we finally had the show we had always imagined. It was wonderful and funny and audacious, and we were ready.

The next day, we moved into our assigned venue, the 45th Street Theatre, which we shared with four other shows (as you do in festivals). We had about five hours to tech the show, which meant putting it together with all the elements, including installing our set pieces and backdrops, working out lighting, and managing the many costume changes. As the tech rehearsal was progressing, I noticed that the theater was feeling kind of warm. I asked the manager if the air-conditioning was on. It was over ninety degrees outside, and one old adage in the theater world is "Comedy is cold," meaning people will not laugh if it's uncomfortably hot in a theater. He said that when you tech, the lights staying on for hours will warm the theater, but hopefully by opening it'd cool off. Hopefully. Eek.

The sold-out first audience showed up and got seated. The buzz on the show was that it was fun, sexy, dirty, and unlike anything else in the festival. As the lights were going down, I saw people furiously fanning themselves with their programs. I turned to Randy and said, "We're fucked."

And we were.

The show opened with Jim appearing center stage to no applause as he started to sing. Normally, an audience will clap at the entrance of a name actor. Clearly, our crowd was too uncomfortable and sitting in misery already—their hackles were up. Jim was dripping with sweat due to the temperature backstage and the flurry of preparation. The opening number, "Fancy Boys," continued and the actors were doing fine, but there was a curious detachment between them and the audience—not a lot of laughing, more fanning, and the show just did not have the zing from the night before. Worse, I could sense the actors pulling away from the material. Instead of full-tilt shamelessness in presenting some of the more blue material, they tended to say things with apology in their voices, as if they were embarrassed, because they weren't getting the reactions they had the night before.

Meanwhile, they were all schvitzing from the high-energy dancing and characterizations. The show was just not working. The heat was bringing everything down; the material never had a chance. The evening went from bad to calamitous during a sketch I wrote specifically for Jim called "Big Daddy Rick and His Amazing Baby Dick." I wanted to give him a Fanny Brice "Baby Snooks"–type character in the person of a baby with Tourette's. His dad, the soothsayer played by the wonderful Tom Stuart, would point to an audience member and "read their mind" about a problem they were having, and the baby would solve it in a suggestive, dirty rhyme. He buttoned each bit by sucking on an oversize baby bottle with nipple.

The sketch was inspired by a line of greeting cards I had written with witty, raunchy rhymes attached to vintage photos from the '40s. I had gotten tired of trying to find birthday and holiday cards that actually made me laugh, not just smile, so I came up with these. The contrast between the conservative images and the bawdy word play was the kind of funny I had been looking for in a card. I had a contract to produce them, but it fell by the wayside, so I decided to see if I could adapt them into sketch comedy.

The bits got a lot of laughter in all the readings we had done and in the run-through the night before, each rhyme landed gangbusters with Tom's droll setup and Jim's razor-sharp character and comedy timing. It was a true burlesque sketch, and I was really proud of it. However, on this hot night, the audience wasn't having it and I could tell the material was beginning to offend. The actors couldn't seem to find their timing due to the lack of audience enthusiasm, and the sketch was even getting hisses at some of the saltier rhymes.

What made it even worse was that the Big Daddy Rick bit was a recurring sketch. The night before, it was met with applause every time they came back, as intended. Not on opening night. In the second appearance, Jim ran through his lines so fast you could barely hear him, and his microphone got so wet from sweat that it went out—just died (like the sketch). I ran backstage as he was changing clothes to give him some positive reinforcement. As he hurriedly changed into his next costume, he was miserable and furious. "I HATE THIS! I FUCKING HATE THIS! IT SUCKS!" I just kept saying, "Jim, please,

please. I know it's hotter than fuck, but you have to play it fully. That's why it's not working. Be the vaudeville guy who doesn't let an audience get to him. Please!" And then he was gone.

By the third entrance of the characters the audience was done with it. Jim and Tom continued the sketch, no laughs, no hisses, no tomatoes thrown, nothing—which felt even worse. When Jim got to the most egregious (though funniest, in my eyes) rhyme, suddenly the audience outright booed him. Instead of going into vaudeville mode and snapping back, "Hey! It played in Poughkeepsie!" he said, "Well, I didn't write this shit."

The audience applauded.

I was in the next-to-last row and I was dying. Randy, in shock, dug his hand into my thigh, but I didn't even feel it. And as the cast continued the show to about the most negative audience reaction I can remember, I had an epiphany:

I have my particular point of view as to what is funny about sex, and I can't expect the world to fall in line. I thought back to my NY musical director friend's reaction after reading the show. He brought his own attitude about sex to the material and didn't see the humor at all.

But *I* knew, if the show was played with the right tone and fearlessness, it could work pretty universally (if you have an open mind and it's not two thousand degrees in the room). I'd seen the material succeed in three workshops and at the final studio rehearsal. It should have worked. There's a craft to the filth, but it had to be executed carefully.

This was not to be my fate that evening, destroyed by heat and abashment. And that's when it came to me: instead of leaving the theater and finding a crosstown bus on 45th Street to throw myself under (as I would have done years before), I thought, Fuck you, Jim. (I love him to death and he was just trying to protect himself, I know, but that was my initial inner reaction. Sorry, mister! I love you and your many talents and I don't blame you a bit!) Fuck you, NYMF, for putting us in a theater that they knew had temperature issues. Fuck everyone but me, I thought, because these were things I could not control. I had the courage of my conviction that the material was funny and would have worked under different circumstances.

I feel that to this day.

So I took the bullets, but I knew . . . I knew it was not all my fault. I remember sitting at dinner with Andy after two agonizing overheated shows and not even being sad or angry, just exhausted and disappointed. We had six performances ahead of us and I was dreading having to sit through two hours of audience hatred each night. I just wanted to cut my losses and escape back to LA, but that was not possible. I needed to vent to someone who loved me and was not involved in the show, and Andy was a great shoulder to lean on. He gave me the wherewithal to continue the process and do what I needed to do.

As the days went by, we did some cutting (including dumping the baby sketch and adding "The Book of Lust" as a recurring bit). Finally, the temperature outside cooled off enough that the air-conditioning actually worked, and the show settled into being a lot of fun, with appreciative audiences. After we had turned things around, Andy came to see it and said, "What were you talking about? It was great!"

However, after so many cuts, *The Fancy Boys Follies* was not the bold, adventurous show I knew it could be. The production received bad reviews early on, and in talking to a couple of producers who saw the first performance, I was told that the more off-color material was the least successful, just there for shock value, and probably would never work. Would *never* work. It never got a fair shot, and if I have one regret in my life, it's that when I saw people fanning themselves, I wish I had run up onstage and said, "Hey, folks! It's gonna get kind of warm in here, so take off your jackets, roll up your sleeves, and have fun!" That might have alleviated a lot of the pain.

When the run was finished, mostly everyone was happy they'd done it, and they had a good time after we cut out the most graphic material. They never really "got" it, but I was glad the show survived and actually thrived in its way. As everyone was leaving to go to the closing party, I had to stick around and break down sets, costumes, and props to put them in storage (I like to quote Mama Rose from *Gypsy* every time I finish a run; as a ritual, I say out loud, "Thanks a lot and out with the garbage"). I ran into our choreographer on his way out, and he just laid into me: it was my fault the show didn't work, the director was too hard on the actors, he was the only one the actors trusted, they all complained to him about how bad the material was, and it wasn't the heat, it was me. My show. My material. No one could make it work.

I was not having that.

I was too tired and deflated to engage in a shoutfest, so we went our separate ways and didn't speak for years. I just wanted them all to go fuck themselves, because I knew how the material really worked, and they didn't.

And that's how one-man shows are born.

SPRING AWAKENING

I was really conflicted about how to continue on as a writer and performer after *Follies*. I felt like a failure when I got back to LA, isolated in my work, which then bled into my personal life.

When what you do becomes who you are, it can be tough, in the low periods, to find the wherewithal to be yourself in a relationship. I've so often thought that if I wasn't succeeding at my work as an actor and writer, if I wasn't making enough money to live well, I was nothing and didn't deserve love, so I just didn't date. It was easier to be on my own than attempt to engage in a relationship when I felt such a lack of worth.

I used to be absolutely impossible to speak to if I felt I'd given a bad theater performance, judgmental of my own work to the point where I would skulk out of the theater hoping to avoid any human contact at all. All my self-esteem was either in my biceps or on the stage, and if I thought a performance of mine wasn't up to snuff, I was inconsolable. Something had to change, because I could not mentally continue this career on that roller coaster.

In 2010, I got to appear in a unique and beautiful production of the James Lapine/Stephen Sondheim musical *Into the Woods* at a really cool downtown LA factory turned theater space, playing the Baker. I hadn't really understood or even much liked the show when I saw the original NY production in 1988, because I hadn't been through "the woods" at that point in my life (I was still idealistic at twenty-nine). But I certainly have been since (and you've been reading about it). Actually doing the show was a revelation for me; being on the inside of it made me realize how complex, deep, and human it is, and I could finally identify with all these flawed characters looking to satisfy their dreams in all the wrong places using all the wrong means. *Into the Woods* is a great and important musical, and I was so proud of my work in it.

I had told friends long ago to not let me know they were in the audience when they came to see me in a show. I had found it distracting and preferred doing my performances without a random face popping up in my head. For a time, this worked for me; I'd do my shows and see friends afterwards, and all was well. I'm not the only actor who feels this way, neurotic as it is, but whatever gets you through. One night, at the top of *Into the Woods*, I said my first line and I heard a familiar laugh and I immediately knew who was out there. I let this new information distract me to the point where I gave the worst performance *ever*. And of course, there's no way it was as bad as I thought, but I not only felt my performance sucked, but I failed as an actor, allowing my thoughts to drag me out of the moment so that I lost that important element of being absolutely present with the character.

After the show, I could barely look my friend Molly O'Leary—one of the best people I know, and also an actor—in the eye, even though she was saying the sweetest, most complimentary stuff. I couldn't hear it. I was in my crazy bad actor headspace and I pretty much dissed her and ran out. Horrible. I was just a horrible person, and yet I was in such pain about my work being distracted and awful and unprofessional, and blah blah bullshit blah, and I hated myself.

A few days later, I emailed her to apologize for my behavior and she messaged back that she understood, but after some wonderful compliments about the show and my performance, she wrote:

> But, my dear, we can only tell you how amazing you are so much. You either have to start believing it or get off the pot so to speak. Also, why do you do this? Why are you an actor? Do you enjoy it? Are you looking for the critics' and your friends' acclaim or are you enjoying the whole journey? *Because if you are not enjoying the journey, then it is time to start thinking about what you want.* You are so talented but if you aren't enjoying it, why are you still here? I love you and I am your biggest fan (besides your Mom) . . .

That was a game changer for me. Of course I loved acting and singing, but as the years went by, I did them with such angst and so much self-critical energy that it was impossible to feel the joy. Molly was absolutely right. I had never really considered myself to be an *artist*, just some guy who acts and writes. An artist puts it out there and doesn't judge it or himself/herself. The work is what's important, telling the story, fulfilling the vision of the writer and making it your own; and if you are the writer, then you do it with honesty and clarity and never once think that you're better or worse than the work you put out.

Shame comes in many forms. I realized how my approach to the work I was doing was loaded with it, how much I cared what others thought of me, and how it was affecting my entire life, being so irrationally judgmental. I believe the early years I spent debasing myself about sex and my sexuality had bled into every aspect of my being, including not just my lack of romance and dating, but my confidence and my work as an actor and writer.

Suddenly, after one email, I felt clear. I was finally understanding: I am an artist. And I can tell you in one word why I'm an artist, why I am here on this earth: connection. I have something to say and want to convey it with as much passion and honesty as possible. All I need to do is give up the control and concern over how it's perceived, if it's a "success." Truth be told, I didn't and don't know how to be a success in the way America defines it. Society doesn't always "get" artists (try applying for unemployment benefits or registering for jury duty as a freelancer and you'll see how an artist's life doesn't fit the norm—those questions!). But I know that we should be measured on our ability to love and create rather than on what's in our wallets.

That epiphany shook things up in a very good way. My acting career took an interesting turn as I began getting nice roles in gay independent films, playing Ebenezer Scrooge in a charming gay musical take on *A Christmas Carol* called *Scrooge & Marley*; portraying James Dean's acting teacher in a very cool fever dream of a film called *Joshua Tree, 1951: A Portrait of James Dean*; and playing the wise but lonely and cloistered owner of a Palm Springs guesthouse whose life has come to a standstill in a sweet little film called *Role/Play*. In that film, I was there mainly to be the voice of wisdom and give advice to the two leads, played by Steve Callahan and Matthew Montgomery, but I thought my character, Alex, should also have a story arc that comes to completion. I (Alex) shut down when my partner passed away, not embracing life or finding joy at all, and unlike other guesthouses that were clothing optional, I enforced a stodgy no-outdoor-nudity rule for my inn.

To show that my character was finally ready to move on and take a chance in life, I suggested to the director, Rob Williams, that he go skinny-dipping in his own pool. That was my first-ever nude scene in a film, and the elation I felt as an actor filming it is blissfully apparent in Alex's reaction to his naked epiphany.

On top of those films, I did episodes of *Grey's Anatomy*, *Law and Order: LA*, and *Modern Family*, and got one of the four leads in the

Web series *Old Dogs and New Tricks*, a gay take on *Sex and the City*. Things were taking off.

But doing the more mainstream TV work, I felt as though I had to take a couple of steps back into the closet, on and off the set. Doing a guest star or day player role on a TV series can be a bit nerve-racking— it's tough to come onto a well-established TV production as the new guy, especially when you're playing a peripheral character—and I felt I had to keep a low gay profile for the little time I was there. Sometimes the crews backstage could feel like an old boys' club, and I always tended to shrink a bit whenever I was the only gay in the room (I was always most comfortable in the hair and makeup trailer).

There were times, playing a doctor or lawyer (my niche), when I felt I had to "pass" and not come off as queer, and I hated that I let myself fall into that trap. When I'm the one delivering the bad news about the disease or informing the client that they're going to lose the case, I'm pretty much hired to bring a no-nonsense version of myself to the character that won't distract from the information at hand. They're usually very straightforward, "here's the way it is" scenes. What I try to bring to those scenes is a committed and educated delivery, as if I'm not playing a doctor but I *am* a doctor. And I have to know my shit and understand the terminology, and if it's a caretaker type, a doctor with a gentle bed-side manner, I tap into that.

As a doctor on TV, I say things like "You're fine" or "You're going to die" or "I'm not saying it *is* colon cancer . . ." which is probably the best worst line in the very Shakespearean TV film *Liz and Dick*. This "biopic" of Elizabeth Taylor starring Lindsay Lohan was just bad and not fun/ bad, so when folks mention that they saw the film, I always tell them I was in it and then they say, "Really? I didn't see you" and then I say, "You didn't watch the whole thing, did you?" and they usually say, "Um. Right." But I digress.

These days, when I play these kinds of characters, though you don't necessarily know it . . . surprise! . . . they're gay. My little secret. Since there's usually not a lot of talk of their private lives in the scripts, I incorporate that detail into the characters' backstories, making them feel more personal and unique to me. Doing this also gives me a greater sense of empowerment than when I first showed up on TV sets and felt like an outsider.

I changed my whole belief system about being an out gay actor on the stage after seeing the actor and playwright David Drake's 1992 one-man show, *The Night Larry Kramer Kissed Me*. I'd met him at a summer party in New York in the '80s thrown by the late great writer David Feinberg. The party was called "The Night of 100 Davids." There were, to be precise, thirty-five Davids in his stultifyingly hot studio apartment.

The Night Larry Kramer Kissed Me is an emotional series of stories about a gay man's journey of self-discovery, and the performance of it was absolutely spellbinding. It was so honest and political, so beautifully acted and written, and I found it empowering that this wonderful artist was blatantly out, making his voice heard, queer as the day is long, and one thousand percent true to himself.

I knew I wanted to express myself in such a raw and honest way, but it took me a while. I was finally able to find that voice in *Party*, *When Pigs Fly*, *Naked Boys Singing!*, *To Bitter and Back*, and the stage version of *Musical Comedy Whore* (more on that in the next chapter).

My mom used to ask me why I felt I had to do so many gay roles. She said I was limiting my career, and I could never quite come up with a satisfying answer for her or, truthfully, for myself. It wasn't until the Q&A after the sold-out premiere of *Scrooge & Marley* at the Music Box Theatre in Chicago that it came to me.

When an audience member asked why I played so many gay roles and if I enjoyed it, I had a spontaneous epiphany in front of this huge opening crowd, and I was able to elucidate to them, to her, to me, actually: we gay folks have a plethora of stories to tell, as many as the straight folks do, and they all need to be portrayed, the full gamut of gay sensibility and experience.

I love that we're having more and better opportunities to tell the stories of our lives, and I continued to pursue these parts onstage, in lead roles in the LA premiere productions of *Fucking Men* (as an asshole businessman in a gay take on *La Ronde* that explores the foibles of gay relationships in ten scenes, written by Joe DiPietro), *It Must Be Him* (portraying a neurotic love-struck writer in a frothy romantic comedy written by Kenny Solms, one of the creators of *The Carol Burnett Show*), and *Bang Bang* (playing a therapist turned crystal meth addict who becomes a serial killer, written by Michael Kearns). How's that for variety?

If I only played gay roles my whole life, I'd be okay with that as long as they were engaging stories and challenging characters, but of course a career is not just roles—you have to put food on the table. So I welcome all kinds of roles, but unless the script dictates otherwise, I'll continue to play those TV characters subversively gay, as I've done most recently on *NCIS*, *I'm Dying Up Here*, and *Silicon Valley*.

I recently came across a strip of paper that I had saved from high school. I can't remember for the life of me what class it was from, but it was a typed response to the question "What do you believe is your purpose in life?" Here's what it said:

DAVID PEVSNER: My purpose is to use my warmth, presence, humor, and craziness to entertain people in order to help them through sad, inert, and lost moments in their lives, and help them enjoy the good times more.

Okay, it's not very eloquent, but it's very earnest and sweet, and though I've sometimes strayed off that path, I think I've been on it or close to it my whole life. I've really tried to keep that purity of purpose as the driving force behind everything I do. Have I been successful? Please. Don't make me even try to answer that.

LEAP OF FAITH

When I originally wrote the screenplay *Puppy Love* (now *Musical Comedy Whore*), I was nervous about giving it to industry folks to read because I didn't want people to know I'd escorted. Friends told me all I had to do was present it as fiction. As proud of the script as I was, as much as it was my baby, as hard as I worked to get it into the hands of those in the industry who could actually get it made, I still had a bit of dread that I would be "found out," and I believe that brought about a reticence to succeed that I was not consciously aware of. Though I've said I felt no shame escorting and how much I loved it, I think that was true as long as it remained separate from the rest of my life, but the screenplay and my journey with it mingled my whole existence into one. And when push came to shove, it did not get made because, as difficult as it is to get any film produced, nothing gets done when fear is involved.

I played the role of Philip the Hustler (how appropriate) in a Los Angeles production of *Corpus Christi*, the Terrence McNally play about a gay Jesus-like character, which was very controversial when it originally opened off-Broadway in 1998. Directed by Nic Arnzen, we performed it everywhere over the years beginning in 2006, from LA to NY to Edinburgh to Dublin, with a wonderful band of LA theater actors. A documentary was made about our production and the play itself called *Corpus Christi: Playing With Redemption.*

To help raise completion funds for the film, I did a benefit performance of *To Bitter and Back* in May 2011 at WEHO Church, a gay, nondenominational, very progressive house of worship in LA. It was really a joy, and it made me remember how much I loved getting up on a stage, telling stories and singing songs that were so personal—entertaining and engaging an audience on my own. With time and distance (and having had the experience of playing a hooker in *Corpus Christi*), I was feeling that I could finally stand up and tell the world my story about being an escort because I was sensing a change within. I was accepting that the part of me that escorted was exactly that—a part of me. In the screenplay, I was hiding behind a character. No more. Time to own it fully and publicly. No holding back.

But if I was going to muster up the courage to tell my story, point-blank, to an audience, I knew I had to go beyond just "Hey, look what I did!" and make sure that the show tapped into the important and relatable themes of dealing with judgment, owning your choices, and that most eternal and internal of conflicts—learning to love yourself. I also knew I wanted it to be musical, like *To Bitter and Back.* So I started to stitch the stage show together.

I needed the musical numbers to do more than just be entertaining. Since most of the songs were inspired by my real-life experiences, the scenes could naturally segue into those songs, heightening the emotional stakes (the key adage of any good musical is you speak until the emotion bubbles up and you have to sing) and providing more depth to the lead character, me. Since I really wanted to explore the sexuality aspect (the whole show was really about that, until I find love with Reid), it was important to focus the material, and anything that did not have a sexual bent was cut. I found it easier to make sense of the story-telling that way.

I did a series of small readings and it took a while for the whole thing to gel, but eventually I did a larger reading in my friend Mark Saltzman's house, and for the first time, it worked. I laid myself out there, fully vulnerable. The members of the audience that night, a combination of supportive friends and judgy industry folks, were laughing and crying all the way through because those universal themes were finally clear as day. And when I got a private email from a young man who'd been at the reading, telling me how much the performance spoke to him, how he had struggled with his sexuality and desires, and how the show made him feel better about who he was—man, what a gift. I knew I was on the right track, and the fact that he was thirty years younger than me con-firmed I was succeeding.

In 2013, I got the opportunity to perform *Musical Comedy Whore* in Rancho Mirage (outside Palm Springs) at a little theater called the Desert Rose Playhouse, wonderfully directed by Randy, and although it was 110 degrees outside, the theater was nicely air-conditioned, so the comedy was "cold." It was great to present the show a little off the radar, and it did very well. Although I was a little nervous about "coming out" as an ex-hooker to a full paying audience, I took the leap of faith with total commitment to the material, and I felt more than at any time in my life that "the truth shall set you free."

I could sense the audiences responding to my brutal honesty. They may not have had my exact experiences, but they had something in their own lives that they'd been judged for or felt shame about or lost loved ones over, and the show touched those nerves. I really hoped my story would provide healing and hope, beyond mere entertainment. A good friend of mine called me a few weeks after seeing it with her fiancé to tell me that watching my show made her future hubby realize that after years of denial, he needed to deal with his alcohol problem.

He put himself into rehab so that they could eventually make their commitment to each other and marry. She tearfully thanked me. I was floored.

I later officiated at their wedding.

I performed *Musical Comedy Whore* at a couple of LA theaters, and then David Zak, who produced *To Bitter and Back* in my hometown, offered me a slot for it at his new theater, the Pride Arts Center in Chicago. Richard Knight, the codirector of my film *Scrooge & Marley*, brought his producer friend Patrick Schaller to a performance, and afterwards Patrick asked if I'd ever thought of filming the show. "Hell yeah!" exploded out of my mouth, because I had been hoping to do exactly that but didn't want to produce it myself after the hell of giving birth to *The Fancy Boys Follies*. He and his partner Clay Ebert produced the film, and in March 2018 we shot the show live at the Colony Theatre in Burbank, with Randy's staging and film direction by Brendan Russo.

During the performance, I show photos of James Darren and Brian Kelly when I gush about them as my crushes to the audience. For a stage production, you don't have to clear the rights to use photos, but you do in a movie, even if it's a filmed version of the show. We were going to bite the bullet and just pay for the permissions, but my production coordinator, Lisa Colangelo, went behind my back and contacted Jim Moret, a correspondent for *Inside Edition* and . . . James Darren's son. She asked Jim to see if James would allow us to use the photo, and he said he'd ask his dad.

The next day, Lisa surprised Randy and me by taking us on a field trip—to James Darren's home. Holy crap. We met James and his wife, Evy, and then spent two hours talking with him in his den. He had some great Hollywood stories, but I had to keep pinching myself that I was in this room, face-to-face, with my childhood dreamboat. James was so sweet and tough and funny and, even at the age of eighty, a total hunk.

He gave us the blessing on the photo as well as a few others just to have.

On our way out, we asked if he'd come to the filming, not thinking he actually would. Guess what? He did. And when I whipped out that photo of him during the show, the audience swooned and clapped, and James was there to see it. Such a great moment. Afterwards, he came backstage with moist eyes, a hug, and kind words about the show—and now I'm friends with James Darren from *The Time Tunnel*. Be still, my little gay heart! (Thanks, Jimmy!)

The film spent a lot of time in postproduction, but my editor friend Mark Dashnaw did an incredible job putting it together, and I was really happy with how it turned out. Because of COVID, the gay film festival circuit in 2020 was pretty much a no-go, so Clay and Patrick decided to go directly for distribution, and sure enough, we got it through a well-respected distribution house called Breaking Glass Pictures. We were thrilled to know that folks in quarantine were going to be able to watch *Musical Comedy Whore!* (we added the exclamation point for the film) at home. It would play on various streaming and DVD platforms, including the largest, Amazon for DVDs and Amazon Prime for streaming.

The day before we were to drop, Amazon Prime informed us that since streaming is available to all ages, the title was inappropriate. This is all done electronically, and the bot objected to the word *Whore* in the title (my friend suggested that it was actually more offended by *Musical Comedy*). We had to scramble to come up with a new name, and that slowed down the distribution process for weeks.

After turning down similar words—*escort, hooker, hustler*—we went with *Musical Comedy Stud!* for streaming; the original title *Musical Comedy Whore!* was okay for DVDs. It was confusing, and I'm sure it affected sales, and though I get their reasoning about the title being family friendly, a part of me still hated the censorship. Whatever, 'zon.

I'm just thrilled and very grateful that we gave birth to it and that it's out there (so take note when you go to rent/purchase it!). At least we didn't call it *Musical Comedy Buttboy!* Hmmm. I like it. That'll be the XXX version. I think I'm gonna start on that script right now.

DREAM

Pre-Google, I'd always wondered what happened to Brian Kelly, my biggest TV crush—"Flipper's Father." Whenever there was a "Whatever happened to . . . ?" on *Entertainment Tonight* or in *Us* magazine, they'd focus on the kids from *Flipper* but not the dad. It was a mystery that I thought I could never solve. In 1997, I was coming home on the 9th Avenue bus one night after a performance of *When Pigs Fly* and the new *Playbill* had come out. I always enjoyed poring over it, especially if a friend was being profiled, and sure enough, there was an interview with Brian d'Arcy James, who was appearing in the musical *Titanic* on Broadway. He's married to Jennifer Prescott, with whom I did *Fiddler* on Broadway, as well as a production of *The World Goes 'Round*. (The latter is a Kander and Ebb revue that they try to sell as "a series of mini-plays, each fully realized with a beginning, middle, and an end" etc., but as I drily said to Jen opening night backstage at the prop table: "Look—a bar stool, a bowler hat, and a feather boa. It's a revue.")

I love Jen and her hubby Brian. So I was reading this *Playbill* article and the interviewer asked him if he had show business in his blood; did he have any family in it? He said that, yes, his uncle had been an actor in the 1960s. His uncle—*Brian Kelly*. Holy shit. As soon as I got home, I called Brian. I knew he would be onstage, but I left a message: "Call me! ASAP! Emergency! CALL ME!"

Brian called me back the next day and I found out that, indeed, his uncle was Brian Kelly and that he was still alive. He told me that, back in 1970, Kelly was being primed to be the new hot leading man in *The Love Machine*, a film based on the Jacqueline Susann novel. However, right before filming, he had a motorcycle accident that ended his acting career. Although the accident did damage to one side of his body, he was able to function without the aid of a wheelchair or walker. Brian said his uncle was an extraordinarily tenacious man, and despite the challenges that came with the accident, he was still able to have a fantastic family (including a son and a daughter), and he went on to work in film production, most notably as an executive producer on *Blade Runner*.

Brian ended by saying his uncle was a terrific mentor, always extremely supportive as Brian began his own successful theater and film career. Though I was so shaken and sad to hear about the accident, I was touched by Brian's palpable love and respect for his uncle, and it made me appreciate Kelly's beauty even more, inside and out.

This bit of news made me think of Montgomery Clift. After I read Patricia Bosworth's bio of him, I wanted to save him even though he was long gone. Clift apparently was so tortured and so internally fucked up about his sexuality. When I read how his car accident changed his outward appearance and brought him such pain, it felt like tragedy to me. There was something about such beautiful men that touched me. It went beyond superficiality. Especially in the case of Brian Kelly and Monty and James Darren, they were so stunningly beautiful in my eyes that it was almost overwhelming. As a gay boy, they stirred something in me that I couldn't describe. Back then, these attractions were kind of the reason I felt I was gay even before I knew what that was. I was in love with them and yet I knew I could never have them. They were my own personal fairy tale, if you will, and they inspired me to search for beauty in my own life, although they also set up impossible standards in my head and heart for what I wanted, and certainly the gay community has a tendency to glamorize, sexualize, and celebrate only the beautiful men. I learned that lesson too well.

It's great that, finally, our definition of what's "hot" has expanded past model beauty, what with the bears, the otters, the twinks, and many more tribes that appeal to so many factions. However, I treasure having had those boyhood crushes, and even though Brian Kelly was a fanboy love, he has come to mean more to me over the years. He was truly the first man in all my history who made me understand there was something different about me, and though it was scary and confusing, it also made me feel warm and happy, and in a strange way . . . loved.

When I read in 2005 that Brian Kelly had died of pneumonia, I kind of shut down for a bit. There's that moment in *Musical Comedy Whore!* where, just as when I show James Darren's photo, I get an audible wave of appreciation when I show Brian's picture; it's kind of a bonding moment for those who know who he was. We all had that little secret crush on him, even though he wasn't a teen dream or iconic movie star. He was my first "daddy."

ROCK OF AGES

I was always attracted to older guys but rarely acted on it. When I was in my early twenties, I met a very handsome fifty-year-old man who was the artistic director of one of the regional theaters I had performed at, and though you're not supposed to shit where you eat, we slept together a few times during the run. Whenever he came to NY, we'd hook up at his hotel room and have a great time, but he tended to be a little staid.

One night, he took me to see *Irma Vep*, an off-Broadway play written by the amazing Charles Ludlam, in which he starred with Everett Quinton—two actors playing eight characters, cross-dressing, very Victorian. It was really fabulous, inventive, and funny. My older date kept leaning over to me, not really laughing but commenting, "This is crazy. Heh Heh. Crazy!" That's when I became aware of the age difference. He just wasn't getting it, it was way too campy for him, and I was starting to realize that, even in our shared love of the theater, we didn't have much in common. We went out a few more times and then it was done, but I still had that attraction to older men. As *I've* gotten older, however, I find that it's gone the other way.

I'm still attracted to men my own age, but it seems the only guys who come on to me are in their twenties and thirties, guys who are just like I was, attracted to older men. I don't know when I became a "daddy," but I'm okay with that (and some would say I'm even too old at this point to be a daddy—call me Gramps). I'm not saying I necessarily want a twenty-five-year-old boyfriend, but I've found that some mature men can be very set in their ways; it's an abyss that's very hard to avoid. I'm older, but that doesn't mean I'm dead or homebound. Younger guys can be more open and adventurous, and I like when they drag me out somewhere I've never been. Sometimes, when I'm home in the evening and just working on the computer or watching some TV, I feel as if the world is passing me by—like I'm the Cat Lady without the cats—so I appreciate anyone trying to wrestle me out of Netflix and chill and Scotch.

Why is there that older man–younger man pull? When I was in my twenties, getting validation from someone more mature and experienced made me feel stronger in a certain way, more stable. They knew who they were, were more secure and solid, and were able to comfort and take care of me when I needed it (Christopher Plummer from the film *The Sound of Music* became my pillow).

Guys my own age were usually flailing around just as I was. Plus, I loved a hairy chest, some wrinkles in the face, and a masculine demeanor. I realize now what an internalized homophobe I was, being so romantically and sexually dismissive of men who were more effeminate than me. I was always looking for what I called a "Man," and believe me, I was never even close to the epitome of butch. I just cringe at how shallow my thinking was.

As I've said, Carnegie Mellon didn't help at all, making all of us gay boys feel less. Now, as a "daddy," I feel very protective toward these younger guys who are trying to make their way and live their lives authentically. My paternal instincts kick in sometimes when younger guys come on to me, and sometimes it does cross over into the sexual and romantic. I used to think that was kind of creepy, but it can sometimes be part of the dynamic—part boyfriend, part lover, part dad. I don't think there's anything wrong with that, especially when it's a mutual feeling. Not all young guys want "daddies" and not all older guys want "sons" (in the gay vernacular), but it can be a really complex dynamic, and I think it should be what it needs to be.

THE FULL MONTY

There's a problem with nudity today!
Yes, we have a problem with nudity, much to our dismay.
"Cover up those hoohahs!" and "Put that thing away!"
"Only pigs' and hussies' doodahs should be put on display!"
We hear that from so many, so it's time that we got tough.
The problem . . .
with nudity . . .
is we don't think there's enough!!!

Don't be afraid of the penis,
a healthy strong expression of sexuality.
No shame in what it stands for,
or what it stands to do!
Don't be afraid of the penis!
—from "Nudity: A Problem"

After my first nude shoot with Tom Bianchi in 1989, I posed for other photographers in NY, but some of those shoots were not as successful.

One session was with a photographer who shot for a glossy exercise magazine, and though I had a fit body, I wasn't classically handsome and chiseled like the fitness models he usually photographed. He put me in all the same poses and attire as those muscle gods, the tight little gym shorts and string tanks that I enjoyed wearing in real life, but the resulting comparison in my head was disastrous—I felt like the ugly stepsister. Another photographer wanted erections, but I was still not ready to go full-tilt erotic and "cross over" to what I perceived as porn. I was trying desperately not to get hard in front of him, and you can actually see the struggle on my face. I hated those photos.

It wasn't until I moved to LA in 1998 and embraced the erotic photography community—wonderful artists who told sensuous and exciting stories through their work—that I wanted to do more. I met photographers at art fairs and exhibits, and I ended up shooting with a bunch of them; some I approached, some approached me.

Jay Jorgensen was the first to take me on. His black-and-white images had so much life and drama to them, with beautiful men and their chiseled bodies. I didn't think I was that kind of model, but I knew I had something that could spark on camera, and Jay and I both believed that erotic photos could go beyond just nudes to tell a story, to have some context, and we worked together many times. He's a wonderful, gentle, creative guy and we always got intriguing images that went beyond just dick pics.

As I was over forty, I knew not every photographer would be interested, but I worked with a slew of really talented guys who were happy to photograph me, and I had some fabulous collaborations. I accrued an extensive portfolio over the years that lived on CDs and JPGs on my computer but nowhere else, because there were no venues to put them except in the odd coffee table book, calendar, or gallery exhibit.

Then, in 2013, I discovered Tumblr, a personal place to post on the Web that allowed full-frontal everything. Compared with the more

PG-rated Instagram, it was a way to express yourself in any way you wanted: the dinner you made, the flowers you arranged, the dick you sucked last night. And while scrolling through some of the naked man Tumblr feeds one day, I saw my picture, a shot by photographer Michael Stokes that had been published in a 2010 photo book called *Jewels*. Michael had shown me that photo before he submitted it for the book, and though there were others I liked better, it's the one he preferred. I decided to get over myself and trust his judgment. I gave him the go-ahead to publish it with my face showing—the two Bianchi photos were anonymous or veiled—because I thought the book would have a small, exclusive audience. I embraced it and felt proud to be a part of it. The idea of any publication beyond the book didn't cross my mind at the time, so seeing it online three years later was a bit of a shock.

It was me in a suit sitting in a wingback chair in his library, tie thrown over my shoulder, dick sticking out of the fly of my pants, my face in ecstasy. When I saw my erection on the Internet, I had a moment of panic, as if my secret had been found out. I had given Michael absolute freedom to choose and publish as he liked, but neither Michael nor I posted it on Tumblr; someone must have copied it from the book and put it up there. I was now exposed to the world in this most public, cyber way. It initially unnerved me. I wondered if I should tell my agent about it, but frankly, it aroused me knowing that my non-anonymous hard-on had gone global, so I didn't feel the need to mention it to her. It felt provocative and dangerous, way beyond that little boy's fantasies of showing off for the neighborhood.

After that photo went online, I never again requested anonymity in the results of photo shoots. I wanted to fully express myself, screw the consequences. Another photographer I shot with on a trip back to NY, Walter Kurtz, published one of my photos on his website, and there I was again, fully nude and hard, licking my bicep as my erection stretched upward, my skin a golden tint to fit with the series. Once again I had a moment of distress over it, but only a moment.

I experienced such a sense of freedom when I saw those pictures, and then again when I discovered them reblogged on others' Tumblr sites. I found it highly flattering that people wanted to share them. I relished knowing that some would love the photos, some would be scandalized, some would criticize. It played into the best and worst of my narcissistic tendencies: on the one hand, I wanted to show off my naked body for validation and attention; on the other, I believed I could use that body and my erotic flow to make a statement on sexual freedom. Even though I wasn't a typical model type, the photographers found a beauty in quirkiness—a big nose, a chunky butt, an average (well, maybe above-average) size cock—not to mention my age, which at the point I discovered Tumblr was fiftysomething. The photos reflected my refusal to feel I was done, irrelevant, or unattractive because of my age.

That "woo-woo" from my childhood still rang in my ears every time I read of someone feeling terrible about their body in a world where unreal depictions of beauty are everywhere. It makes men feel crappy about their shells, with gay men having the added stigma, instilled in their brains from birth, that they are less than straight men, who are viewed as the "normal" ones.

I started to notice young men in the locker room at the gym wrapping towels around their waists before removing their gym shorts or underwear. I was seeing it more and more, and it puzzled me. I wondered if it was a size-insecurity thing or shyness or what. Someone told me it was to protect themselves against phone cameras, but a photographer friend gave me a much more astute hypothesis. He said that since young guys have been on the Internet practically their whole lives, they've been exposed to porn from a much earlier age than any previous generation, and much of the nudity they've taken in has been sex-oriented. Nonsexual nudity certainly doesn't get the attention or hits that actual sex images do, especially when you're a young gay man trying to figure out what you want and what turns you on. So to them, nudity = sex, and sex is private. I thought that was an interesting point of view.

I used to go to the JCC with my dad when I was a boy. I remember all the older men in the locker room roaming around, barefoot or in flip-flops and nothing else—bellies bulging, dicks hanging soft, face-to-face, having long conversations about sports or business or Judaism, shuffling from steam room to shower to locker with no embarrassment whatsoever, no attempt to cover up. It made me so uncomfortable, but I was fascinated that they were all so nonchalant about their nudity, that to them it was the most natural thing in the world. I couldn't do that, just hang around that locker room naked and social. I always managed to have either a towel around my waist or a bathing suit on when my dad would introduce me to those guys, and I had to work hard not to stare at their flaccid penises, just hanging free, while we made chitchat.

When I was growing up and becoming more aware of sex and sexuality, like many kids my age I was taking my signals from movies and TV shows: boy meets girl, boy loses girl, boy gets girl, they kiss. *That's* what was "normal." There were no gay characters anywhere in all that TV I watched. The stolen moments with naked and shirtless men in the media (*Playboy*, *After Dark*, *GQ*, and later *International Male*) that filled me with innocent lust (did I even know what lust was?) embarrassingly translated into sexualizing nudity in gym class and made me want to die rather than expose myself. So when I see these young guys changing at the gym in such a covert way, it makes me sad and dispirited that for all the more overt sexuality we witness in the media and online, we actually have not progressed at all (at least in America) when it comes to a healthy acceptance of male nudity in the real world.

Once I started to pose nude, way back in the late '80s, I began to seriously consider: What is art and what is porn? A photographer told me once that if the model has an erection and is looking directly into the camera, it's porn; if his eyes are averted, it's not. Really? And is a hard-on porn but a soft dick is not? Does the backdrop matter, the composition, the size of the model—both his body and his penis? And what is the standard for beauty? Should only the *GQ* model type be depicted naked? Is anyone else not beautiful? What about age? Should I not be posing for photos at fifty-five because some millennial leaves a message that says, "Grampa, you're fugly, put it away"? At a certain point in life, are you "done" sexually? Invisible?

And what's wrong with porn, anyway? Nope nope nope. I was not having it.

I felt our country rapidly moving in a dangerously conservative direction regarding sex and nudity. The worst of the right-wing bigots were rearing their very ugly heads, adamantly pushing their unenlightened agendas, spreading hatred and divisiveness against the LGBTQ community and our bodies and what we do with them. The cockroaches had come out into the light to declare war on us and what they consider obscene.

The Internet had made it easier to access images that we could enjoy, but these homophobic, stick-up-their-ass prudes declared everything porn, whether it was a naked body in repose or an orgy. To these folks, there seemed to be no difference or nuance; it was all shameful and awful. So even though there was a lot of content out there, the attitudes toward it were becoming more harsh, judgmental, and negative.

On a global level, we were hearing more and more stories of men in foreign countries getting their heads cut off or thrown off buildings for being gay, and women being raped into heterosexuality—so tragic.

This demonization of our naked bodies and sexuality had always made me crazy, but as an adult of a certain age with a point of view and a desire to express myself as an artist, it made me want to take action. Every moment those photos I had taken remained hidden, it was as though I was holding them back out of pure shame. One thing I learned when I finally embraced the fact that I actually *was* an artist: an artist does not hold back. I thought, you have a problem with "gay"?

I'll fucking give you gay.

With the bit of notoriety I had accrued in off-Broadway theater and gay independent films, I knew it was time to make a stand, that maybe I could use my narcissism and exhibitionism for the greater good: a mission to fight body shame and ageism, and to champion nudity and sexuality. At this point, what did I have to lose?

Well, possibly my acting career . . .

ARTISTS AND MODELS

The pleasure and satisfaction I derived through erotic photography overrode any hesitancy I may have had when I started, and I felt there was a message in that—to indulge rather than hide. I continued to do nude shoots, sometimes once a month, sometimes less; sometimes with new photographers, sometimes repeat; sometimes the shoots were themed, sometimes not; sometimes they were more on the erotic, suggestive side and sometimes more blatant and hard-core.

The more I shot, the bolder I became, and I explored more and more aspects of nudity and fetish. I had amassed a pretty extensive portfolio over the years, and in 2013, I figured it was time to put the photographs out there myself, acting career be damned. First off, I was an older character actor; I figured, who the fuck cares? I mean, I know people care about that kind of thing—anytime anyone of any level of celebrity has a naked pic or video leaked, the Internet blows up, the scandal begins, and the repercussions follow.

In 1984, when Vanessa Williams's *Penthouse* photos were published and she got stripped of the Miss America crown, I was all up in arms. Furious. I heard she was giving a press conference at the Sheraton

Centre Hotel in Midtown Manhattan, and I had to be there. I don't remember her denying, decrying, or apologizing for the posing she had done. The photos were pretty explicit. She wasn't having inter-course, but she was naked with another woman and—horrors!—giving and receiving tongue in places society frowned upon with someone of the same sex.

In making sure my memory served me correctly, I googled the whole situation, and it turns out she was quoted as saying she regretted doing it, that young people do stupid things. However, she also said she had not committed an act of "moral turpitude." So at least she didn't back away and say it was disgusting and awful, and she did not apologize. She said if the pageant wanted to take away her crown (which they did), so be it. She focused more on the legality of posting photos when she was promised they would never get out. She handled it well, and I believe the fact that she addressed everything head-on without apology is why she continues to have a successful career and this did not ruin her.

Today, it seems that whenever a celebrity has nude pics "leaked" on the Internet, it's a huge deal, gigantic, an incredible violation of pri-vacy, a travesty, a crime, an emotional nightmare. I contend that, though it may be exciting for the viewer to see a celebrity in the altogether or copulating, maybe for the subject of the photos it ain't such a big deal. Once it's out there, why are they so concerned that America, the world, is watching them naked, hard, having sex, what-ever? My take is the Vanessa Williams Rule. Own it. Don't apologize. Do not say the words "I'm sorry." Say yup, that's me. I look pretty good, don't I? And if you own it, I believe they cannot come for you. My friend Steve, who worked in high-profile public relations for years, says the cardinal rule in his business is always: "Take control of your own story." Prime advice. It's when you cower and apologize and put yourself on their level of screwed-up morality that you get in trouble, and as I earlier noted, that screwed-up morality was coming at us fast and furious and I was done with it.

All of this was my inspiration and motivation for beginning my own Tumblr blog, to begin posting photos from all those shoots and create my own gallery. I got tired of holding my cards so close to my chest. However, I'm a bit of a techno-idiot. When I had a PC, I found it difficult to figure out anything but getting online and writing in Microsoft Word, but when I shifted to Mac, everything was easier and clearer. The iPhoto app on the computer opened up my world to editing the photos, getting them off the CDs to make lighting and coloring changes or to sharpen them up if a photo needed some supplemental zhuzhing.

Most of the photos were given to me by the photographers with permission to do as I pleased with them, so I started to look through them with a curator's eye. I set up my Tumblr blog, and although I would have liked to, I was still a little apprehensive about using my name and calling it *David Pevsner: Shameless*. So the blog became simply *Shameless* . . . which isn't totally shameless, I know, but baby steps. I wrote this on the intro page:

> Why am I posting these pictures? I posed for them, I'm proud of them, and they are no longer my "dirty little secret." I want all of us to feel good about our physicality and our sexuality, and not ashamed or embarrassed the way so much of society dictates. Over that. So over it. I hope you enjoy the pics. 18+ Please!

I added the 18+ later, when I had a better sense of the legalities of posting. Of course, kids ignore that. They're going to look if they're going to look. However, it takes responsibility off the poster. I know teenagers shouldn't be watching—I would have—but if they do, I want it to be positive and nontraditional, and to work on more than just a sexual level. No shame.

I posted individual photos to start, always crediting the photographer. As time went on, I started posting photo sets, because I realized I could create a narrative with multiple photos, even if they were simple portraits. I would name the shoot something clever or fun to give the photos another layer of context. For instance, I did a covert shoot posing nude in an underground garage that I called "Auto Exposure." There was another collection in which I was photographed in the backseat of a car flashing my cock as if I was an older hustler selling my wares, called "40 Bucks a Pop" (get it?); another shot where I'm in a suit jacket with open shirt and tie on top with legs splayed open and a floppy dick was called "A Gentleman."

I didn't post everything right away, because some of the earlier shoots were more extreme and I didn't know if I was ready to present them publicly. Years before, I did another shoot with Tom Bianchi that was meant to run the gamut of all my fetish wear, from leather and Speedos to a pair of fishnet hose. I can't remember if Tom provided the fishnets or if I already had them in my gearbox, but whatever, it really aroused me to wear them for the camera.

We had an epic shoot, and afterwards the only doubt I had was about those fishnets. I started to feel hesitant due to how I perceived them—so feminine, even though I was hard as a rock posing in them. Although I gave him full consent to use the photos, I remember thinking that Tom would never use all of them, and I wasn't sure I wanted him to. Jay Jorgensen was browsing Tom's site and told me that Tom had posted some photos of me. I asked if there were any fishnet stocking shots. He said no. I breathed a sigh of relief.

The next week, Jay contacted me and said, "Fishnets are a go." I went on Tom's site and, sure enough, the whole rest of the shoot was there, including the fishnet photos. At first I felt flush with embarrassment, but I did tell Tom that I wanted to explore *everything* in this shoot. It was meant to feel fully rounded, a total portrait of my sexual psyche. But actually seeing those photos online gave me a little agita.

I let it go because they were on his private pay site, not for general consumption, but I was secretly aroused by the fact that the photos existed. When I began my own blog, I eventually put them out there because they were part of my journey. I also posted an earlier set of Jay's that I had kept under wraps, in which I was dressed in lingerie, hosiery, and garters. I remembered how much of a turn-on it was to wear them for the camera, and I thought about those times I wore my mom's pant-ies and how they brought me pleasure, and I could now acknowledge at least on film that though it wasn't a regular thing for me, it was a fetish to explore, shame be damned.

Once I started posting, I found my shots were getting reblogged on other Tumblr pages, which then linked them to *Shameless*, and since I also had my gay indie film cred, more and more folks started joining Tumblr, following me by the thousands. I got notes from all over the world from men, young and old, applauding what I was doing, saying that it was brave, defiant, and inspirational, and set them thinking about their own relationships to sex and nudity, how it made them feel, how they judged themselves or others.

In doing this blog, my message was never to say, "Put your dick on the Internet!" It was just to express your sexuality at any age, in any way that brings you joy and comfort and lust and love and all the good stuff. (But if you want to put your dick on the Internet, think it through first and know that, once it's there, it ain't going away. If you're com-fortable with that, have at it!) I made a joke in my song "The Perky Little Porn Star" that the character singing it could never be president. Maybe we won't ever have a porn star as president of the United States, but I wouldn't be surprised if, at some point, we have a president whose dick is online.

I eventually expanded the name of the blog to *Shameless: David Pevsner's Personal Photo Blog*. I could have come up with a porn name, something cheeseball like Peter Harden or, according to the formulas for creating your porn name, Elliott Tripp (middle name, street I grew up on) or Maish Elliott (first pet, middle name), or I could have gone off the formula and taken street name and middle name—Tripp Elliott. Now *there's* a porn name! I even thought about using the name Ross Stein, the character I played in the Web series *Old Dogs and New Tricks*, who has a sex tape leaked, turning art into life into art. But I wanted to finally get to the place where I was being totally honest about how I represented myself in this project, and the use of an alias would have supported the shame I was trying to divest myself of.

One thing I couldn't control was where the photos went after I posted them on Tumblr. Besides getting reblogged on other Tumblr pages, many were posted on Twitter and gay cultural or sex sites, which was A-OK with me. I wanted them out there. Google "David Pevsner XXX" and loads of pictures that I've posted over the years, individually and in sets, will come up, but they're just a fraction of the entire range of photos I posted on Tumblr. Taken in toto, I have hundreds and hundreds of nudes shot through so many photographers' eyes, and I'm really proud of how vast and diverse the collection is.

Funny story: I usually get an agreement from photographers that if I really hate a photo, they won't use it. They know I'm very bold and jump right into what the moment brings, so we agree that if I put it all out there in the shoot, we can pull it back a bit in the final choices. I worked with a lovely man named Vance Trancygier who lived in Salt Lake City. He was a huge fan of *Old Dogs and New Tricks* and a fetish photographer, as well as a security guard as his day job. He asked if he could shoot me, and as I found his work intriguing and disturbing, I agreed.

Vance came to LA after saving up to travel, and we shot in a hotel room, with ropes and nooses and skulls and sex toys. Although it took him a while to get over his nerves, we had a successful shoot that gleaned some terrific, provocative images—autoerotic asphyxiation, a Hamlet-esque sensual shot with a skull, and even some lonely, albeit romantic, photos in and out of a mussed-up bed.

I liked Vance a lot and we stayed in contact. One day, though, he posted a photo that I had *not* agreed on—a shot of me sitting, totally relaxed, goofy smile on my face, and a blubbery paunch. I don't know how long it had been up before I caught it, but I asked him to take it down. He said he liked it because it was very me, and I said thanks, that's great, but as any model will tell you, those shots where you're relaxed or where the lighting sucks do not show the body off to the best advantage. I was feeling in particularly good shape that day, so I didn't think it was a fair depiction. I get why he wanted to use it—I guess it had an endearing quality to it—and I think today I wouldn't make a stink about it, but I was determined to show that men of fifty-plus could hold it together and stay in shape, and that photo did not fit with that idea. He took it down, but even a few minutes on the Internet can make it multiply, so it was out there. I had seen it on one or two blogs over time, but . . .

I have a wonderful fan who lives in Japan. In the past he has sent me gifts, made DVD compilations of my photos, and started "The David Pevsner Fun Club" (membership of two, I think). We kept in touch by email and he really appreciated the blog and what I'd set out to do. He just seemed to be an agreeable, hardworking guy who was maybe a teeny bit obsessed, but I felt no danger, and his gifts ranged from Calvin Klein underwear to T-shirts and book bags with my face illustrated on them, as well as traditional Japanese garments (*fundoshi*) and Asian candies and cookies. Sweet gestures.

One of the DVDs was marked *A David Pevsner Tribute*. I popped it into my DVD player, and it was a slew of photo images prefaced by "I love David . . ." Then it would say, for instance, "in leather" and some shots of me in a harness or chaps would go by as a gentle, flowing montage; "I love David in briefs" was followed by tighty-whitie and Speedo shots; "I love David with muscles" led to shots of me flexing or looking kind of pumped. Toward the end, that photo of Vance's that I nixed went floating by, and the caption read "I love David fat." *SEE???* I was not crazy. I called Vance and we had a good laugh about it.

Not long after our conversation, Vance had a fatal accident. He had broken his foot and was on crutches when he took a bad fall, and a blood clot from the break went to his lung; a pulmonary embolism killed him. He was so young and such a good guy. I found out about his death when his sister posted a notice on his Facebook page. I was heartbroken. I wrote a eulogy for him on my blog and linked it to Vance's Deviant Arts page of all his photography (under the name Wreckles; it's still there). I know he would have liked to be remembered for the wonderful, wicked, sometimes twisted, and absolutely fearless work he put out there, as a photographer and fine artist. I made sure my guys on Tumblr knew about him beyond what we shot together.

That's the other part of the blog that I loved. It was kind of a community, and I always welcomed messages and questions, all of which I answered. There were men following my page who lived in parts of the world where being gay could get them killed, so I messaged back and forth with them and tried to help however I could, but mostly I think they just needed to vent and know that someone was listening, that they were not totally alone.

MR. WONDERFUL

I know the word that's probably going through your head. The other N-word.

Narcissist. David's a narcissist. In my eyes, that word has such negativity attached, but there are so many more layers to it, both positive and negative. It's complicated.

Sure, let's talk about the ego and its hunger for attention. Though my narrative seems to be driven by it, I like to think of myself as a recovering narcissist. No, really. I know I'll always be narcissistic to an extent, that there's a part of me that needs attention and adulation—"It's about *ME*."

The older I get, the more aware of it I've become, and I try to control these tendencies because I find having conversations with heavily narcissistic people a losing battle. Let's face it—I'm in an industry filled with narcissists. Sometimes, after running into an acquaintance and getting a half-hour-diatribe answer to my question "How are you?" I would absolutely drop dead if that person then said, "How are *you*?" Not being asked the question back used to bring out the neurotic worst in me. Unprompted, I would go into my own monologue of "I'm doing this" and "I'm doing that" and just babble on to show that hey, I'm popular and successful too! I've finally learned not to engage in that way because I know the other person isn't listening; it's a waste of air. Instead, I say, "Great to see you!" and move on. There's a glaze in the eyes of narcissistic folks when they have to stop and listen to you talk— the dead-eyed stare that says this was not meant to be a dialogue, I'm not interested in your little life, so *Sha!* And I know that as a fact, because that's how I used to be.

When I first came to LA and was trying to get *Dog Days* made, I had a pad and pen on me at all times (before smartphones) so that I could keep a record of all the networking I was doing. That's fine because, as they say, it's all about who you know. However, I found that if the potential connection wasn't interested in either helping me or fucking me, I quickly moved on. It was kind of obnoxious (kind of?), and after a time I could see people literally back away from me, as if they were thinking, "Oh, shit. Him. Run!" That is not a good feeling. I don't believe being opportunistic is a bad thing—it's how we get things done—but mixing it with desperation isn't pretty, and people can smell it. I never wanted to be *that* guy, but I think I was, because my ambition got the best of me, being new to Hollywood. I said earlier that in trying to get *Dog Days* produced, I maybe held back a bit subconsciously out of fear that I might one day have to publicly acknowledge having been an escort, but I was actually pretty pushy about getting into initial conversations with anyone who had even the tiniest toe in the door of independent filmmaking.

Through a lot of soul-searching, therapy, and faking it until I made it, I think I've changed. I hope I have. Now, when engaged in a conversation, I try to keep my spoken résumé to a minimum when asked and then respond with a sincere "How are you?" As Dale Carnegie said, "To be interesting, be interested." I've found the latter to be so much more engaging and just, well, human.

So that's one kind of narcissism, but now let's talk body. When I was a skinny boy looking in that mirror in my parents' bathroom all those years ago, I fantasized about my body looking like what it would eventually become. When naked in the gym class locker room, something in me wanted so badly not to cower and cover up, but to walk around the communal shower as if I owned it and knew every eye was on me, the way some of the jocks did. I just wanted some confidence. I had none. When I was with my first boyfriend, Stan, I deemed him so much more worthy than me in terms of beauty, especially because he had this lean muscularity that made me look like a twig next to him. I never reveled in the pure joyous outlet that sex could be because I was too self-conscious, and not just about how I looked. I couldn't give in to the sheer pleasure and passion of it because it felt covert and verboten, as well as constrained and by the numbers, all about trying to please him, to do it "right."

As I got older and had more experience with men, I got more comfortable with sex, and I can say for a fact that porn certainly helped. I remember there was a lot of "Oh, THAT's how you do that" in my head as I watched the sex gods go about their business, taking note of their techniques (like the good student I always was) as I jerked off. There were no gay XXX movie houses in Pittsburgh that I can remember, but when I visited my family in Skokie on college breaks, I sometimes escaped to Chicago and the Bijou Theatre. When I got to NYC in 1982, I saw a few films on the big screen at the legendary 55th Street Playhouse, a gay porn movie theater in Midtown Manhattan, but most of my viewing was via the newer technology called the VCR.

When I first started to look at gay porn in my teens and early twenties, many of the bodies on display were more "real guy" types, lightly muscled, not overly built, sometimes with more body hair (Al Parker, Kip Noll, Casey Donovan, Richard Locke). And though the films presented these beautiful men as ideals and fantasies, they never made me feel bad about my body. The idea that I could look like them someday wasn't so remote. In actuality, they gave me something first to fantasize about and then to aspire to (although I could also appreciate the more muscled Jack Wrangler and Peter Berlin, whose bulging crotch and tight clothing always turned me on, and later inspired my desire to flagrantly flaunt my assets).

In the '80s, the porn stars were more muscled and smooth: Bill Henson, Mike Henson (no relation), Brian Maxon, Eric Stryker, Michael Christopher, Rick Donovan, Joe Cade, Matt Ramsey. They were the "types" that guys were looking for in the bars. That level of physicality seemed impossible for me to achieve, and I'd find those guys so intimidating, setting me on the road to failure when I tried to connect with one of the bodies beautiful. But in the late '80s, developing my physique gave me more confidence not only in myself but in approaching the men I was attracted to. Their bodies were my main priority, and in turn my body was usually what attracted them to me. When I started to wear leather, it was the Colt Men photos and videos that really did it for me, those big, beautiful bodybuilding buckos shot by photographer Jim French, some oiled up and smooth, others hirsute and swarthy, but all stunning. The Ultimate Men.

As the muscles developed, my narcissism kicked in big-time. I loved how I looked and I loved being looked at, wearing next to nothing in public—tight jeans and tank tops on the street, tiny tight shorts with no undergarments and string tanks to the gym. It was partly that I wanted to be able to see my progression as I pumped my body parts, but it was more about the thrill that I was bulging out and displaying my physique for everyone to see.

I've always been a "give credit where credit is due" guy, and in this case I worked hard for what I achieved physically and I wanted to show it off. I felt no reason to cover up when I could feel the eyeballs on me. It wasn't all approval: I know some folks were disgusted and thought

I just looked like a whore, even at the Chelsea Gym where, ironically, more than most were sucking dicks in The Low Self-Esteem Room. But there was a part of me that relished irritating them; if they felt they needed to judge me and shoot me some snark, I was happy to give them something to judge me about and then return the snooty look. That was fine; I was getting plenty of carnal attention and I reveled in every second of it. We talked about this when I was in therapy, that my self-worth was so attached to what I was presenting physically to the world, especially when I was not working as an actor. It wasn't enough for me to be just a good person with some talent, brains, and humor that people seemed to like for myself. I wanted to present myself as healthy, successful, and, well . . . hot (or what I perceived to be hot). Inside, though, it was a different story. I was very up and down with self-esteem. Sometimes I was self-assured and content with myself, and other times harshly judgmental about my looks, doubting my abilities as an actor, and punishing myself as to why I wasn't more "successful," even though I had just come off two national tours and a Broadway show. But though my insecurities may have manifested into shame-lessly (shamefully?) displaying my body, I also loved being so brazen about putting my sexuality front and center.

These days, next to most of the guys wearing the standard baggy shorts and oversize tank tops on the gym floor, I see some men in tights, tiny shorts, no undergarments, dicks bulging and pecs uncovered, and though I see eye rolls from some patrons of the gym, I respect the show-offs, the rebels, the fact that they don't care they're being judged and just go about their business. As for me? I don't give a crap anymore what anyone thinks. I wear my tights and short shorts (with a G-string underneath to reel in the goods), and there's still a part of me that's thrilled that I can inject some sexuality into my daily workout just by what I wear, and it pushes me to work harder. Besides, I don't like wearing baggy clothing in or out of the gym; I feel as though I'm being swallowed up by the ensemble. I go to the big gay Gold's Gym in Hollywood, a porn star-palooza, so what I choose to wear is not an issue. If I go to a more "family-friendly" gym when I'm visiting Chicago or on the road for work, I adjust and cover up because I don't want to get kicked out. And guess what? I actually do wear shirts with sleeves (unless it's hot out). I collect Ben Sherman button-down shirts and I love them.

But let's be honest: working out isn't just about health. I believe that everyone has some degree of narcissism, and I believe very strongly that a little bit of narcissism is a good thing if it keeps you pursuing a healthy lifestyle, watching what you eat, staying active physically and mentally. It's okay to put a little makeup on or to do a quick *zhuzh* of the hair in the mirror as you run out the door, whatever will make you feel a little better about yourself and what you put out into the world, as long as it's not excessive, more balanced, what I'll call "measured narcissism."

As I've aged, my health has definitely taken priority over the shape of my body, but I'm talking mental health as well. Lord knows, working out keeps me sane and gives me a bit of a routine. As a freelancer, it's nice to have somewhere to go five or six times a week to really push myself and clear out the cobwebs. And I can finally acknowledge that I'm okay with how I look—big nose, chunky butt, creasy face, and all— but also that my face and body are just a part of who I am, and that the whole package, inner and outer, is fine but constantly needs upkeep as I age. It's important to keep learning and improving oneself but also to have humility, grace, and gratitude to put out into the world. Balance.

I think about when I've been on beaches overseas and saw plus-sized men and women in Speedos and bikinis, not giving a fuck what anyone thinks. Just living their lives, enjoying themselves. Not covering up because some magazine says they're not beautiful. It comes down to confidence. Confidence is sexy. Confidence is loving who you are, no matter what your body looks like. My confidence has been shaken so much throughout my life, from the skinny boy in gym class, to Carnegie undercutting my talent and self-worth, to eventually feeling that no one would love me if I wasn't built and "pretty."

I've manifested those insecurities in various ways throughout my life: as a boy, I covered up, and as a man, I've stripped down. But as I've gotten older, I've begun to challenge those insecurities and unrealistic expectations about everything from my work as an actor and a writer to relationships that ended in disappointment, because they've only served to make me physically ill and depressed. I've also had to come to grips with the fact that aging is inescapable, but here's the good news: the older I get, the easier it is to let the crap go. I like to think I've gone from young and stupid to mature and more aware. I've worked hard to put that insufferable person I was when I moved to LA behind me, although lord knows you may still think he's alive and well and yapping in the pages of this book.

I've tried to find the balance, to love the man in the mirror both physically and emotionally, dressed and not. I think a lot of us need to feel more confident, more loving and accepting of ourselves. I know I'm not alone. It's an ongoing struggle for me, a journey that continues. But can I give you a little tip?

Sometimes—why not?—just get out there and strut. It feels pretty good.

TABOO

When I hit my fifties, I came to the point professionally where I just didn't give a shit anymore. Between my nude photos and my hooker show, no secrets. *Hey, that TV doctor guy's hard cock is on the Internet! He fucked guys for money!* As someone who was building a public persona but nowhere near "famous," I figured my honesty could go either way: kill my acting career or push me forward in a different, more intriguing way that I could shape for myself. I always had a choice, to either explore my deeper fantasies or not. I chose to pursue them. Have there been professional consequences? Well . . .

My commercial agent left a message for me one day: "[So-and-So] Casting told me that they would not see you because you apparently have a naked picture on the Internet? Can you get it taken off? Call me." First off: *a* naked picture? Second, good luck getting anything off the Interwebs once it's up and shared.

I didn't hear from my commercial agent much or go out on commercial calls very often. I think I was a bit of an in-betweener. I can be "the doctor" and "the lawyer," but I didn't have the silver hair or the paunch that those labels bring to mind for the type of commercials

I went in for, and I would usually see ten other guys in the waiting area who looked the part more than me. In commercials, to be an effective "salesman," you have to be a strong, immediately recognizable type as there's so little time to establish character.

I did a few and made some good coin, but I hadn't broken through as one of those recognizable commercial faces. You'd think that the guy who incessantly sang product jingles and acted out TV ads as a kid would want to avidly pursue that kind of work as an adult, but the more time I spent going to commercial calls, the more I realized what a crapshoot they are compared with all the other aspects of the biz I was involved in. Plus, my least favorite words in the English language became "You have a commercial audition in Santa Monica at three thirty on Friday." Anyone who lives there knows that at that hour, you can't get the fuck out of Santa Monica.

So I called the agent back and she asked, "What's up with that photo?" I told her I most likely had put it up myself. Silence. Then (and I had to move the phone away from my ear), "WHY WOULD YOU DO THAT?!" As I let the tinnitus subside, I calmly explained, "I have a blog displaying all the erotic photos I've posed for over the years, and it's my statement about taking back my body shame and maybe inspiring others my age to feel better about themselves and their sexuality, to help erase the stigma on nudity that our culture preaches . . . " blah blah and blah-dy blah. She listened quietly. I ended by saying, "Look, I take full responsibility for it, but if you need to drop me, I understand. I hope you won't, because I think you're great, but if that's the way the biz goes, totally understood."

She said, "No, no, I'm not going to drop you. But you have to know that it could negatively affect you sometimes with casting. If you're okay with that, we'll just continue as we have. I applaud what you're trying to do." I said, "Thank you. Let's just soldier on!" She laughed, and I laughed, and two weeks later she dropped me by email, at first saying she was sorry they hadn't done a better job representing me, but then:

> At this time we are releasing you from commercial representation
> so that you may have the freedom to pursue a better fit for the future
> jobs that are to come.

Since the agency didn't have a porn department, I assumed she hoped I'd find representation elsewhere for those "future jobs." The fact that this happened just weeks after I told her about my pics, after I'd been with the agency for six years, made it pretty clear to me that it was a dig. I'm not the least bit bitter. I totally understand, and as I said, I take full responsibility.

Commercials are not like other forms of television. They're brands, and it would be hard to convince a company to cast me as the doctor face of their product if they don't agree with what I put out publicly on social media. Employers have the right to hire or fire folks based on how they represent them, and if you don't want my easily googlable hard cock attached to the face of your product, fine.

Personally, I think it's silly, as commercial actors are usually name-less representatives (even when you're as big as "Flo" from Progressive Insurance or the "Can you hear me now?" guy from Verizon—quick, tell me their real names!), but I get it. I don't agree, because it shouldn't be a big deal, but I get it (even though the publicity should it be discov-ered could be golden). It's America, and America has a problem with sex and nudity. However, with TV and film . . .

After this exchange with my commercial agent, I realized I should probably talk to my TV/film agent. I'd been with her for about seven years, and although I got a lot of my work myself, she did get me in the door for some TV spots, including *Modern Family* and *Law and Order: LA*. I liked her a lot, so I figured I'd better give her the heads-up about my nude Internet presence. I asked to meet with her, and when we sat down in the conference room, I opened by saying, "This may be the weirdest meeting you've ever had."

She laughed and said, "What's up?"

I explained to her about my photo blog, my mission, the commercial agent's reaction to casting inquiries about my nude photo, and she listened quietly, nodding consistently throughout like those ever-present bobbleheads. I ended with the same proposition of "If you need to drop me, I get it, but I hope you won't." TV and film are different from commercials, and I honestly didn't (and don't) think the directors whose work I love and respect most would give a crap. If anything, it might make me more interesting to them.

I asked if she had ever heard from any casting directors about my pictures. She said, "No, and I'm not going to drop you. I just have to think through who I can sell you to. I can't do the Disney or Nickelodeon kids' shows"—that was fine with me—"and I know sometimes casting can be very exclusive and this doesn't help. But I like you. I always have, and I think you're talented, so let's see how we can make this work."

Great. I felt encouraged and supported when I left. And at the end of my contract, they dropped me, saying I hadn't been bringing in enough to warrant keeping me on, that they were sorry, and they wished me well. That email came two weeks after the commercial agency email. Honestly, I expected that and I felt no ill will. Maybe I wasn't bringing in as much as before, but I find it hardly a coincidence that after all those years with them, some pretty lucrative, the end of these particular contracts came about after I came clean about my pics. And if that is indeed the case, it shows that nudity makes people uncomfortable and that it can still affect your bottom line. I don't care. Making my statement and putting it out there trumped my desire to continue my career "in the closet," so to speak.

ON A CLEAR DAY
YOU CAN SEE FOREVER

Social media has afforded me a lot of opportunity to express myself. While Tumblr allowed me to explore the sexual aspect of my life through photos, Facebook let me express myself politically. I have a nice community of friends and "friends" who share, comment, and keep the dialogue going. I'm pretty loud on that platform, especially about gay issues, but I try to balance it with fun life stuff. I call myself The Angry Homosexual Who Likes Cat Videos. I know I'm not changing the world through Facebook postings, and some would say it's now passé and greedily corporate, but it has forced me to be as current as possible on world events and politics. I want to hear what folks have to say about the daily news, and if I can spur a conversation about the issues of the day, fantastic.

Between Facebook and Tumblr (and now Twitter and Instagram), the platforms helped me find the voice that I'd been seeking, modes of self-expression that felt right and relevant and 100 percent me. What was weird, though, and made me feel like a bit of a hypocrite, is that I didn't talk much about my anti–body shame mission on Facebook. I kept Facebook and Instagram a little "cleaner" as I'd nearly gotten kicked off

Instagram multiple times for posting cropped versions of the *Shameless* photos. I'd also heard that casting people refer to your social media if they don't know you well, so I figured I should tone down the skin. Double life. Still.

Please don't think I have a sense of self-importance about any of it. It's just Facebook and nudies, after all (I call my photos nudies in deference to the great Neely O'Hara from *Valley of the Dolls*). But sometimes I get feedback that makes the whole thing worthwhile and puts to bed any doubts I may have about social media and having any kind of Internet presence. In January 2014, I got an email from a young man in high school, random and out of the blue:

> Dear David,
>
> I'm not quite sure how often you receive fan mail—or if you even read it, but I thought I'd write a message because I think it's worth the chance of you seeing it. I grew to know your existence through Tumblr—and while watching "Criminal Minds" a few days back I had to do a double take when I saw your face in an episode.
>
> I began looking into your background and realized that not only are you a good-looking actor, but a gay-rights activist. I'm a senior boy at a Catholic high school in IL. Accepting my sexuality in regards to spirituality, friends, and family was a nightmare that I wouldn't wish on the worst of mankind.
>
> Last year I was hospitalized a couple of times for severe depression and becoming a danger to myself. It's hard to say, but I admit that there were so many times that I didn't want to live anymore because of my conservative family or the horrible things people said at school. I'm happy to report that I'm currently doing great—and although I'm stuck in a rut at home, college is just months away.
>
> Although I didn't know of you last year, the people like you that aren't afraid to speak out really inspire me. When I was up at 2 a.m. scanning

blogs and videos with dried tears on my cheeks for a reason to live,
I found videos and interviews of adults telling me that I was special
and worth it. That life is going to improve. And aside from opera and
vocal performance, I want to speak for the LGBT community too,
and human rights in general.

I think lots of activists focus so much on changing people and forget
how many people look up to them. So if you ever feel like that, remember
that there are people being inspired by what you do every day. Whether
it's a young boy who sees your picture and realizes for the first time that
he's gay, or someone that's finally learned to accept him/her/them-self, it
could have been you that saved the tears, the scars, or the life. I've already
begun brainstorming, and some day I hope to release a novel about teen
sexuality and mental illness. I think the world is changing for the better—
and your generation has kicked the snow that will become an avalanche.
Maybe some day you will see my name in the newspaper and I can join
the amazing team of human-rights activists.

Fondly,
Mitchell

I was so moved by Mitchell. This note was eye-opening to me
in many ways, and it touched me that this young man had succeeded in
getting past what so many of us have gone through in varying degrees
of desperation. His experience sounded horrible, yet he was surviving
and thriving through the help and inspiration of those who came before
him. I do think it's important that we gay folks who have any public face
at all speak out and not cover up, so that young people in small towns
and small-minded communities and families can feel hope and know
that they can get past the internalized shame and fear of being gay that
can not only cripple but kill. To be that young and living an out life is
just so damn brave; it was unthinkable when I was their age.

Mitchell and I corresponded back and forth for a while, and he got through that last year of high school. He went to college, formed a band, engaged in a real relationship, and, best of all, found happiness and comfort with himself and his work as an up-and-coming out recording artist. I never take it lightly when someone says that I'm a role model, whatever the role is. I wish I'd had access to folks I looked up to when I was growing up.

Things have certainly changed for gay kids today, with more positive representations of queer people in the media and online. But there are still bashers and haters and bible beaters who want nothing more than to see us dead. And now, the hate has found a place online. Cyberbullying is increasingly prevalent, and as a result, gay kids keep secrets about their sexual identity that inhibit their ability to develop natural relationships the way their straight counterparts do. Secrecy is soul destroying, it's the devil, and that really doesn't seem to have changed much from when I was a teenager.

Young people today may have more information and role models than ever, but all it takes is one stupid bully to make a kid feel shitty about themselves. I want every young person in the LGBTQ community to know that they are loved, if not by someone in their immediate sphere, then by me and all their brothers and sisters around the world. We have your backs, and if you can just get through the tough times, the humiliating, painful internal wrestling matches, you will not only survive, but thrive.

I recently rewatched *Trevor*, the short film that inspired the creation of The Trevor Project, a hotline for gay kids who might be considering suicide. It's about a thirteen-year-old boy whose gay crush on a schoolmate is found out and the ostracism that ensues, to the point that he attempts suicide—by aspirin. The film is so charming and heartbreaking and funny, and in experiencing it again, I identified with it even more. Trevor's Pinky Faraday was my Joe, his Diana Ross was my

Barbra, and we both had the same love for theater and drama, with aspirations both personal and professional. It's a perfect little film that really is a must-watch for any gay youth, and I was charmed and moved to tears all over again by its message of hope. The Project has saved so many lives, but it kills me that even though we gay folks have greater visibility, the number of suicides has gone up among young people in our community.

We all have to continue to speak out. We all have to BE out. There are now enough out gay actors and celebrities enjoying great success that there's no need anymore for closets, beards, veils, or excuses. Visibility can save lives, and we need to support our gay and trans kids. I've been there, so many of us have. It has to stop. Celebrities, A-list and otherwise: come the fuck out.

CURTAINS

In June 2017, Tumblr was bought by Verizon and the platform announced that it was going to censor adult material, anything with nudity or sexual content. Apparently, some child porn was found on Tumblr and this led Apple to discontinue carrying the Tumblr app, and that became an issue for the company. So when Verizon bought it, the CEO announced they wanted to create a "more positive Tumblr," and in December 2018 the Tumblr Purge occurred.

Here's what I found out. Yes, child porn was found, which is a terrible thing. But the fact is that Tumblr employed lots of people and technology that were supposed to be monitoring that kind of stuff. So some folks or bots weren't doing their jobs. Tumblr had been around a long time and a nominal percentage of it was adult content (around 11 percent of the top two hundred blogs), but this content was provided by less than one percent of Tumblr creators, including bots. That said, around 22 percent of Tumblr consumers were there for the adult stuff (all of this info gleaned from websites such as Vice, Vox, and ValueWalk). And there were a lot of people who grew to depend on the artistic freedom that Tumblr provided, not just for expression but also as a way of making money—gathering advertisers to their blogs, getting folks to click to their product, linking to affiliates, finding sponsorships. I wasn't monetizing the site; for me, it was strictly for self-expression and the mission. And now, with the changeover, they wanted to pull the rug out from under us all for a "more positive Tumblr." I interpreted that as meaning that, in their view, sex and nudity and eroticism were negative and bad, and not in a good, naughty way— just bad. Tumblr was at the forefront of a nasty censorship wave that had started to infiltrate the Internet and continues to move forward.

HBO's Vice News contacted me after they saw an interview I did for the Naked Sword porn site and asked if I would talk on camera about the purge. At first I said no. I had been dividing my two lives: actor/organizer David Pevsner and the erotic model David Pevsner. I wasn't sure I wanted to meld the two so openly, and yet—what a platform for my anti–body shame, anti-ageism, pro-sexuality and -nudity mission. So I said yes.

They came to my place in LA and stayed for three hours, and it became a five-minute piece about how Tumblr was censoring an important means of self-expression. It was a bit couched in "Sixty-year-old man posts naked pictures of himself and now what?" but I was able to make my case—to an extent. I chose not to get screamingly angry about it so that I wouldn't seem like some crazy banshee exhibitionist, but in retrospect I wish I *had* gotten angrier.

Because I was/am angry. Tumblr had been a terrific venue for creative expression and reached a pretty large audience—25,000 followers for me (it's not 25 million, I know, but it's still a lot). Having that many eyeballs and ears allowed me to put expression into action, providing a vehicle by which I could encourage people to vote or see my shows and films or spur them on to get out and fight for LGBTQ causes.

It was all good until it wasn't and my work got censored. I tried testing them. I would post something that was totally G-rated—shirtless, but nothing sexual—and it would get tagged as adult content, and while not deleted, Tumblr made it invisible to my followers so that I was the only one who could see the post. So, five years of consistent posting, a fully curated gallery of my work as a model and provocateur, was essentially gone. I can still see the photos there, but you can't. Hundreds of stories, hidden from your view. I made sure to back up all the posts I had put so much time and care into composing.

I began a search for new platforms, as I was even more determined to get the photos out there and push the envelope—more depictions of sexual activity, maybe some video. I was appalled by the censorship, but also confused that there were Tumblr posters who were not at all affected by the purge, posting dick and sex pics to this very day, flying under the radar. WTfuckingF? In any case, I still wanted to post from an artier standpoint, but if it's porn to you . . . oh well. Fuck it. America's point of view when it comes to sex—especially gay sex and the penis—sucks. And not in a good, slurpy way. It just sucks. And I was and am resolved to do something about it.

"A Gentleman." I think it's my favorite shot of all. I wish I could show you the whole photo, but it was decided that erections were a no-no for this book. We couldn't take the chance of some retailers shutting us out due to a few woodies, but who knows? Maybe all penises are verboten. We'll see. However, I think my most intriguing and sensual shots include arousal, and you can easily find a whole slew on the Internet. But for the next eight pages, you can follow some of my journey as an erotic model. Or, if you don't want to look at me naked, feel free to move ahead. We're adults and we all have the right to choose.

Me being censored.

"All-American." My first published nude in Tom Bianchi's book *Out of the Studio*. Too nervous to show my face, but later not too nervous to put the magnet on my refrigerator.

On the beach, on the rocks, on the make. I love posing outdoors. You never know who you'll run into.

I so wish you could see this in color. Forget my ass—it was fall and the leaves were gorgeous.

Daddy.

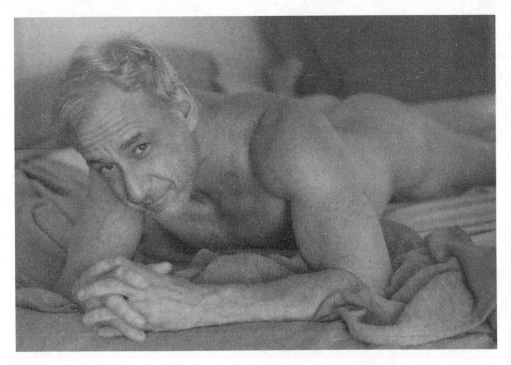

Boy.

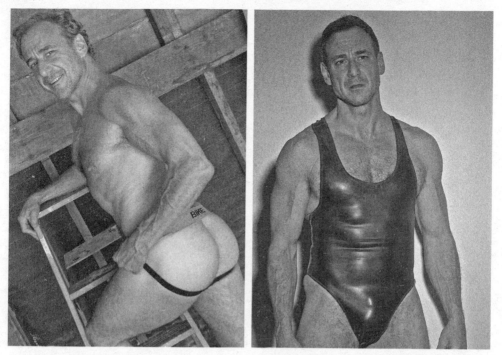

A jockstrap is a man's (and a butt's) best friend. I like my rubber leotards snug. How about you?

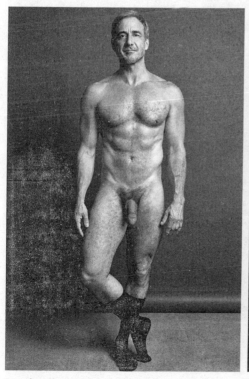

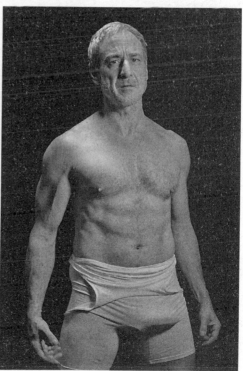

I can't tell you how many requests I get for wearing dress socks and nothing else.

Ready to rassle.

Between the leather and the ladder, I never felt more butch.

Tie me up and I'm a happy man. There are about four hundred other bondage shots if you ever want to see them.

Did you think I wasn't going to have a Speedo pic?

Feeling quite saucy in lingerie.

Moody, like me.

Sometimes, you go with the classics.

Suit and tie shots are my most popular, especially if they eventually come off.

From a photo session for my 55th birthday. A little daddy-tude.

I do enjoy life in front of the camera.

ANYTHING GOES

I searched for other venues that not only allowed adult material but also would be as easy and convenient as Tumblr for a computer idiot like me. I looked into sites that allow you to build your own web page inexpensively or for free, such as Squarespace and Wix, but they didn't allow adult material. I took note of some of the places that were advertising as taking emigrants from Tumblr, and I landed on New Tumbl. Though not as well traveled as Tumblr, it looked and worked almost exactly like it. So I started posting there. It was an easy transition.

I originally liked the idea of portraying the erotic without full-on sex in my posts. I tested the waters over the years that I'd had the blogs, but after getting cut off at the knees on Tumblr, I decided to go beyond my previous limits. I began taking masturbation, bondage, fetish such as leather and water sports, and duo and trio shoots to greater extremes, while continuing to shoot less provocative portraits as well. I ran the gamut from playful and erotic to explicit.

Meanwhile, I had a friend who had been shooting small, arty sex films for his own online production company, Fae Films, and he asked if I might want to take part in one. I had shot some very low-tech personal sex stuff on a Flip Video camera just for fun, but I never used the footage for anything because my sex partner didn't want it out there. I sent the clips to him just for his own enjoyment. This seemed like a good next step, so I made the video. Fae shot me jerking off in front of a white screen while video of rushing water from the ocean was projected on me. That became *Wave Ritual*, the first of our collaborations, and it felt amazing to be in it. The film was very dreamy and poetic.

The next film I participated in was *Sons of the Moon*, a five-minute short in which three guys have sex while the phases of the moon are projected on us. The result is really gorgeous and erotic. There was an NSFW (Not Safe for Work) short film festival featuring videos that would never get into other festivals because of their sexual content, and Fae wanted to submit *Sons of the Moon* there, which I thought was great. We were then asked to add a little extra to the event: a live depiction of the film at Highways, the performance space in Santa Monica at which the festival was taking place (I had also performed *Musical Comedy Whore* there).

After the screening, a good number of the audience came back to the greenroom, sat in a semicircle against the walls, and watched the live show. It started with me entering alone in a jockstrap, joined one at a time by the other two guys in a few stitches of clothing, and then we began to have sex, eventually stripping down to nothing, all while the same footage of the moon's phases was projected on us.

It was an amazing experience, and I don't think I have ever felt such power over an audience as when I was naked and having sex while a circle of clothed men watched. I had had sex in the open at bathhouses and parties, but not this publicly. When I did *Broadway Bares* all those years ago, I'd felt a little of that power, but this was much more extreme.

The audience was absolutely rapt, and the sexual tension in the room fed my desire to let my inner porn star out and just enjoy showing off, kissing, eating ass, sucking dick, engaging in faux fucking that looked very real (actual fucking could have gotten a bit messy in those environs), and then ultimately shooting a huge load all over the naked torsos of the two guys.

Even though the room was small and the situation kind of intimidating, the audience clapped (which made me chuckle, but I stayed "in character," and though I didn't bow, I took a curtain call in my head). I fucking loved it and it felt absolutely right, because I was letting go of any judgment and was just free to be myself, no matter how I might be perceived. In retrospect, it was beyond anything I'd aspired to when I watched the dancers on a Saturday night at the Gaiety Theatre all those years ago.

I continued to make videos with Fae, but the experience made me want to take my photos even further.

Meanwhile, my New Tumbl blog was building slowly, and I felt I wasn't getting the traffic I'd had at Tumblr. I started to look into subscription-oriented personal sites that were more high-profile, and I landed on OnlyFans, where you can pretty much present whatever is important to you (not just sex), and you can either make it free or charge a subscription. Since my photos on Tumblr and New Tumbl were free, I decided to continue that on OnlyFans, but figured that if I ever decided to bite the bullet and start posting the videos, I could charge. Meanwhile, I continued to post on New Tumbl as well.

I uploaded all my previous photo shoots onto my OnlyFans page, but I got even bolder and began shooting and posting photos like the ones that turned me off when I was younger, confronting the camera with close-ups of my hard cock and spread asshole. I wanted to face head-on anything and everything that made me feel shameful or embarrassed, specifically for OnlyFans. I tried to click into my inner Mapplethorpe. And though one would not refer to graphic pics like that as classy, I knew that they could garner some kind of emotional reaction. I just wanted to be sure that each shoot had a different creative and sexual vibe from the previous one, and the photographers and I relished letting go of the reins. I also began doing even more explicit shoots with photographers and other models. I posted a duo shoot in which the model and I were artfully photographed flip-flop fucking, each top and bottom, and the photos did not shy away from capturing the actual penetration. I called the resulting photo set "They Call Him Flipper." It was kind of an ode to Brian Kelly. I thought it was sweet and witty, but I'm not sure he would appreciate the homage.

These photos made me feel intensely vulnerable, but I reveled in the freedom, the sheer audaciousness of what I was posting. I felt fearless on OnlyFans. To see the photos, you just needed to create a free account, and though I didn't amass the same size of audience I had on Tumblr, I still accrued thousands of followers.

Then came COVID and quarantine. One positive outcome of the pandemic was that the less time I spent around people, the less I cared about their opinions of me. My instincts were telling me it was time to start posting the videos, and to charge for them as a way of making money during this period when everyone was losing their livelihood.

Not knowing how long the pandemic was going to last made me extremely nervous about my immediate financial future. Although I was still bringing in residuals and royalties from my TV and film work, as well as from *Naked Boys Singing!* and the eventual film they made of it (the less said about that, the better), all TV production pretty much came to a standstill. I couldn't go into people's homes anymore to do my work as a personal organizer, and even if I had wanted to find work doing any of the other stuff I'd done in the past, such as bartending, cleaning homes, or even hooking, it would have been a lousy and ultimately dangerous idea to risk mingling with others.

On top of that, I had a conversation with a film producer friend about my sexual presence on the Internet, and I asked him point-blank: "Would that affect your ability to hire me?" Since he worked a great deal for Disney, he admitted that yes, it would, but he also offered encouragement, saying that if my "sexual activism" was important to me, if I felt I could make a difference, then I shouldn't hold back. I considered it long and hard (whenever anyone says that, I just think cock) and finally decided that yes, I do want to make a difference, I want people to look at nudity and porn and sexuality in a different way, to normalize it, to destigmatize it, to take away that mucky stench that's projected onto it.

I didn't want to just generally put out sex videos on Pornhub or XTube because I thought that was maybe a bridge too far in terms of my acting career, but I wanted to give my followers what they had been requesting for years—video—plus I was enjoying making those arty little sex films. I figured charging the subscription would attract the folks who really wanted to see them, because I wasn't interested in playing to the lookie-loos and haters.

So, in March 2020, I went live with XXX video content (the first being *Wave Ritual*) and began to charge a subscription. I lost a lot of followers who didn't want to pay, but there were plenty who stuck around as I began to curate this new gallery, a combination of erotic videos and photos.

Fae and I treated videos very much the way I did photo shoots—finding humor or enacting role plays, using more artistic camera angles and tricks. He also created musical scores as an effective supplement to the onscreen action. Eventually, because I couldn't mix with other artists during COVID, I had to begin shooting my own solo videos and photos to keep up with the demand for content.

I did some DIY videos, including showing guys how to do that sock/plastic bag fucking technique that Jerry Feinberg taught me years ago (still surprisingly effective). I instructed them how to take a two-foot dildo up their ass. (Did you know you have a second rectum inside you? You have to find it and push past it to get it all in. Fun facts to know and tell!).

There are also Q&A videos, livestreams, lots of different kinds of masturbation footage with themes like "Crazy in Quarantine" (letting the deprivation play out with some intense jack-off sessions), "Cockcentric" (various ways to present my penis to the camera; sometimes I felt like Andy Warhol), fondling my bulge in Speedos and tights ("Bulge Play"—perhaps I should trademark that), character role plays (the college football coach seducing one of his players, the actor getting casting couched, the handyman catching me pleasuring myself, the absolutely inappropriate Skype job interview, all leading to jacking off for my invisible scene partner), alfresco nude photo shoots in the nooks and crannies of local LA parks and forests, and a whole lot more—any creative, fun way I could find to present myself sexually.

Eventually, I was able to engage with a few of Fae's other models who were "bubbling" so that we could film duo and trio shoots. I began to write dirty, detailed stories to set up the videos and photo collections, behind-the-scenes dish about the shoots and what inspired them. I tapped deep into my salacious brain and fantasies to write witty and provocative narratives, from naughty and erotic to XXX and very explicit. It was a lot of fun (and, may I say, well-written) smut, and I was having a ball releasing the filthy ruminations from my head and getting it all down as prose.

Financially, OnlyFans got me through the toughest times of the pandemic. I felt so fortunate. So many people were hurting, losing jobs and homes. I stayed afloat with OnlyFans, and it pulled the trigger on my finally putting up and not shutting up.

All of my content is meant specifically for the subscribers to my page, but I tease moments on Twitter to attract potential new followers. Being exclusive to OnlyFans has given me freedom to really explore and post the most explicit and cathartic stuff I can, and since it's considered copyrighted, it can't be shared unless I'm the one doing the sharing. So I guess you can now add "pornographer" to my long list of occupations, and I love it. Down the line, I may still be there, I may move on. But it's been a fantastic and freeing experience.

I continued to post cropped versions of photos on Instagram as a way to marry the two Davids a bit. A friend messaged me once to say that if I kept posting shirtless photos there or on Facebook, no one would take me seriously as an actor, that I needed to "put on a shirt." Why does any of that not make me a serious person? I know that some folks think, because I'm naked on the Internet, I've totally crossed over and am now doing porn and have no credibility and there's no turning back and that eventually there will be no further possibilities for me to make a living except to get peed on in fetish videos. Although I appreciate the concern, I don't see it that way. If I'm being perceived as nothing but a porn person (hardly a "star"), then you're just not doing your homework. If you've never seen my work as an actor or heard my songs or used my personal organization services or even had a conversation with me about life at two in the morning, then you really have no right to judge me at face value. I actually take this mission of mine very seriously, and I want to change that attitude about sex. And unless you intended to pay my bills during COVID, shut the hell up.

By the way, when I worked as an escort, I did my damnedest to make sure I was the best companion possible, both sexually and emotionally. So if I were indeed doing nothing but porn, I'd still do my utmost to be the best goddamn daddy porn star out there.

ROCKY

Okay, I got a little defensive in that last chapter, but oh dear, I opened that can of worms and I feel the need to delve a little bit more. Indulge me? Just this one chapter? I really need to say this. But I warn you—I've got my boxing gloves on.

We all have sex. More than half the population has vaginas, the rest have penises. That's all a given. Yes?

Many many many of us watch porn. Admit it.

Even the Crazy Christian fundamentalists do. In a study by the *Journal of Sex Research* with stats provided by Google and Pornhub, the Bible Belt has the largest rate of porn consumption in America. They watch. Not all of them, of course, but I'll bet a lot who don't, want to. Especially the men. Their desires are so covered over in layers of bullshit and guilt that they don't even know that they want it, and I'll wager 90 percent of the anti-gay ones are closet cases. They're more obsessed with what goes up my asshole than I am.

And then there are the evangelical hypocrite lawmakers who would *never* watch porn, but they're busy passing legislation to punish old people, women, African-Americans, gays, trans people, you name it, which is even more obscene. How Christian is that? Meanwhile, they're tapping their feet under restroom stalls and getting blow jobs from hookers in dirty motel rooms thinking no one's watching, but they confess it to some child molester in a booth and everything's fine.

The fundamentalists judge us because they think they're on a higher moral ground. They're afraid of their Lord judging them, that they won't make it into heaven if they "sin," so they want to take us all down and dictate how we should live our lives. It's actually kind of selfish—because you're afraid God is going to shortchange you in the afterlife, you have to make the rest of our lives a fucking nightmare?

If we could all live and let live, say hey, that's not for me but have at it, in sex, in life, in politics, everywhere we're just regular folks trying to get through the day without loudmouth buttholes making everything we do a miserable chore, maybe, just maybe, we could sit down and work it out.

But the word *fundamentalist*—the very definition of the word—refers to people who want nothing to change, and they won't shut up about it. They believe in the word of God (which is a translation of a translation of a translation—from Latin) that was (supposedly) sent down thousands of years ago and now there is no wiggle room for discussion. We're up against the wall, folks. They're not going to adjust, update, or reboot, and I wouldn't care so much if they weren't such a driving force in a war against the gay community and sexual freedom. "Love the sinner, hate the sin"? Screw you, bitches. Sex and nudity ain't no sin.

Many of them claim they've never met, don't know, or in fact have never even seen a gay person, but of course, everyone has, whether they know it or not. There's a clever song in *When Pigs Fly* called "Color Out of Colorado," about how the gays exist in every aspect of the community—entertainment, politics, everywhere—and you can't and won't get rid of us. "You can't take the Mary out of Maryland!" It's a very clever lyric that shows that everyone rubs elbows with gay folk every day, and most often in your own family. I'm the "funny" uncle to my niece and two nephews and the grand guncle to their kids. Eight of them! And I love them all and they love me and accept me and I'm so grateful to have a family that does.

We're all over, ya bible beaters, surprise! And though you may be making inroads into higher levels of our government, you will not take our rights away, treat us like fifth-class citizens, make us feel crappy about our bodies, and vilify our sexuality.

Just as you do, we have the right to live our lives freely, to figure out where we belong in this cray cray confusing world. I took the journey I needed to take to live my authentic life and it's *my* story, not yours, and I hurt no one. You deal with shame, desire, need, and lust by a lot of contrite and hostile mea culpas. Fine. Have at it, kids. Don't judge mine, I won't judge yours (actually that was pretty judgy, but you do what you need to do). Boom.

Wait. Nope. Take that back. I judge you for judging yourself *if* your negativity wedges into *my* life and results in extreme measures, from bullying to lawmaking, that impact the rest of us who are just trying to get through the goddamn day. Stay out of my bedroom, my politics, my Internet, with your boring-ass vision of what you think the world is supposed to be. Get the fuck out of our way.

We all have desires, we all have experiences that maybe we're ashamed of or hold close to the vest or live in fear that someone's going to find out about, and I'm here to say no. No. These experiences, these desires are part of who you are, and if you squelch them, you're not living your truth. I'm not saying post your dick on the Internet (which I do a lot) or go be an escort (which I did) or get penetrated by a dozen cater waiters in a bathroom after the Oscars at the Governors Ball (relax, I've not done that, but fantasizing about it just made my penis tingle), but don't *not do* what you really want *to do* if it's manageable, you're aware of possible consequences, and no one gets hurt.

You've wanted to pose nude for photos but you haven't because you're ashamed at even the thought of it? Get past that. You're afraid that maybe the photos might get out, or you feel that your body is not one to be photographed? Fuck that. Listen to Dr. David: posing nude is such a freeing, cathartic feeling. I highly recommend it. Get out a camera and take some pics. Or have someone shoot them for you. Whatever. You don't have to post them, you don't have to show them to anyone, you don't even have to keep them. Delete them. It's the experience of doing it that I would advocate to anyone and everyone. After that, it's different strokes for different naked folks in terms of what you do with the photos.

I've shot a few guys myself, and they love it, and they either keep the photos to themselves or post them wherever, but the decision is in their hands. When that power is taken from you, I'm sure it's frustrating. When actors'/actresses' nude photos are leaked, they receive so much criticism in the media, saying if they'd never posed for them at all, they wouldn't be in "trouble." Bullshit. That's like saying don't ever have sex and you'll never have to worry about STDs. In a way that's true, but . . . fuck you.

I sometimes have heated conversations with invisible adversaries in my head who challenge me for putting myself out there with my nudies, the photos and videos. "They" say that it's all a career killer and that I'll never get another acting job, at least in mainstream TV and film. The word that I keep yelling to "them" is . . . *why*? Why should that be? Why should being naked and/or sexual publicly ruin a career? Though there are still agents, producers, and managers who don't want their gay actors even to come out, being out and gay doesn't kill a career anymore, so why should any of it be an issue?

I know America has a problem with sex, thinking it should be a "private" thing, "private parts" (ugh), all that, but . . . really? We all have sex, many watch porn, we all know what's going on between the legs, so why all the coyness? I get so bored when I see male models bend over backwards to hide their genitalia in photo shoots, or how "clever" filmmakers are in their efforts to avoid showing anyone's dick (in my opinion, vaginas and female breasts are less and less taboo, and less likely to affect a woman's career).

And in the editing of this book, we had many conversations about just how many and what kind of explicit photos we were going to be able to include. Was I going to offend the customers and booksellers by including photos of my hard cock in it, possibly even inciting them to ban the book or cellophane it shut, when what I'm saying is that those nudes are part of the story and the total point of my entire mission? The book's in your hands now, so let me know.

Oh, and here's a random thought: Why is it supposed to be so calming, when engaged in public speaking, to imagine your audience in their underwear, as if it's some kind of reverse humiliation? Just asking.

Though we've caught up a lot regarding male nudity thanks to HBO on shows like *Oz*, *Westworld*, and *Euphoria*, it's insane to me that we still have issues with showing actual unsimulated sex (especially gay sex) when it would really help the story, atmosphere, and character development. (Brownie points to the HBO show *Girls* when Allison Williams's character got rimmed by her boyfriend. Hmm . . . perhaps "brownie points" was an unfortunate choice of words.) Sex can say so much about us, how we express ourselves, physically and emotionally. It's such a joyous element of life, and I don't accept the notion that it should be disparaged or ruinous.

SAG-AFTRA, the actors' union for TV and film, has rules regarding sexuality and what actors are allowed to do. There has to be a nudity rider in their contracts, stringently laying out whatever specific sexual activity the consenting actors and creatives agree upon in the scenes. If, in the heat of the moment at the shoot, the actors agree to push beyond the sexual activity laid out in the rider, they later have the right to request in the final edit that anything that was not in the contract be nixed.

Though there's nothing at SAG-AFTRA that says graphic, unsimulated sex isn't allowed at all, no mainstream American studio films have the real thing. Some indie films do, most notably Chloë Sevigny fellating Vincent Gallo in *The Brown Bunny*. I've seen unsimulated sex used to great effect, as in the aforementioned *Shortbus* (American, non-union), directed by John Cameron Mitchell, who said, "Sex, like music, is a universal language. We want to use it to introduce character, evoke emotion, propel the plot." It's a wonderful film. More dramatically, it's used in *Intimacy* and *Nine Songs* (both British). When Kerry Fox put Mark Rylance's hard cock in her mouth in the opening scene of *Intimacy*, I almost dropped my Diet Coke. How intensely hungry the real sex was in that film, and when Rylance's character follows Fox home and sees her shitty life, we realize that "casual" sex was the only real human connection she felt, and as portrayed, it was so emotionally palpable and it revved up the dynamics of that relationship. More, please.

I'd love to do a film like *Intimacy*, *Nine Songs*, and *Shortbus* that addresses and portrays sex and sexuality head-on without all the reserve. I've been approached to do porn films, but that's not quite what I want—studio porn that's just about the sex. I always knew, if I did porn, I'd want to do it my way, and as I've been experimenting with video, I'm feeling freer and freer about expressing myself sexually on film. And as I look back on all the erotic work I've done, I think I've been pretty diverse in how I presented myself, sometimes artsy and esoteric, sometimes much more explicit. But yeah—sometimes I'm just shoving my dick in your face. Oh well. Get over it, America. I know that there's an audience for what I do, because the numbers on my social media add up to tens of thousands watching.

Is it affecting my legit career? I don't know. I'm still getting auditions and still building up my IMDB. Conventional wisdom has always been that if you've done gay porn, you can't cross over to the mainstream. Why? If a casting director won't call me in because I'm naked or getting fucked on the Internet, why? I'll speculate their reasoning: the director won't give me the time of day, my credibility is shot if the character is a doctor or lawyer, the Bible Belt or the studio will get all up in arms, I'm not manly enough if I'm seen taking it up the ass . . . Why? Why? To all of that. And as a side note, I think the directors I really want to work with wouldn't give a crap. Now, having said all that, things do seem to be changing a little bit thanks to more explicit sexual content produced for HBO, Starz, and the like, so who knows?

It's just nudity. Or sex. Maybe it's porn. Sometimes art. But it's all part of life, so why shouldn't it have a place at the table?

I obviously feel the need to justify my choices, and that's what this chapter has been all about. The trip gong has rung; the round is over. I thank you for listening. Moving on . . .

NO STRINGS

After years writing only dirty *Naked Boys Singing!*–type ditties, I wanted to see if I had it in me to write something lovely and heartfelt. As sexually oriented as I am, I'm that love-struck teenaged gay boy inside, and I always have been, and yet you would never have known it from my musical oeuvre.

One night, I challenged myself to find that ballad within. What is a ballad? Usually a love song, but I had never had that one man who I felt loved me as much as I did him. Could I write about that kind of profound, intense love? I thought, what if I wrote a ballad about a guy who can't write a ballad? Maybe that's the song. So I poured myself a Scotch, went out on my balcony, I worked all night, and as the sun came up, I pushed "Save" on the computer. I had written my very first ballad . . .

I could never write a ballad,
emotional and free,
melodious reflections of what someone means to me.
I guess it hasn't happened yet.
It cuts me like a knife.

But till then I'll dream the ballad
of the great love of my life.
—from "Ballad"

Pretty melancholy stuff. But I am hopelessly romantic. I've met guys who only know me from my photos and think I'm some kind of serial sex guy who could never settle down. I think I'm a perfectly nice, fairly smart, somewhat attractive fellow, and every so often friends or coworkers tell me what a catch I am, and I always say thank you as I roll my eyes, because I'm very rarely, if ever, attached.

That may not surprise you. Perhaps I come off as superficial, but what I really respond to is warmth, humor, talent, and especially smarts, not just physical attraction. However, there can be so many wired fences and brick walls on the road to making a connection.

For instance, when I meet a guy, a sexual undercurrent often comes immediately to the fore, whether it's emanating from him or me or both, and it can skew a "get to know you" kind of conversation and make the connection go off the rails rather than let it flow. I remember an evening a few years ago at the Eagle in LA. It was packed and I was trying to inch my way through a sweaty gaggle of tank top–clad gays. I noticed an older guy coming toward me through the throng, warmly smiling at me with really kind, intelligent eyes. I shyly returned the smile. "Okay," I thought, "possibilities." I was looking forward to chatting, to seeing what he was like beyond the obvious attraction. Just as he slipped by me, he brought his face right up to mine and made a long-drawn-out, saliva-engorged, highly off-putting mouth sound—*sluuuuuuuuuuurrp.* What does one say to that? I know, I know, I was in a bar, what did I expect, but . . . really?

Then there's this: How many times have I started to hit it off with someone, really in sync about a lot of subjects as we chat, a little of that sensuality beginning to happen, and ten minutes in I get "Well, my boyfriend and I . . ."? *Goddamnit*. One thing has not changed about me: I can still fall in love in two minutes. And the other guy gets to be all flirty because he's in a boring relationship and it's just fun! For *him*. I may be old, but that doesn't mean I don't melt when I meet someone who seems terrific, and there go those raised expectations again. So if this is you, I beg you—stop it.

Oh, and here's another barrel of fun: I'll be at a party and start chatting with a guy I'm attracted to and the conversation flows and we're really hitting it off, and it sometimes takes that same ten minutes or so before he says, "Well, my girlfriend and I . . ." *Fuck!* Or "My wife and I . . . " And the air goes out of the tires and the lead goes out of the pencil. I get this plastered smile on my face for a second as it registers, but I soldier on and just try to enjoy the conversation. In that situation, I think it's actually easier for me to chat with a straight guy, as they don't put out that sexual aura; we just talk about stuff, which I love (although I do have to shake that residual fantasy of fucking the straight guy . . . sorry . . . focus, David). Whatever. New rule: if you have a boyfriend, husband, girlfriend, or wife and you start connecting with a single guy or gal at a party, YOU ARE REQUIRED TO REVEAL YOUR RELATIONSHIP STATUS WITHIN THE FIRST TWO MINUTES OF THE CONVERSATION. Either stop being so great or reveal, ASAP. This is a public service and I approve this message.

And speaking of straight men, sometimes it gets even more complicated when you run into this guy . . . which I have . . .

I'm a straight guy until I get drunk.
I'm a straight guy until I get drunk.
Just a few sweet sips of cognac, I'll be slidin' down your bone, Jack.
Salt up that Margariter, I'll take any Dick or Peter.

Guzzle down a dry martini, use my buns to hide your weenie.
I'm a straight guy until I get drunk!
—from "Straight Guy"

You may be reading this book and thinking a) kudos to him, he's brutally honest and self-effacing, and maybe his thoughts on sexuality are kind of inspiring or amusing; or more likely b) he's nothing but a narcissist and full of shit and he's single, he's been single most of his life, and his choices are keeping him from the very thing he wants most, what we all want most—love. Real love. Unconditional love. That person who is your partner, your lover, your best friend. So let's hit on that for a bit.

You'll note I don't spend too much time on relationship stuff in this book, because I've admittedly not had many. Reid was the longest, at fourteen months. But after that shit show, I really didn't want another one. They say relationships take work; that one was a *job*. Since Reid, I've met a couple of guys who I thought were great and I engaged with them for a time—this is it, I thought, he's the one. But having raised my hopes and expectations, both went nowhere and I fell into depression. One just wanted to get in my ass and then it was done, and the other was intimidated by how open I was about sex and I think I scared him away.

Before Reid, when I fell for someone, I'd lose track of who I was and become someone else, the one I thought they would like better than the guy in front of them. I had always felt there was some secret to successful relationships that everyone seemed to understand but me, some "love club" I never belonged to. But I knew and I know that I have a huge capacity to love, to empathize, and to feel so deep down to the point that it's painful. When I fall in love, I'm done. I'm gone. If I like someone and it seems that it might go somewhere and then it doesn't because they've chosen not to continue, I have taken to my bed for days. Stan, Kalani, The Editor, Reid—all were devastating in their way.

I know how to be a friend and a lover, and can go from romantic to sex pig. But I find guys are attracted to one or the other, usually not both. And being someone who creates the kind of material I put out there is not an easy row to hoe (ho! See what I did there?). I think there's still a part of me that looks at myself as separate beings that don't quite come together. Who will love me as a man and an artist, but also a "porn star," an ex-hooker, a narcissist? Most importantly, can I even love myself?

Or, can I just live alone and be satisfied? Because my body is so public, people think I have men falling all over me, but I just don't (at least not that I'm aware of). They also think I'm very extroverted, but I'm not. I read a piece that talked about introverted people in extroverted situations, and that's me to a T. As an actor, a model, an escort, and even as a personal organizer, I have thrown myself into work that compels me to be outgoing and engaging, but I'm really someone who likes to be alone. Or maybe I just think I like to be alone.

Even back to eighth grade, I was a pretty affable kid, but I struggled with feelings of loneliness and being different. In a speech I delivered at eighth grade graduation (all in rhyme) I talked about how hard it might be to make new friends in high school and if I should even bother. To address that, I said:

But no, that's just not like me.
I'm not like an old crone.
I'm not like Greta Garbo,
I don't vant to be alone.

Oh, that sweet little gay boy. Me, standing at the podium, wearing this huge, fashionable paisley bow tie that was bigger than my face.

I can tell you, he was a really good boy. But he was lonely. And now, I sometimes still can't tell if I'm alone or lonely. Maybe I'm just meant to be on my own. I don't know. I still live with hope that it will happen when it happens.

In 2005, I went to see a show at the Geffen Playhouse and I was seated next to playwright/actor George Furth, who wrote the librettos to *Company*, *Merrily We Roll Along*, and many other works. I had known him for about five years, and we were actually pals. I loved him to death, irascible and blunt as he could be. Let's just say you never wanted to be on his bad side. If you were in conversation with George and said that you found something "interesting," he would stop you mid-sentence and just lay into you. "Interesting? *Interesting*? That tells me nothing! *Nothing!*"

We were chatting before curtain, and he told me he had a boyfriend. I was surprised, because I'd never known George to have a beau. He went on enthusiastically about "my new long-distance relationship with this guy in Chicago, and I travel there to see him, and I've never had someone like that in my life, it was never in the cards, but lo and behold, here it is, what a surprise at the age of seventy-two, and oh, David—that's how it's going to be for you too!"

Aaaaand the lights started to fade and the play began. And his words hung in the air and I went numb. I didn't even hear the first ten minutes of the show. I was only forty-seven years old. Really? And I thought, yeah. Really.

I started to dwell on some of the missed opportunities I'd had over the years, how exclusive I could be when it came to connecting with men.

The Spike and the Eagle were the two leather/fetish bars on the West Side Highway in the '80s and '90s, and I spent many a weekend promenading between the two, one long block away from each other, cruising guys coming back and forth, each of us on an endless parade, drinking and flirting enough to almost always ensure a hookup. Since

I lived just a few blocks away, I was usually the host, and many a good buttfucking and cocksucking time was had, almost always of the one-night-stand variety. One evening, I ran into a young man at the Spike whom I had met earlier at a party. He introduced me to the friend he was talking with, the activist and playwright Larry Kramer.

We all chatted for a good long time and I was transfixed by Larry—so brusque, smart, honest, and a little prickly—but I was also attracted to the young guy and we did a lot of flirt flirt, but in a very noncommittal way, as if neither of us was going to be the vulnerable one who admits he's attracted. Finally, Larry said, "Jesus, would you two go home and fuck already? You young guys. All games." We laughed, but still didn't complete the pass, and we all went our separate ways. I do think about what Larry said to us, his slightly bluer version of "Youth is wasted on the young."

The problem is, I'm still a time waster, and I ain't young. Just a few years ago I was in a show and the playwright came to see it one night. We chatted briefly after the performance, and I was so taken by how intelligent and funny he was. We kept in touch, and a few months later a new play of his was opening at one of the most acclaimed theaters on the West Coast, and he invited me to the premiere and said I could stay over. I wasn't sure what "stay over" really meant, but I gladly agreed to drive up.

We had a terrific evening watching his wonderful play and then hanging out at a lovely opening night soiree. We exchanged smiles during the party as he mingled, humbly and sweetly taking in the plaudits. I kept looking at him thinking, "Is he the one?" When we got back to the hotel room, we got ready for bed. We were both wiped out and got into the king-size bed and just kind of said good night and turned off the lights.

I didn't know what to do. I lay there, eyes wide open, unable to breathe. Part of me wanted to make a move on him, but I didn't know if that was rushing things and maybe it was best to take it slow and not force sex just because we only had one night plus he lived in NY and this would then turn into a long-distance thing which I didn't really want although I would definitely have moved back to NY for the right guy which is never a good idea actually and he was such a nice guy but was he too nice and maybe he wasn't interested at all and that would be kind of humiliating and there was really nowhere to go if I had to leave because it was his hotel room and what if he had a boyfriend and *Jesus fucking blah blah blah . . . !!*

Why didn't I just pull him closer to me to find out? Why did I not take that moment? I don't have many regrets in life. This was one of them. Who knows how it would have turned out? He might have rebuffed me, we might have fucked and then never have seen each other again, but we might have become lifelong lovers. I don't know. I couldn't know. But I let the moment go by. I was going to ask him about this a few months later, to see if he would have been interested, but he had since found a boyfriend, tight as can be. Good for him. No, really.

That little boy making love to his pillow is still so present inside me. And I've hooked up enough in my life to know that sexual trysts can be a lot of fun but empty in the end. Not always, but more and more. When I'm on the verge of just a hookup, I try to envision the denouement, and if I see myself doing a lazy, slovenly walk of shame after, feeling empty and unsatisfied, I'll usually decline.

I'm on various sex and dating apps and I guess I get hit on a lot there, but a few bad pictures and a brief profile aren't always enough for me to want to take the time to engage with someone. Plus, it's hard to communicate in that space with just those little chat balloons, where it is so easy for everything to go wrong. Once, on Grindr, a guy messaged me all the naughty things he wanted to do to me, and I typed "Mmmmm," but when I sent it, auto-spell turned my reply into "Mom." Hot.

I know, I know, I should get off the hookup sites altogether. But what are the other options? As much as I used to love them, bathhouses seem to be more a hotbed of tweakers and unsafe sex these days, and I'm getting to hate bars, standing there with a drink and a stupid painted-on smile on my face. I would love to get fixed up, but the couple of times that happened, it amazed me that my friends thought the other guy and I were a match. I love going to parties and meeting guys face-to-face, but as I always have, I put too much stock in those gatherings and my expectations never get met. Expectations are the death of everything. And as Ann Reinking said in *All That Jazz*, "I have no more small talk."

Meeting guys through work, Match.com, volunteering, they're all legit, I've done 'em all, but they still haven't gleaned *him*. I'd like someone in my life, but after all these years, maybe I really have become that guy who's too set in his ways and used to depending on himself. There are times I catch myself eating dinner in my apartment like a caveman, shoving salad in my mouth with my fingers, because no one's there to have manners for.

I do want a partner, to be in love and make a home, to pay bills together and drive each other to the doctor's and the airport, but I don't even know if I'm capable anymore. And is there such a thing as unconditional love at this age? Whatever, Myrna. The heart wants what it wants, so . . . who knows?

But then, I still have an AOL account, so maybe I'll never learn.

Do I have to wait until I'm seventy-two, if I even make it there? How do I change that? George only lived a couple of years after I saw him at the theater, and although we fell out of touch toward the end of his life, I hope he died without regrets. I'm only sixty-two as I write this, so there's time. But is there? If a relationship is something I truly want in my heart, it has to happen, right? But I'll tell you one thing: I hope I don't die before I actually do find the great love of my life.

MERRILY WE ROLL ALONG

Here's where I'm at: The filming of *Musical Comedy Whore!* and the first CD of my original songs, *Most Versatile*, are available right now, and you're holding my book in your hand or reading it on your tablet. And beyond my two one-man shows, there's a musical about bullying for kids called *Fully a Bully* that I'm working on, two narrative films I'm trying to make, a cabaret show of my naughty ditties called *Schwingin' My Songs*, a stage piece incorporating graphic sexuality that I'm curating called *Bawdeville*. I have also narrated audiobooks, which I love; I hope to do many more. I've done a few mainstream ones, but I especially enjoy doing the gay erotic books. I used to narrate those under the pseudonym Darren Douglas, but not anymore; I'm happy to read both the legit books and the smuttier ones under my very own name. And speaking of that, I've been asked if I was sullying the Pevsner name by not changing it for my erotic work the way porn stars do.

No. That's the point of all this.

Though I lost my representation a while back, I found new agents and managers who know about my erotic Internet presence and are on my side, and pre-COVID I continued to appear in films, on the Web, and on TV. I did notice right before quarantine that network TV auditions had fallen off a bit, possibly due to the blog but more, I believe, because the roles I usually go for, the fiftysomething doctor or lawyer, are now cast with more diversity. Asian, African-American, Indian. I get it. We white guys have had our time being the caretaking doctor, the slick and sharky lawyer, the courtroom judge, so I respect the shift. It's important. It has cut into my own bottom line, though, but what can you do? So I take things into my own hands and write.

What I miss most, though, is being in the theater. I was one week into rehearsal for *Little Shop of Horrors* playing Mr. Mushnik in a small theater in Hollywood when the plug was pulled due to COVID. The arts have taken such a hit, but I believe by the time you read this book, we'll all be back on the boards and you'll have your tickets for that play or musical or ballet or concert you've been dying to see. And once again I'll have the privilege of standing on a stage in front of a live audience, telling a story alone or with a bunch of other artists, connecting with each other and the folks in the dark, taking them on a journey with us that maybe changes their lives a bit as it enriches ours and gives purpose to our existence as purveyors of empathy and humanity. We entertain, but we also enlighten, and I truly believe that's magic.

BRING IT ON

So, what am I still working out for myself in my sixties? Why is it still important to be "shameless"? You'd think society would have progressed into a more liberal atmosphere about sexuality, but I don't think so. In the 1980s, AIDS was used as a way to slut-shame gay men for having sex, and it took years to break free from that stigma and be able to go about our lives freely. As someone who came of age in that period, who lived in New York at the height of the crisis, the fear and self-loathing that we felt in connection to that virus is so deeply embedded in my brain that to this day it still influences my choices and behavior. Maybe it always will.

But posing nude, posting photos, and putting my body and sexuality out there satisfies me in a strange way. I have always been someone who has dived into the eye of the hurricane. I have tremendous fear of being judged, and yet I constantly put myself into that position by the choices I make. Look, I've done all the therapy, but I've come to grips with the fact that this exhibitionism, this desire to express myself so publicly, is a part of me. Call me a "sensualist." A "provocateur." And I think there was something unconscious in my putting myself out there— I needed to learn that in this life you have to own everything you do, good and bad, and if there's judgment to be had, you must never let anyone make you feel like crap.

From being an escort to posting dick pics in middle age (I say middle age even though I'm still doing it, which means I'll live to be 120, and that only happens in Russia), my activities have felt sexual, artistic, *and* political, yet they have also opened a door for a different kind of slut-shaming. I have inadvertently invited people to look at my behavior and say their piece, and they do. At the risk of giving oxygen to a segment of cynics, for all the positive feedback I've received, there's always going to be the big thumbs-down.

There's a popular gay website that provides a forum to discuss all aspects of gay gossip, politics, and news, all in a bitchy, no-holds-barred way. A friend told me that I was the subject of many a discussion there. Early on, the comments on the site were more positive and supportive of my photos and such, and then gradually things got nastier and nastier. Here's a sample of some of the anonymous poison posts (think Jimmy Kimmel's "Mean Tweets"):

"Sad Old Gay, David what's his name? That gay singer who likes being fisted."

"God, life is unkind. Beautiful young men turning into shriveled leather."

". . . rapidly aging Jewish grandpa masturbating in public is for some reason not attractive to me. Time moves on and youth is gone and we all lose our charms in the end." (How could I not present you this reference from *Gentlemen Prefer Blondes?*)

"Ewwww, dirty Jew, and OLD." (Anti-Semitism reared its head a few times.)

And then, simple and to the point:

"Puke."

At first, my feelings were hurt, but eventually the condemnation thickened my skin and made me stronger and more determined, more resistant to criticism, so I thank them for that (not to mention that I actually found some of the comments pretty funny since they were so over the top). It led me to say, good, have at it. Talk about it. Why am I "gross?" My age, my body, my demeanor, my audacity, my nose? And apparently it's not enough to say, hey, that's not my cup of tea, and different strokes; some folks just have to come right out and viciously attack when they don't see the appeal; it's fun for them to dismiss people in such a bitchy, judgmental way. And usually, when it's that critical and mean, it says more about the person slinging it than about me.

But hey, guys, you're not alone: I have even tried to make *myself* feel bad about what I've done, both the escorting and the blog, and when I'm tired or down, I can be all self-judgy and pretty hard on myself and my choices. I read an interview in which the actress/comedian Sandra Bernhard quoted another comedian named Lotus Weinstock: "Never judge your life when you're exhausted."

When I'm thinking clearly, though, I try to apply a bit of the Vanessa Williams Rule—to own the choices I've made, but also to be proud that I had the guts to explore my sexual desires with conviction and empathy. I still have a bit of a double life (not so much anymore with this book you're holding) and maybe that leaves the door open to attack me. Maybe. But not all the comments on the forum were so mean, and this one poster kind of "gets" it:

"I knew too many people who did not reach the age that I am now.
I would have felt cheated had I died at the ages that many of these
people did. Life is beautiful—as long as you live it. I think that what
David and others do by posting their images is very inspirational.
Life isn't over until you close your eyes for that final time."

Amen, buddy. Amen.

DEAR WORLD (THE ELEVEN O'CLOCK NUMBER AND FINALE)

The last few years have been tough. I lost both my parents to cancer. Fucking cancer. I've joined the Orphan Club. It's a pretty shitty club to be in. I somehow thought my folks would go on forever. My mom was little, barely over five feet tall, a real lady, and as she was in her eighties, she was undoubtedly old, but she was never a little old lady, and my dad was stubborn and strong to the end. They were extraordinary people who led incredibly full lives with absolutely no regrets. Kids, grandkids, great-grandkids, travel, activism, entertaining—Marcia and Sheldon were the hub of the extended family and of an enormous social network.

At eighty-three (Mom) and eighty-seven (Dad), it still felt too soon, and after my mom passed, I thought my dad would continue on, but as so often happens when couples have a lifetime together, he followed her only thirteen months later; they had had sixty-five anniversaries together when she died (they certainly beat my fourteen months by a million miles). I'll write more about them in the future, but for now I can tell you that I'm a bit at sea. Everything feels . . . different . . . and I've never heard the clock ticking stronger than I do now.

I needed to work out that growing awareness of mortality, so for the year I turned sixty I wrote a song for myself called "Happy Birthday to Me." It has all the trademark narcissism and filth you might expect from me, but also the bittersweet sense of a guy who is a bit lost, has always had to depend on himself, and has no idea where he's going.

I did an interview about my blog with David Hiri Feign, the cofounder of Bateworld, a website for guys who are into masturbation (and who isn't?), and he mentioned that he produced erotic videos centered around the music he composed, and as he knew I was a songwriter, he said we should collaborate sometime. I told him about "Happy Birthday to Me" and he got really excited and asked if I'd like to use that as the backdrop for a video. I told him it was meant to be a wistful piece about aging, but he decided to turn it on its ear and gave it a James Bond-ian feel, and rather than being melancholy, the video became a celebration of age and self-love (both physical and emotional), with presents and cake and champagne. It was weird but fun, and was shown exclusively on Bateworld.

> *Happy Birthday to me.*
> *Another year I didn't die, I'm thrilled as I can be.*
> *Gonna shower some affection on my favorite devotee.*
> *That would be me.*
> *That would be me.*
>
> *I spent my whole life dreaming*
> *I would go kicking and screaming,*
> *that the time I quit the earth was a millennium away.*
> *But the moment's getting nearer,*
> *can see it in my rearview mirror,*
> *so yeah, it's getting closer but good news, it's not today.*
> —from "Happy Birthday to Me"

I'm in my early sixties and still posting photos and videos, but will I continue into my late sixties, seventies, eighties, beyond? When I'm a big bag of brittle bones or soft, flabby, and paunchy, will I want to keep doing this? It sure is a great incentive to stay in shape. I do wonder if I'll want to post when time and gravity have their way with me. That would be the true test of my commitment, to put my body out there and have no shame even when I'm not the ideal model.

But I've never been the ideal model. I've never been a *GQ* body beautiful guy with a huge cock. Will I have the guts to put out photos with all the stuff that maturity can bring? The last five years or so, I've seen how quickly I'm aging—the body is softer, the face has age spots and wrinkles. But I want to convey the message that you should love your body whatever state it's in at any age, and I hope I have the courage to reflect that as I continue to mature.

My photos get reblogged onto sites with guys way older than me, and they're showing off, fucking and sucking, and getting thousands of "likes." Hey, kids, we old folks do all the stuff you do! Why not show it? Screw the negative nellies, the ageists, the small-minded prudes. Society needs to catch up; it's not for us to temper our self-expression. Sex and nudity are natural, fun, and beautiful, and there is no age limit on that. If I'm still having strong erections at eighty years old, with or without a pill—wheeee!

But will I one day wake up and regret any of this? I don't think so. I'd like to think I'll be one of the guys who looks back and feels proud that I had the guts to fucking say what I wanted to fucking say, and didn't let the haters sway me from doing what my heart and cock were egging me on to do. I'm always trying to stay in the moment with this art project. When it's not fun anymore, if my creativity gets tapped out, maybe I'll move on to something else. Or maybe I'll continue to keep the mission going in a different way. As the song says, I intend to go kicking and screaming into old age. Fuck the numbers.

Most importantly, I want my friends and family to remain a loving presence in my life, even after I've revealed all of this; I want them to see and to understand the roads I've taken. I don't know how much everyone knows about everything I do, but I can tell you I lost a family member when he discovered my photos online. I've known him my whole life and he won't speak to me anymore. Not even at both my parents' funerals. I tried to reach out, but . . . nothing. Oh well. Maybe he'll read this book and see the light. Yeah. Right. When pigs fly.

So to all of you whom I love and who love me even though I can be distant and difficult to love sometimes, I want you to know . . .

I'm still the little boy who delighted in entertaining and singing Barbra in the basement and commercial jingles in the car and dancing like no one was watching, and when they started to watch, I knew I wanted to make that my life's work and have much more than what I was so afraid would be a dull, routine existence.

Perhaps the germ of my aversion to Judaism is that I didn't feel I could ascribe to the rules and morality that it seemed to dictate. And I've had to fight the voices in my head telling me that what I really wanted out of my life I could never have, that it was all a pipe dream, maybe even an embarrassment, a "*shonda* for the neighbors."

And as I think about why I've not reached every goal I've set out to attain, it all seems to come down to this: as much of a Warrior as I've been about sex and art, I think I'm still that nice Jewish Doctor inside, and that Warrior and that Doctor have been at odds my whole life, judging, belittling, criticizing each other's desires and choices. I've been so many things: writer, actor, musician, gay man, activist, escort, house-cleaner, personal organizer, romantic, sex pig, shameless exhibitionist, and on and on and on. But there's just so much I wanted to explore, and though it may make me seem like a jack-of-all-trades, master of none, I've chosen to open my arms and take in whatever my curiosity led me to. Maybe I'm not exactly where I want to be at this point in my life, but the journey itself has taken me to extreme places I never thought I would go. That journey has been wonderful and horrible at various times, but also pretty goddamn interesting.

Sorry, George . . . but it has been.

I try my best, learn from my mistakes, and keep pushing forward, and I am not done. Some people my age say they've lived a full life and if they died tomorrow, they'd be okay with it. I can't say that. I have so much more I want to express, more than I can include in this book even, and I intend to continue on as I have been, with one eye looking inward toward creativity and the other looking out into the world with hope, ready to surprise myself with what I learn and pass it on as artfully and passionately as I can.

I believe I'm finally finding some balance between who I am and what I do, understanding that being an artist feeds my soul and gives me purpose. Exploring my sexuality and diving into the deep end with the escorting and modeling has taught me so much about myself over the years, giving me the courage of my convictions that sexuality is not something to bring about shame, but is all about being your authentic self and celebrating it. I think I'm ready to be with someone, fully. To really show up. I think. Anyone? Anyone? I'm not 100 percent there. And until I am, until I'm nicer to myself and fully accepting of who I am, I can't expect anyone else to be. But I'm getting there.

Maybe I wrote this book, my shows, my song lyrics, everything, as a way to make you understand who I am inside, but also to help you to look at your own lives and the people in them differently, to love someone who doesn't do what you expect them to do, to help you "get" them, to explain the unexplainable. I hope so. But here's the thing: maybe, just maybe, the person who really needs to hear everything I'm saying . . .

. . . is me.

It's time. Time to own my story. Time to truly and wholeheartedly give it up to love. No judgment. Just love. Joy. Confidence. Contentment. I'm on my way. I feel it.

> *I gotta give it up to love.*
> *No excuses, no alibi.*
> *I gotta give it up to love,*
> *I found myself . . .*

. . . or at least I think I'm finding myself . . . a fabulous guy.

(Curtain. End Act Two.)

ACKNOWLEDGMENTS

To my sisters, Janet Pevsner and Linda Margolis, I only talk about the difficult moments I had with you, but it wasn't always that way growing up. And as adults, we get along great. You are both spectacular and supportive, and I love you. And Michael Margolis, Linda hit the jackpot with you.

To Ari and Rachel Margolis, Lori and Adam Barbag, Brian and Shana Margolis, and all the kidlets: Laila, Adaya, Eliora, Derek, Josh, Benji, Maya, and Sadie, I am a proud guncle and grand guncle, and I love having you all in my life. I sure hope you feel the same.

To Scott Sellers, well . . . there would be no published book without you. You always dream you'll find someone so supportive, so as-one in their thinking, who really "gets" you and your work, but who will also push you to dig deeper and go beyond the text to get to the real truth. It wasn't always easy, but when you trust someone as much as I trust you, you know you can leap and the words and the story will catch you. I got lucky with you, Scott. A gazillion thanks.

To Anne Collins and Sue Kuruvilla of Random House Canada, I can't thank you enough for throwing your support behind my story, and seeing beyond any sensationalism to the heart beating underneath.

To Andy Baseman. Oh, Mr. Hole. We've sure been through it together, all these years. Even though we're officially old, we can still have BFFs and you are mine.

To Paul Zappala, my late roomie and first writing partner. I miss you every day.

To Anne Allgood, Randy Brenner, Melissa Josephs, Nic Arnzen, Molly O'Leary, Steve Callahan, Matt Montgomery, Jim Bullock, Jennifer Lynch, Demian Wyma, Mark Dashnaw, Patrick Baca, Jennifer Prescott, Brian d'Arcy James, Rob Marshall, Dan Shaheen, Barry Kramer, Robbin Slade, Jay Corcoran, Debbie Pollack, Suzie Ritter, Kent Gash, Jordan Thaler, Jeremy Mann, Jeff Calhoun, John Scherer, Mary Moran, my *Corpus Christi* family, the *When Pigs Fly* guys, and anyone I may have missed . . . always supportive in so many ways over the years, but most importantly . . . all funny. I have funny friends.

And speaking of funny, to the late Ted Bales, who after listening to us bitch and moan about the producers of *Party*, took a huge drag off his cigarette (when you could still smoke in the dressing room) and said, "Honey, they don't call it show fun." That little tidbit of wisdom has stayed with me over the years and I have found it intensely helpful, along with his other gem, "Funny always wins." Yes, it does.

To Mark Saltzman for giving my shows a home to work them out.

To Karen Berry for suggesting I turn my story into a book. At the time, I vehemently said no, impossible, forget it, don't know how, don't want to. Well, here it is. Thanks, doll.

To Norman Buckley and Kim Powers, who got me on the way to telling my story way back when.

To Steve Bolerjack for being the first to assure me this book has resonance beyond myself, and for starting me on the road to a publishable manuscript. There were lots of red marks for my run-on sentences and questionable punctuation, and though it was sometimes maddening, it was also greatly appreciated.

To Mark Smith, Glenn Hughes, and Stella Alex for sticking by me professionally, even while knowing about my Internet presence.

To Connie Silver, Lee Kassan, Connie Wynne, and Randy Smith, all terrific and supportive therapists—unlike the first guy.

To Mitchell Kinn and all the LGBTQ youth who are out there trying to live their lives authentically and without fear, you so inspire me. Stay strong. We older LGBTQ folks have your backs.

To Jerry Proffit, my high school drama teacher who gave me a chance to express myself on the great stage after the mean girls shut me down.

To Carnegie Mellon University and the faculty there, thanks a lot for the homophobia and for bolstering my lack of confidence and low self-esteem. I had to fight that every day of my life post-college, and though it has always weighed on me, it also gave me a reason to keep fighting to be creative and get your voices the fuck out of my head.

On the other hand, to Carole D'Andrea, who gave me the shot of confidence I needed to act and sing when it was all breaking down. Your class was a safe and creative haven to develop my work as both actor and writer. Carole, I have so much love and appreciation for you and your work on behalf of all your students. Thank you

For Sheldon Pevsner, my late dad: even though you were the quiet one, I never doubted you loved me and I hope you know that I love you always.

And Marcia. Oh, Marcia. Mommy. Mom. When you told a story, you had us rapt, usually laughing, most often left to muse on your wisdom. And you were always maddeningly right, goddamnit. My friends loved you and Dad, sometimes more than I did when you had to be "parents," and you had so many loyal friends who stayed in your life for eons. If I'm at all clear in telling a story, it's because of you. I don't think you liked a lot of my subject matter, but you knew I had to be me. Mommy, Dad. I miss you both so much.

PHOTO CREDITS

Section One

Page 1
All photos courtesy of the author.

Page 2
Clockwise from top left: Photo courtesy of Alamy; Photo courtesy of Alamy; Photo courtesy of Jason Stanford; Photo by Kenn Duncan, © Billy Rose Theatre Division, The New York Public Library for the Performing Arts.

Page 3
All photos courtesy of the author.

Page 4
Clockwise from top: Photo by and courtesy of Ken Lustbader; Photo by and courtesy of Scott Ewalt; Photo by and courtesy of Rodney Allen Trice.

Page 5
Clockwise from top left: Photo courtesy of the author; Photo by and courtesy of Reed Massengill; Photo by and courtesy of Nigel Teare.

Page 6
Clockwise from top: Photo courtesy of the author; Photo courtesy of the author; Photo by and courtesy of Gerry Goodstein.

Page 7
Clockwise from top left: Photo courtesy of the author; Photo courtesy of the Desert Rose Playhouse; Photo by Norm Palley. Courtesy of Leon Acord; Photo courtesy of the author.

Page 8
Photo by Tris Beezley. Courtesy of Lucid by Proxy; Photo by Hank Baim. Courtesy of Tracy Baim; Photo courtesy of the author.

Section Two
Page 1
Top photo by and courtesy of Johnie Thornton; Bottom photo by and courtesy of Jay Jorgensen.

Page 2
Top photo by and courtesy of Tom Bianchi; Bottom photo by and courtesy of YogaBear Studio.

Page 3
Photo by and courtesy of Jay Jorgensen.

Page 4
Top photo by and courtesy of Taylor Imagined; Bottom photo by and courtesy of Dexter Brown.

Page 5
Clockwise from top left: Photo by Michael Liberatore. Courtesy of his estate; Photo by and courtesy of Jay Jorgensen; Photo by and courtesy of John Mar Photo; Photo courtesy of the author.

Page 6
Clockwise from top left: Photo by and courtesy of Dexter Brown; Photo by and courtesy of Domasan (https://twitter.com/TheeDomasan); Photo by and courtesy of Jay Jorgensen; Photo by Michael Liberatore. Courtesy of his estate.

Page 7
Clockwise from top left: Photo by and courtesy of ©Daniel Rarela; Photo by and courtesy of YogaBear Studio; Photo by and courtesy of Liam Jager; Photo by and courtesy of John Orbit for Real Men Real Life.

Page 8
Photo by and courtesy of Austin Wondolowski.

David Pevsner is an LA-based actor and writer, with a little modeling on the side. His film appearances include *Scrooge & Marley* (as Ebenezer Scrooge), *Spa Night, Joshua Tree 1951: A Portrait of James Dean, Role/Play*, and *Corpus Christi: Playing with Redemption*. His guest starring roles on television include *Silicon Valley, NCIS, I'm Dying Up Here, Modern Family, Grey's Anatomy, Liz and Dick, Law and Order LA*, and he starred in the popular web series *Old Dogs and New Tricks*.

David has had a diverse stage acting career, from regional theatres to Broadway. As a songwriter, his work has been featured in the global hit show *Naked Boys Singing!*, his CD of original comedy songs *Most Versatile*, and his two one man musicals, including *Musical Comedy Whore!* which is currently streaming and available on DVD. He continues his anti-shame, anti-ageism, and pro-nudity and sexuality mission with his work in erotic photos, videos, and writings. He also helps people unclutter their lives and environments through his personal organization business "Address the Mess."